Travels with My Scarf

by

Mark Dabbs
Walsall's Running Ambassador

Grosvenor House
Publishing Limited

All rights reserved
Copyright © Mark Dabbs, 2015

The right of Mark Dabbs to be identified as the author of this
work has been asserted by him in accordance with Section 78
of the Copyright, Designs and Patents Act 1988

The book cover picture is copyright to Mark Dabbs

This book is published by
Grosvenor House Publishing Ltd
28-30 High Street, Guildford, Surrey, GU1 3EL.
www.grosvenorhousepublishing.co.uk

This book is sold subject to the conditions that it shall not, by way of
trade or otherwise, be lent, resold, hired out or otherwise circulated
without the author's or publisher's prior consent in any form of binding or
cover other than that in which it is published and
without a similar condition including this condition being imposed
on the subsequent purchaser.

A CIP record for this book
is available from the British Library

ISBN 978-1-78148-895-9

Dedicated to Sophie and Scarlett

"If I had a flower for every time I thought of you, I could walk in my garden forever."

Alfred Lord Tennyson

Also by the same author

Untoward Occurrence

The story of The Saddlers

Walsall were formed as Walsall Town Swifts in 1888 when Walsall Town F.C. and Walsall Swifts F.C. amalgamated. Walsall Town had been founded in 1877 and Walsall Swifts in 1879. Walsall Town Swifts' first match was a draw against Aston Villa. Two players from this early era received international caps; they remain the only Walsall players to be so honoured. In 1882, Alf Jones won the first two of his three caps (against Scotland and Wales) while with Walsall Swifts, and in 1889 Albert Aldridge received the second of his two caps while playing for Walsall Town Swifts. The club was first admitted to the Football League in 1892, as founder members of the new Second Division, but in 1894–95 finished 14th out of 16 teams and failed to be re-elected to the Football League. In 1896 they changed their name to Walsall F.C. and joined the Midland League. A year later, they returned to the Second Division, three teams having failed re-election in 1896. The team finished in sixth place in 1898–99, but once again failed re-election two years later, dropping back into the Midland League. A move to the Birmingham League followed in 1903, and in 1910, the club were elected to the Southern League. With the expansion of the Football League after World War I, Walsall became a founding member of the Third Division North in 1921

Walsall's highest "home" attendance was set in 1930, when they played in of front of 74,600 fans against Aston Villa in the

FA Cup Fourth Round. Although a home match for Walsall, the tie was played at their opponents' Villa Park ground, and it remains the highest attendance that Walsall have ever played in front of.

In 1933, Walsall won 2–0 in the FA Cup against Arsenal at Fellows Park. Arsenal went on to win the First Division that season, and the cup defeat to Third Division North side Walsall is still regarded as one of the greatest upsets in FA Cup history.

Following a reorganisation of the Football League, in 1958, Walsall became founder members of the Fourth Division. Under the management of Bill Moore, the club achieved successive promotions, scoring 102 goals on their way to winning Division Four in 1959–60 and finishing as Division Three runners-up in 1960–61 to reach the second tier of English football for the first time since the early 1900s. Players such as Bill 'Chopper' Guttridge, Tony Richards and Colin Taylor were intrinsically important to the success of the side. After just two seasons in the Second Division, the club were relegated back to Division Three in 1962–63, and remained there until a further demotion to the Fourth Division, in 1978–79.

The club has always had a rich history of producing players who go on to play at the top level. Allan Clarke went on to win the League Championship under Don Revie at Leeds United after beginning life at Fellows Park. Bert Williams and Phil Parkes both became England goalkeepers in the years after they progressed from their roots in Walsall. David Kelly had a long career at the top level after leaving Walsall in 1988, representing the Republic of Ireland at the very highest level of international football. More recently, Michael Ricketts represented England after blossoming at Bolton Wanderers. In recent years, Matty Fryatt and Ishmel Demontagnac have both represented England age-groups.

The club moved to the Bescot Stadium in 1990. At the time it was a state-of-the-art arena, and was only the second new

Football League ground since the 1950s. A Morrisons supermarket was built on the site of the old Fellows Park ground. The arrival at Bescot Stadium saw some stability brought back to the club after two successive relegations. Ex-Wolves star Kenny Hibbitt managed the club for four years, setting the groundwork for a golden era for the club that would follow soon after his dismissal in September 1994.

New manager Chris Nicholl led the club to promotion in his first season, building the nucleus of a strong and under-rated team. Two seasons of stability followed, before Nicholl resigned in 1997.

Ex-Ajax and Danish international Jan Sorensen took the helm after departure. Whilst 'The Saddlers' finished 19th in Division Two that season, the club reached the 4th Round of the League Cup (beating Nottingham Forest and Sheffield United along the way), as well as rampaging through the early rounds of the FA Cup. Lincoln United were dispatched in the first round, whilst league newcomers Macclesfield Town (who until then had been unbeaten at home in all competitions) were beaten 7–0. Peterborough United, who themselves have a rich cup pedigree, were beaten on a bitterly cold Tuesday evening to set up a tie away at Manchester United. Walsall lost 5–1. Sorensen's tenure was marked by the signing of two of the finest players ever to pull on a Walsall shirt. Ivorian-born striker Roger Boli started the season in superb form, becoming a marked man for much of the season which dampened his predatory instincts. However, Boli's fellow Frenchman, Jean Francois 'Jeff' Peron was a shining light in an otherwise poor league. Despite being 32 when arriving in England, Peron's reputation grew, and Bescot increasingly became the home for scouts from the Premiership and Division One. Though he only scored one goal in his solitary season for the Saddlers, he is best remembered for his mesmerising ability with the ball at his feet and the exceptional performance which tore Macclesfield Town to pieces in the aforementioned FA Cup tie.

In 1998–99, ex-Aston Villa winger Ray Graydon took over as manager and led the club to a runners-up spot in Division Two. They were relegated on the final day of the following season, despite derby wins over local rivals Wolverhampton Wanderers, Birmingham City and West Bromwich Albion earlier in the campaign.

WALSALL FOOTBALL CLUB

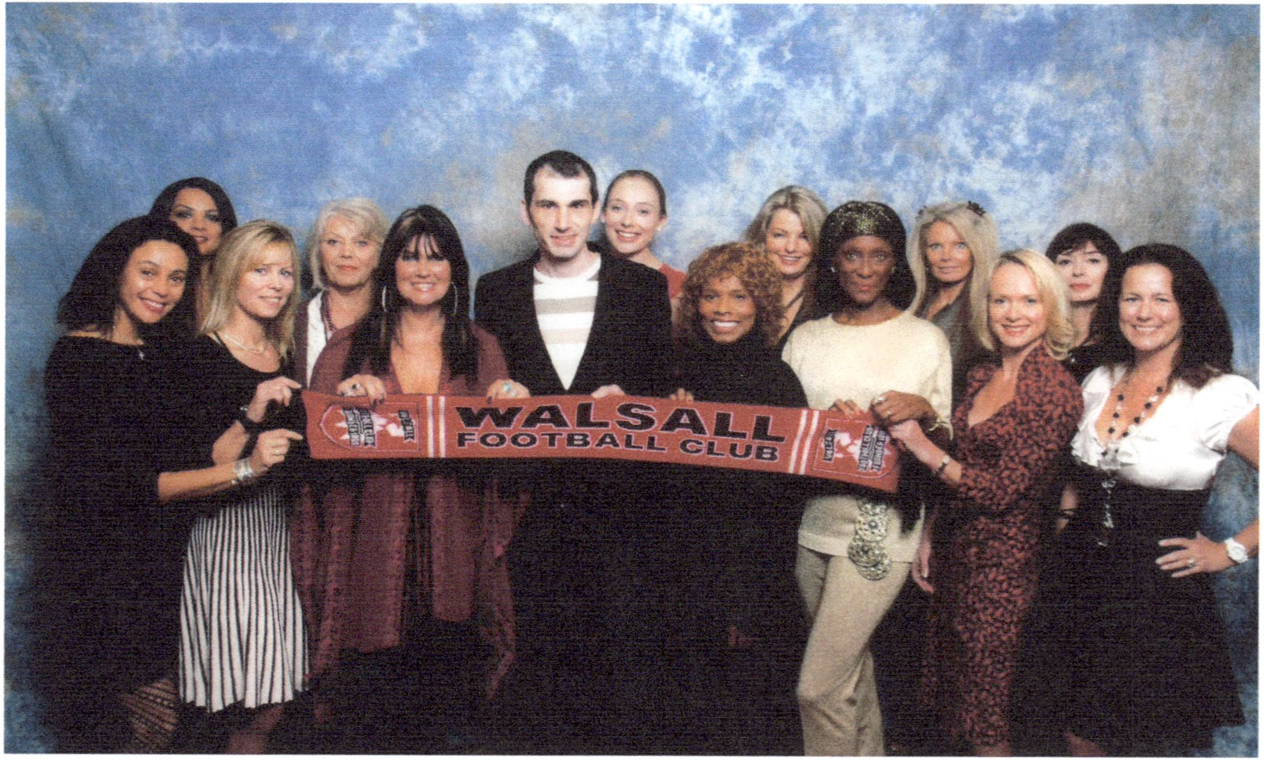
WALSALL
FOOTBALL CLUB

Bond Girls

A Bond girl is a character (or the actress portraying a character) who is a love interest of James Bond in the films made by EON Productions. The girls occasionally have names that are double entendres or puns, such as Pussy Galore, Plenty O'Toole, Xenia Onatopp, or Holly Goodhead, and are considered a "ubiquitous symbol of glamour and sophistication."

There is no set rule on what kind of person a Bond girl will be or what role she will play. Some have been allies whilst others are enemies of Bond. They are often pivotal to the mission or can be simply eye candy. That said, there are female characters such as Judi Dench's M and Miss Moneypenny, who are not romantic interests of Bond, and hence not strictly Bond girls.

The role of a Bond girl, as it has evolved in the films, is typically a high-profile part that can sometimes give a major boost to the career of unestablished actresses, although there have been a number of Bond girls that were well-established beforehand. For instance, Diana Rigg and Honor Blackman were both cast as Bond girls after they had already become stars in England for their roles in the television series, *The Avengers* (in an unusual twist, an unknown Joanna Lumley played "The English Girl" in *On Her Majesty's Secret Service*, and went on to play the lead in the television series *The New Avengers*). In addition, Halle Berry won an Academy Award in

2002—the award was presented to her while she was filming *Die Another Day*. Teri Hatcher was already famous for her role as Lois Lane in the television series *Lois & Clark: The New Adventures of Superman*—and for a photograph in which she is wrapped in nothing but a cape, which became an internet sensation—before she was cast in *Tomorrow Never Dies*. A few years after playing a Bond girl, she became one of the most highly paid actresses on television, starring in *Desperate Housewives*. Kim Basinger had perhaps the most successful post-Bond career. After her break-out role in *Never Say Never Again*, Basinger went on to win an Academy Award for her performance in *L.A. Confidential* and to star in the blockbuster films *Batman* and *8 Mile*.

In this group shot we see many of the girls from the official EON Productions film series included are: Alison Worth, Carole Ashby, Gloria Thomas, Gloria Hendry, Caroline Munro, Caroline Hallett, Toni White, Helene Hunt, Cheryl Anne, Jane Spencer and Margaret Nolan.

They were more than happy to kick off my tour starting in London at the film museum.

WALSALL FOOTBALL CLUB

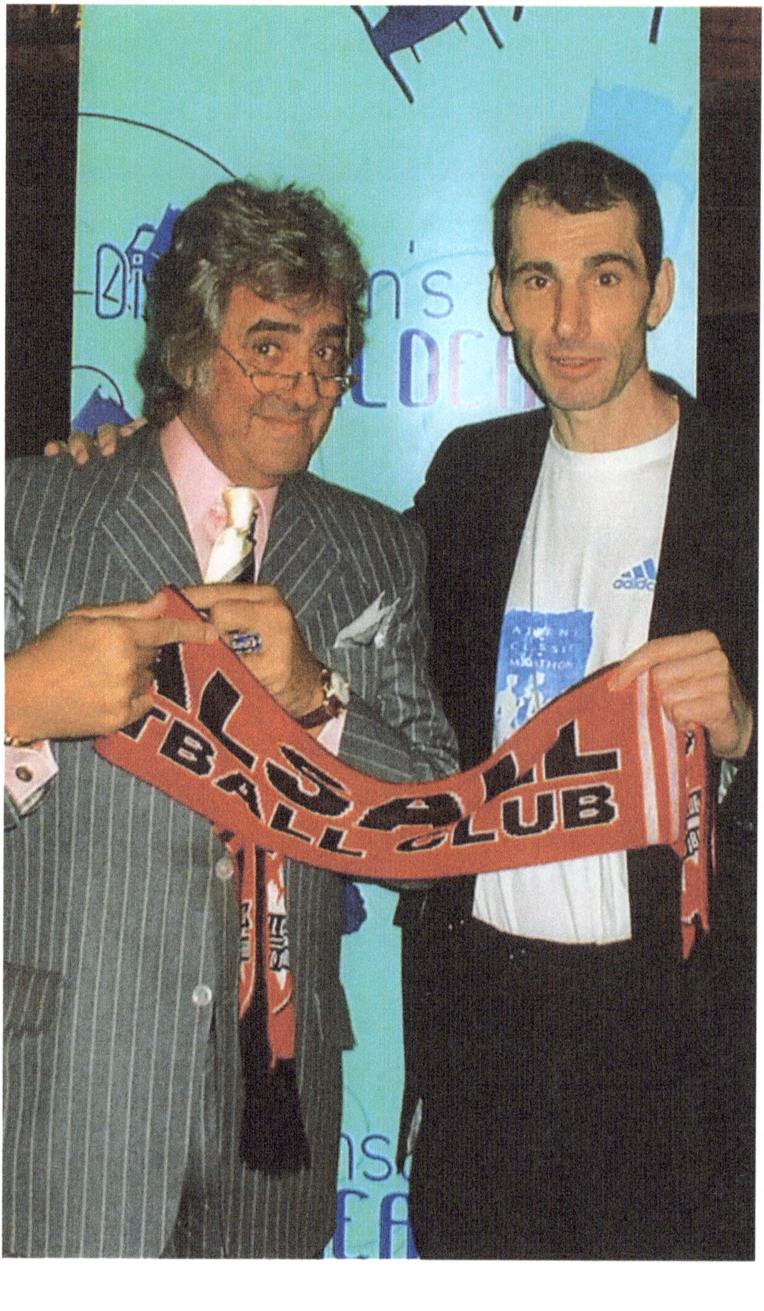

David Dickinson

David Dickinson was born in Cheadle Heath, Stockport, Cheshire, to Eugenie Gulesserian. Eugenie was a member of an Armenian textile trading family, whose father Hrant Gulesserian, had moved from Constantinople to Manchester, England in 1904. Dickinson had corresponded with his biological mother in her later life in Jersey, but they never met. Dickinson's biological father is unknown.

David was eventually adopted by the Dickinsons who were a local couple. Mr. Dickinson died when David was 12, and as his adoptive mother worked hard to keep the family together, David was in part brought up by his French adoptive grandmother Sarah Dickenson. Dickinson began an apprenticeship at an aircraft factory when he was 14, but quickly left to work in the cloth trade in central Manchester. At 19 Dickinson was convicted of fraud and served three years of a four-year sentence in prison, the majority being spent at Strangeways in Manchester.

In 1998 a chance meeting led to Dickinson's TV appearance in a two-part documentary for the BBC made about him and his preparation for a show at Olympia. His dark complexion (often implied to be a fake tan, but he claims that it's because of his Armenian ancestry) and numerous catchphrases quickly caught the viewers' attention. He often describes particularly excellent items as "real bobby-dazzlers", poor items as "a load of tat," and bargains as being "as cheap as chips"

Dickinson came to public attention as an antiques expert on *This Morning* and BBC Two's *The Antiques Show*. His career break as a TV celebrity came from presenting the game show *Bargain Hunt* on BBC One at lunchtimes which gained a keen following amongst daytime viewers including students.

He went on to present a reality show, *Dealing With Dickinson* on BBC1 in 2005 which was cancelled after only one series. Dickinson left the BBC once the primetime editions of *Bargain Hunt* were cancelled.

Dickinson moved to ITV in 2006 to present a new daytime antiques programme, *Dickinson's Real Deal* which is broadcast on daytime weekday afternoons. The show visits locations around the UK where people come in and either sell their antiques to a dealer for cash. Alternatively, they take a gamble and go to auction if the dealer's offer is refused or no offer is made to buy the object. Dickinson's job is to act as a mediator to help the sellers obtain the best prices from the dealers or to help them with the decision about whether to refuse the offer and to take the item to auction.

Seen here on a visit to Walsall Town Hall for a recording of the show Dickinson was a particularly amenable gentleman who spent much of his time mingling with the crowd.

WALSALL FOOTBALL CLUB

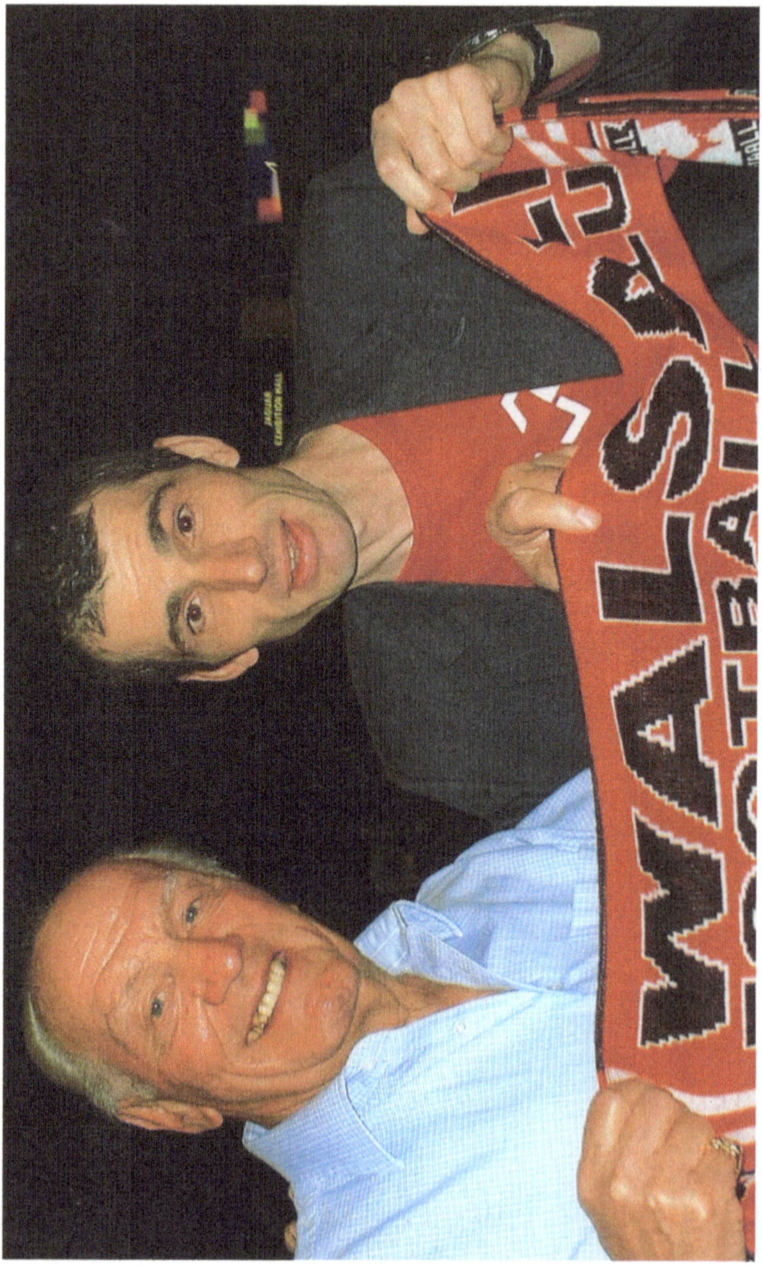

Sir Henry Cooper

Sir Henry Cooper was an English heavyweight boxer known for the effectiveness of his left hook, "Enry's 'Ammer", and his knockdown of the young Muhammad Ali. Cooper held the British, Commonwealth and European heavyweight titles several times throughout his career, and unsuccessfully challenged Ali for the world heavyweight championship in 1966.

Following his retirement from the sport, Cooper continued his career as a television and radio personality and was enormously popular in Britain: he was the first (and is today one of just three people) to twice win the public vote for BBC Sports Personality of the Year Award and is thus far the only boxer to be awarded a knighthood.

Although Cooper is best known for knocking down Muhammad Ali, he defeated a string of well known heavyweights during his career, including; Zora Folley, Roy Harris, Karl Mildenberger, Alex Miteff, Wayne Bethea, Brian London, Joe Erskine, Jose Manuel Urtain, Piero Tomasoni, Dick Wipperman, Dick Richardson, Billy Walker, Tony Hughes, Jack Bodell, Jefferson Davis and Gawie De Clerk.

After his retirement from boxing Henry Cooper maintained a high public profile with appearances in the BBC quiz show *A Question of Sport* and various advertisements, most famously in those for Brut aftershave, which have been credited with removing a lingering suspicion among the British that men who wore cologne were effeminate. Although generally a traditionalist, Cooper abhorred racism; his grandfather was an Irish immigrant and Cooper became the first celebrity sponsor of the Anti-Nazi League, a largely left-wing campaign against far-right groups which were agitating against immigration. He was also active in charity events. He appeared as boxer John Gully in the 1975 film *Royal Flash* and in his later years featured in a series of UK public service announcements urging vulnerable groups to go to their doctor for vaccination against influenza called *Get your Jab in First*

Cooper had become a 'name' at Lloyd's of London, a supposedly 'blue chip' investment, but in the 1990s he was reportedly one of those who suffered enormous personal losses because of the unlimited liability which a 'name' was then responsible for, and he was forced to sell his hard won Lonsdale belts. Subsequently, Cooper's enduring popularity as an after dinner speaker provided a source of income and he was in most respects a picture of contentment until the death of his wife, Albina.

Seen here at The Ricoh Arena in Coventry Henry was as charming and well-mannered as he ever was on our screens. A true gentleman in what can only be described as a brutal sport.

Cooper died on 1 May 2011 at his son's house in Oxted, Surrey, after a long illness, just days shy of his 77th birthday.

WALSALL FOOTBALL CLUB

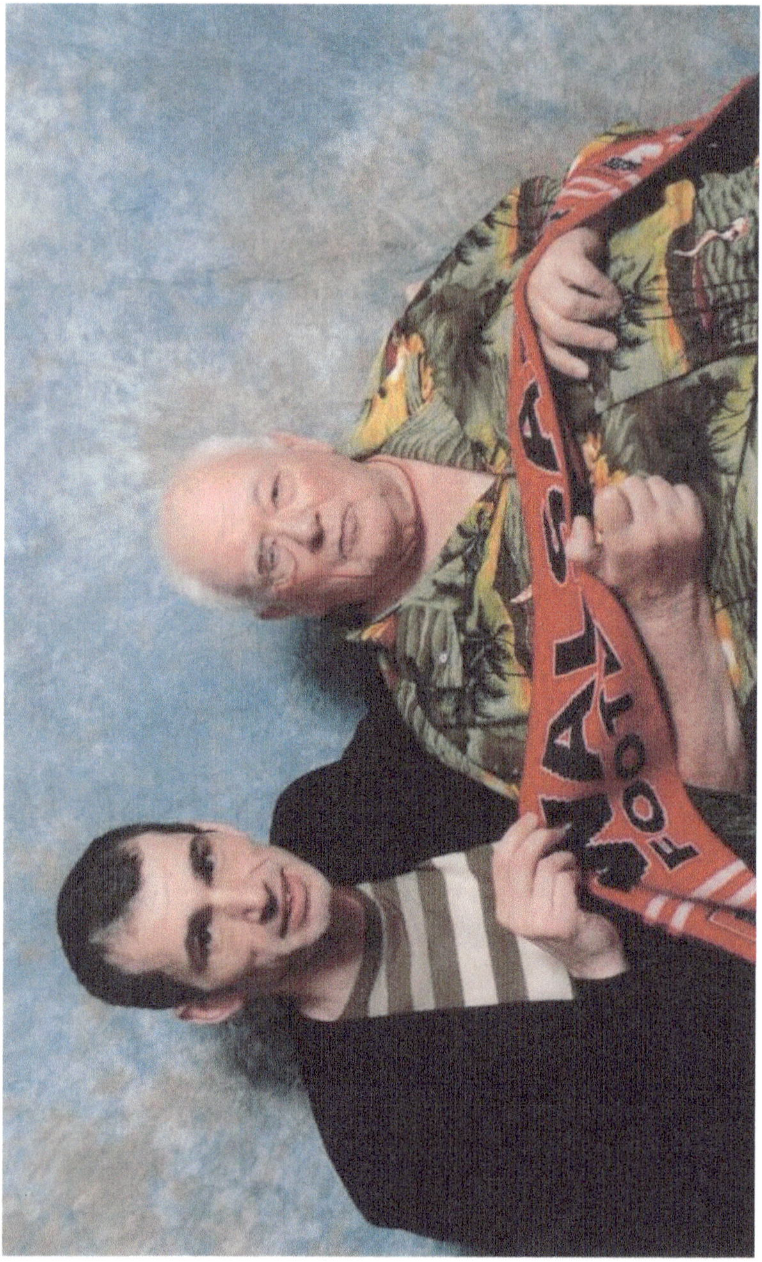

Sir Patrick Moore

Sir Patrick Alfred Caldwell-Moore, to give him his full name, was an English amateur astronomer who attained prominent status in that field as a writer, researcher, radio commentator and television presenter.

Moore was president of the British Astronomical Association, co-founder and president of the Society for Popular Astronomy (SPA), author of over 70 books on astronomy, and presenter of the world's longest-running television series with the same original presenter, the BBC's *The Sky at Night*. As an amateur astronomer, he became known as a specialist in Moon observation and for creating the Caldwell catalogue. Idiosyncrasies such as his rapid diction and monocle made him a popular and instantly recognisable figure on British television.

Moore was also a self-taught xylophone, glockenspiel player and pianist, as well as an accomplished composer. Amongst other sports he played as an amateur were cricket, golf and chess. In addition to many popular science books, he wrote numerous works of fiction. Moore was an opponent of fox hunting, an outspoken critic of the European Union, supporter of the UK Independence Party and served as chairman of the short-lived anti-immigration United Country Party. He served in the Royal Air Force during World War II; during which his fiancée was tragically killed by a bomb. After such an event he never married.

In 1945, Moore was elected a fellow of the Royal Astronomical Society; in 1977 he was awarded the society's Jackson-Gwilt Medal. In 1968, he was made an officer of the Order of the British Empire (OBE) and promoted to a Commander (CBE) of the order in 1988. In 1999 he became the honorary president of the East Sussex Astronomical Society, a position he held until his death. In 2001, he was knighted for "services to the popularisation of science and to broadcasting" In the same year; he was appointed an Honorary Fellow of the Royal Society, the only amateur astronomer ever to achieve the distinction. In June 2002, he was appointed as the honorary vice president of the Society for the History of Astronomy. Also in 2002, Buzz Aldrin presented him with a British Academy of Film and Television Arts (BAFTA) award for services to television He was patron of Torquay Boys' Grammar School in south Devon. Moore had a long association with the University of Leicester and its Department of Physics and Astronomy, and was awarded an honorary Doctor of Science degree in 1996, and a Distinguished Honorary Fellowship in 2008, the highest award the university can give.

Moore believed himself to be the only person to have met the first man to fly, Orville Wright, the first man in space, Yuri Gagarin, and the first man on the moon, Neil Armstrong, and on this occasion had the honour of topping that achievement by holding the Walsall FC scarf.

Sir Patrick Moore died on 9 December 2012 aged 89.

WALSALL FOOTBALL CLUB

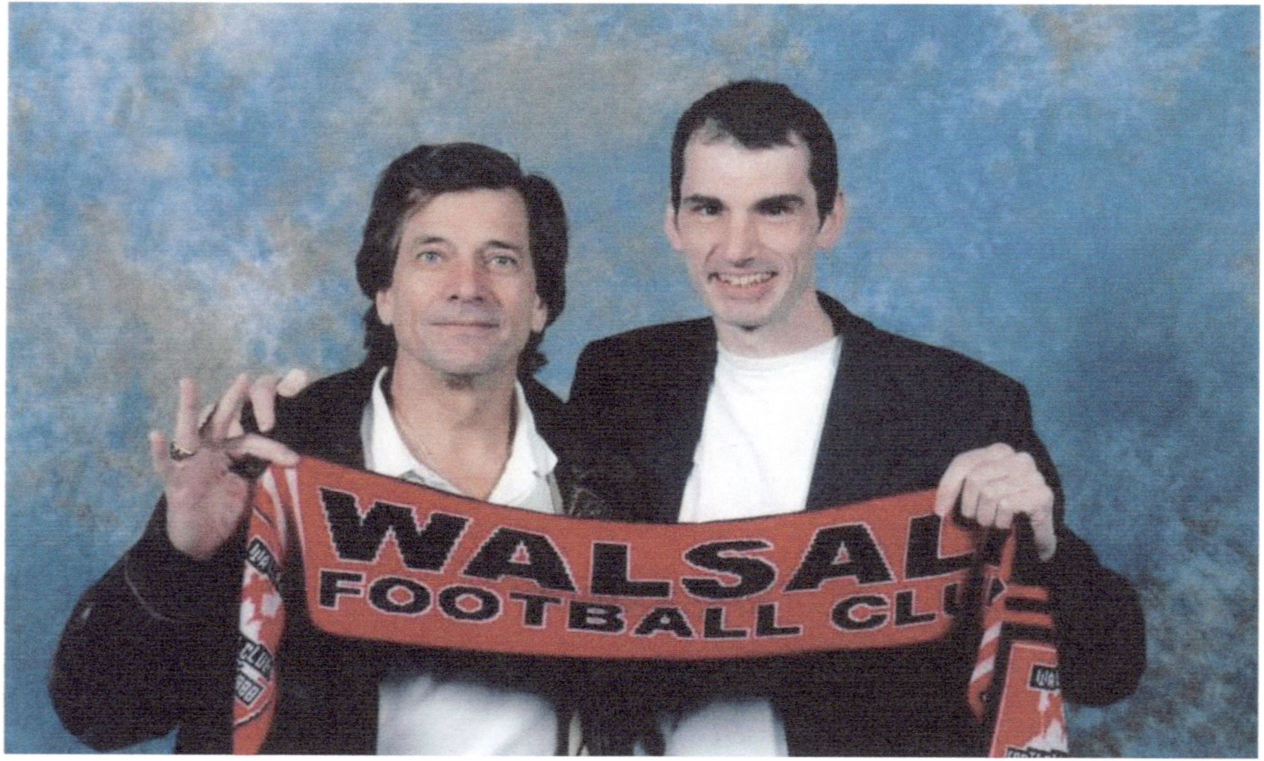
WALSA
FOOTBALL CL

Dirk Benedict

Dirk Benedict is an American movie, television and stage actor perhaps best known for his portrayal of Lieutenant Templeton "Faceman" Peck in *The A-Team* television series and Lieutenant Starbuck in the original *Battlestar Galactica* film and television series.

Benedict was born Dirk Niewoehner in Helena, Montana, the son of Pricilla Mella, an accountant and George Edward Niewoehner, a lawyer. He grew up in White Sulphur Springs, Montana. He graduated from Whitman College in 1967. Benedict allegedly chose his stage name from a serving of Eggs Benedict he had enjoyed prior to his acting career.

Benedict's film debut was in the 1972 film *Georgia, Georgia*. When the New York run for *Butterflies Are Free* ended, he received an offer to repeat his performance in Hawaii, opposite Barbara Rush. While there, he appeared as a guest lead on *Hawaii Five-O*. The producers of a horror film called *Ssssss* saw Benedict's performance in *Hawaii Five-O* and promptly cast him as the lead in that movie. He next played the psychotic wife-beating husband of Twiggy in her American film debut, *W*. Benedict starred in the television series *Chopper One* which aired for one season in 1974. He also made an appearance in *Charlie's Angels*.

Benedict's career break came in 1978 when he appeared as Lieutenant Starbuck in the movie and television series *Battlestar Galactica*. In 1979 Benedict starred in the ensemble movie

Scavenger Hunt. In 1982, Dirk gained further popularity as con-man Lieutenant Templeton "Face" Peck in 1980s action television series, *The A-Team*. He played "Faceman" from 1982 to 1986 (although the series didn't air until January 1983, and the final episode wasn't shown until the 1987 re-runs). The second season episode, "Steel," includes a scene at Universal Studios where Face is seen looking bemused as a Cylon walks by him – an in-joke to his previous role in *Battlestar Galactica*. The clip was also incorporated into the series' opening credit sequence from the third season onward.

In 1986 Dirk Benedict starred as a low-life band manager "Harry Smilac" in the movie *Body Slam* along with Lou Albano, Roddy Piper, and cameo appearances by Freddie Blassie, Ric Flair, and Bruno Sammartino. His character Smilac ends up managing the pro-wrestler "Quick Rick Roberts" (Piper) and faces opposition by Captain Lou and his wrestling tag-team "the Cannibals".

The scarf had a few near misses in trying to catch up with Dirk, before finally meeting him at the Ricoh Arena in Coventry.

WALSALL FOOTBALL CLUB

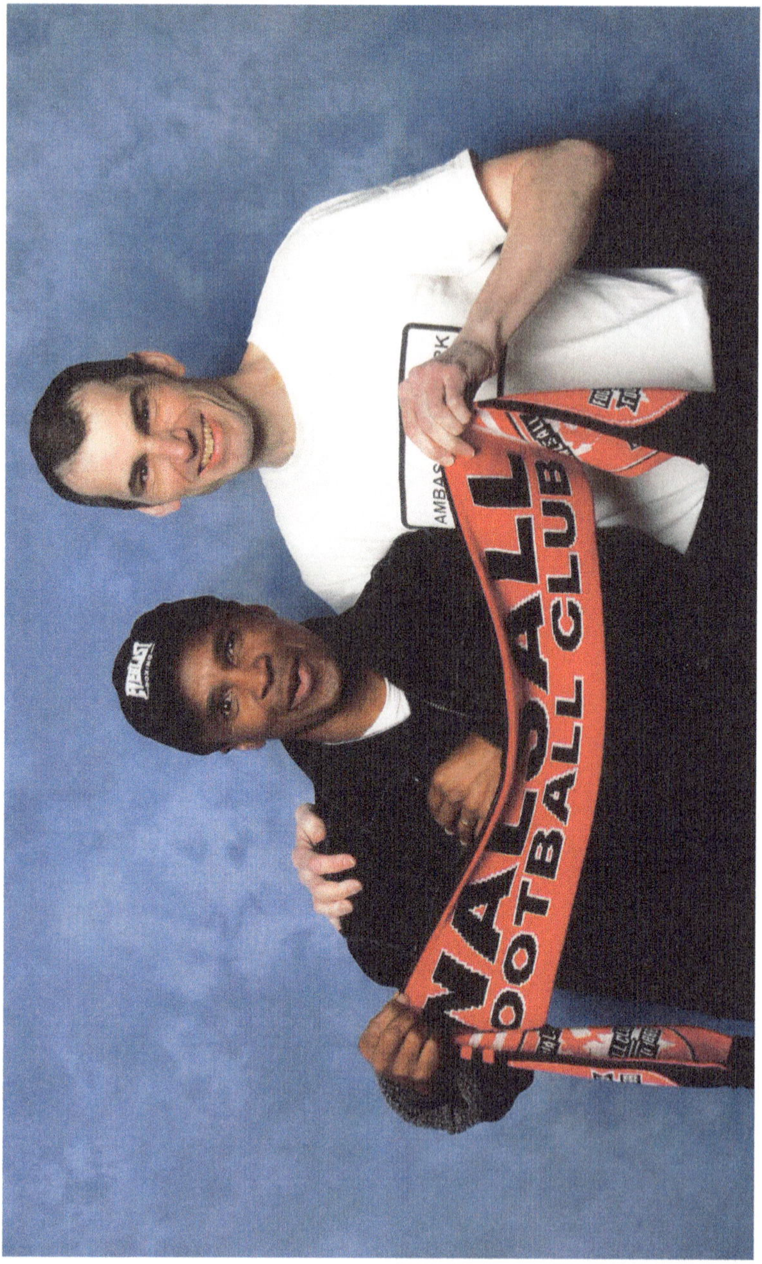
OTBALL CLUB

Sugar Ray Leonard

Taking his name from his mother's favorite singer, Ray Charles, Leonard was the first boxer to earn more than $100 million in purses, win world titles in five weight divisions and defeated future fellow International Boxing Hall of Fame inductees Wilfred Benítez, Thomas Hearns, Roberto Durán and Marvin Hagler during a glittering career which spanned two decades. Leonard was named "Boxer of the Decade" for the 1980s.

Leonard started boxing at the Palmer Park recreation center in 1969. His older brother, Roger, started boxing first. Roger helped start the boxing program, urging the centre's director, Ollie Dunlap to form a team. Dave Jacobs, a former boxer, and Janks Morton volunteered as boxing coaches. Roger won some trophies and showed them off in front of Ray, goading him to start boxing.

In 1976, Leonard made the U.S. Olympic Team as a light welterweight. A team which included Leon and Michael Spinks, Howard Davis, Jr., Leo Randolph, Charles Mooney and John Tate. Surely one of the greatest teams ever put together in the history of the Olympics.

After winning the gold medal in stunning form, Leonard announced, "I'm finished…I've fought my last fight. My journey has ended, my dream is fulfilled. Now I want to go to school."

This changed when his father was hospitalized with meningitis and his mother suffered a heart attack. With neither parent able to work, and a child and girlfriend to support, Leonard decided to become a professional boxer.

Leonard fought Wilfred Benitez for the WBC Welterweight Championship in November 1979 at Caesar's Palace in Las Vegas, Nevada. The victorious Leonard received $1 million and Benitez, a two-division champion with a record of 38–0–1, received $1.2 million.

Leonard returned to Montreal to defend this title against Roberto Durán. Durán, the former World Lightweight Champion, had a record of 71–1 and was the #1 welterweight contender. Leonard was to suffer his first professional loss in this bout and went on to fight Duran again in New Orleans which saw Duran quit the ring in round eight.

Leonard moved up to the junior middleweight division and successfully defeated Ayub Kalule on June 25, 1981 at the Astrodome in Houston, Texas. Kalule, who was 36–0, had been the WBA Light Middleweight Champion for two years.

Forced to retire in 1982 Leonard returned and was successful in bouts with the likes of Hagler, Lalonde, Hearns for a second time and another return match with Duran.

After hanging up his gloves for good, Leonard worked as an actor appearing in numerous television shows, including *Half & Half*, *L.A. Heat*, *Married With Children*, *Renegade* and *Tales From The Crypt*. He has appeared in several movies, including *I Spy*. He also worked as an adviser in the 2011 robot boxing film *Real Steel*. Here he holds the scarf during a visit to Northampton.

WALSALL FOOTBALL CLUB

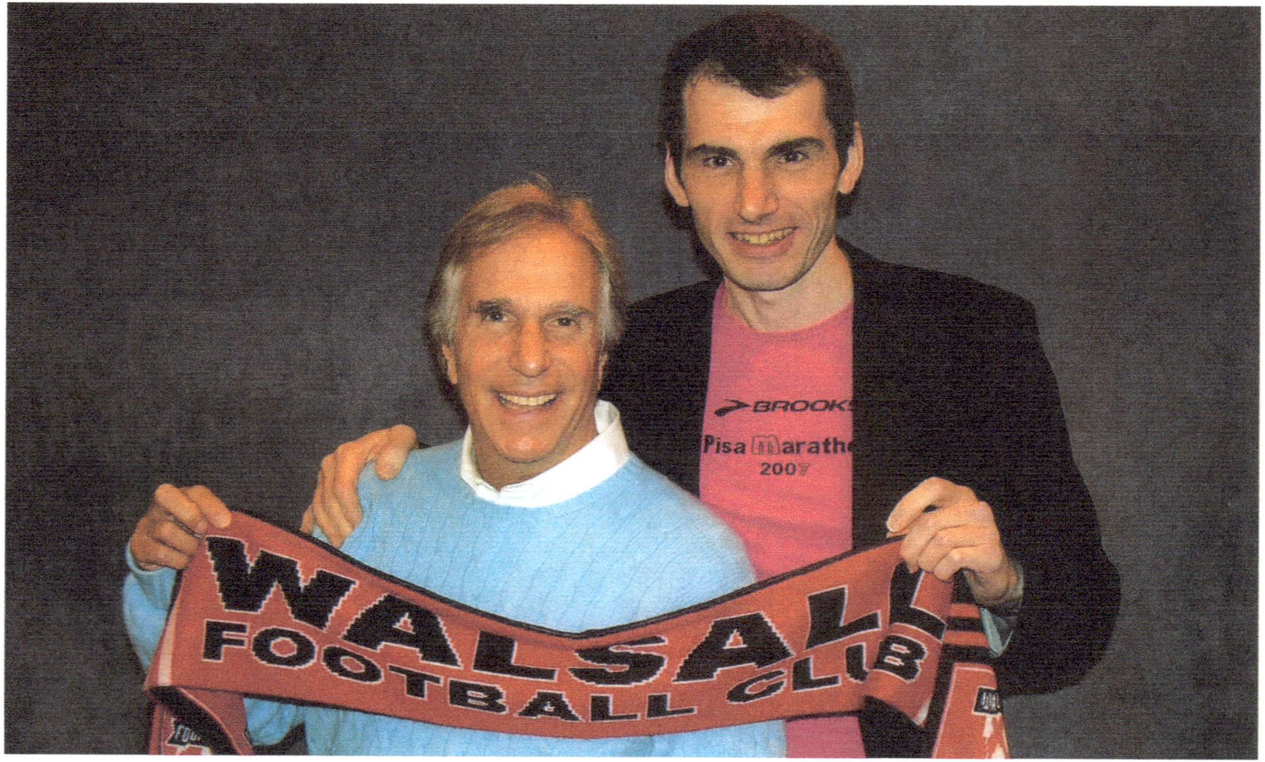
WALSAL
FOOTBALL CL
BROOKS
Pisa Marathe
2007

Henry Winkler

Winkler, is probably best known for his role as Fonzie on the 1970s American sitcom *Happy Days*. As the leather-clad greaser and auto mechanic, who started out as a minor character at the show's beginning, but had achieved top billing by the time the series ended.

He began his acting career appearing in a number of television commercials. He found a niche in episodes of *The Mary Tyler Moore Show* and *The Bob Newhart Show*. However, it was not until October 1973, when he was cast for the role of Arthur Herbert Fonzarelli, nicknamed "The Fonz" or "Fonzie", in the long-running 1970s television series *Happy Days* that his career really took off and gave him his big break.

During his decade on *Happy Days*, Winkler also starred in a number of movies, including *The Lords of Flatbush* (1974), playing a troubled Vietnam veteran in *Heroes* (1977), *The One and Only* (1978), *An American Christmas Carol* (TV movie, 1979) and a morgue attendant in *Night Shift* (1982), which was directed by *Happy Days* co-star Ron Howard. Winkler was also one of the hosts of the 1979 Music for UNICEF Concert.

After *Happy Days*, Winkler concentrated on producing and directing. Within months, he had opened Winkler-Rich Productions. He produced several television shows including *MacGyver*, *So Weird* and *Mr. Sunshine*, *Sightings*, and the game shows *Wintuition* and *Hollywood Squares* – the latter from 2002–2004; occasionally serving as a sub-announcer. He also directed several movies including the Billy Crystal movie *Memories of Me* (1988) and *Cop and a Half* (1993) with Burt Reynolds.

Since 2003, he has collaborated with Lin Oliver on a series of children's books about a 4th grade boy, Hank Zipzer, who is dyslexic. Winkler also has the learning disability, which was not diagnosed until he was 31 and his stepson Jed was tested; the dyslexia was an unhappy part of his childhood. Winkler has published 17 books about his hero Zipzer, the "world's greatest underachiever".

In July 2008, Winkler joined First News on their annual Reading Tour of schools where he read excerpts from his Hank Zipzer books. This has since become an annual tour. In 2011 he donated books to Holy Rosary School PA . The school was flooded out by Tropical Storm Lee.

Winkler married Stacey Furstman Weitzman in 1978; they have two children, Zoe, Max and a stepson, Jed, from Stacey's previous marriage. Henry was the 9th King of the Bacchus Mardi Gras Parade in New Orleans in 1977 the theme was "Happily Ever After".

Here, the scarf caught up with him in Milton Keynes during a signing session for his books.

WALSALL FOOTBALL CLUB

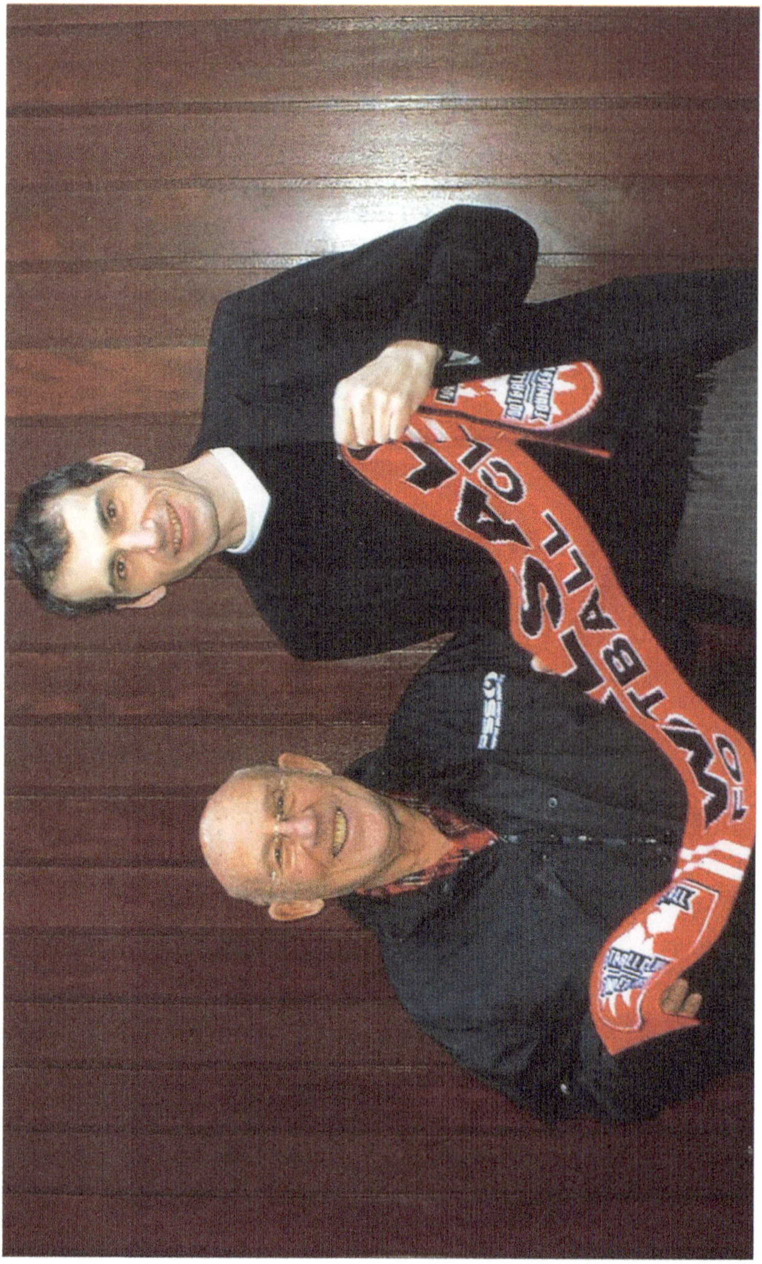

Sir Stirling Moss

Sir Stirling Craufurd Moss, OBE is a former racing driver whose successes in a variety of categories placed him among the world's elite—he is often called "the greatest driver never to win the World Championship".

Moss, who raced from 1948 to 1962, won 212 of the 529 races he entered, including 16 Formula One Grands Prix. He would compete in as many as 62 races in a single year and drove 84 different makes of car over the course of his racing career, including such machines as Lotus, Vanwall, Maserati, Jaguar, Ferrari and Porsche. Like many drivers of the era, he competed in several formulae—very often on the same day. He retired in 1962 when a crash left him in a coma for a month, as afterwards he felt unable to continue driving at a professional level. In spite of this early retirement he has remained a well-known figure.

Away from driving, in 1962 he acted as a colour commentator for ABC's Wide World of Sports for Formula One and NASCAR races. He eventually left ABC in 1980 when he made a brief driving comeback in the British Touring Car Championship with Audi, alongside Martin Brundle. He also competed in the 1974 World Cup Rally in a Mercedes-Benz, but retired from the event in the Algerian Sahara.

In more recent years he continued to race in historic competition, including racing his own OSCA FS 372 during the 2009 season. On 9 June 2011 during the Le Mans Legends qualifying session Sir Stirling Moss announced his retirement from racing to listeners on Radio Le Mans, this time for good.

For many years during and after his career, the rhetorical phrase "Who do you think you are, Stirling Moss?" was supposedly the standard question all British policemen asked speeding motorists. Moss relates he himself was once stopped for speeding and asked just that; he reports the traffic officer had some difficulty believing him. As related in the book *The Life and Times of Private Eye*, Moss was the subject of a less than respectful cartoon biography in the magazine *Private Eye*. The cartoon, drawn by Willie Rushton, showed him continually crashing, having his driving licence revoked and finally "hosting television programmes on subjects he knows nothing about". It also made reference to the amnesia Moss suffered from as a result of head injuries sustained in the crash at Goodwood in 1962. According to the book, Moss responded by offering to buy the original of the cartoon, an outcome the book describes as "depressingly common" for its satirical cartoons about famous people.

Sir Stirling lives in Mayfair London and was more than accommodating when he invited the scarf to his home one summer.

WALSALL FOOTBALL CLUB

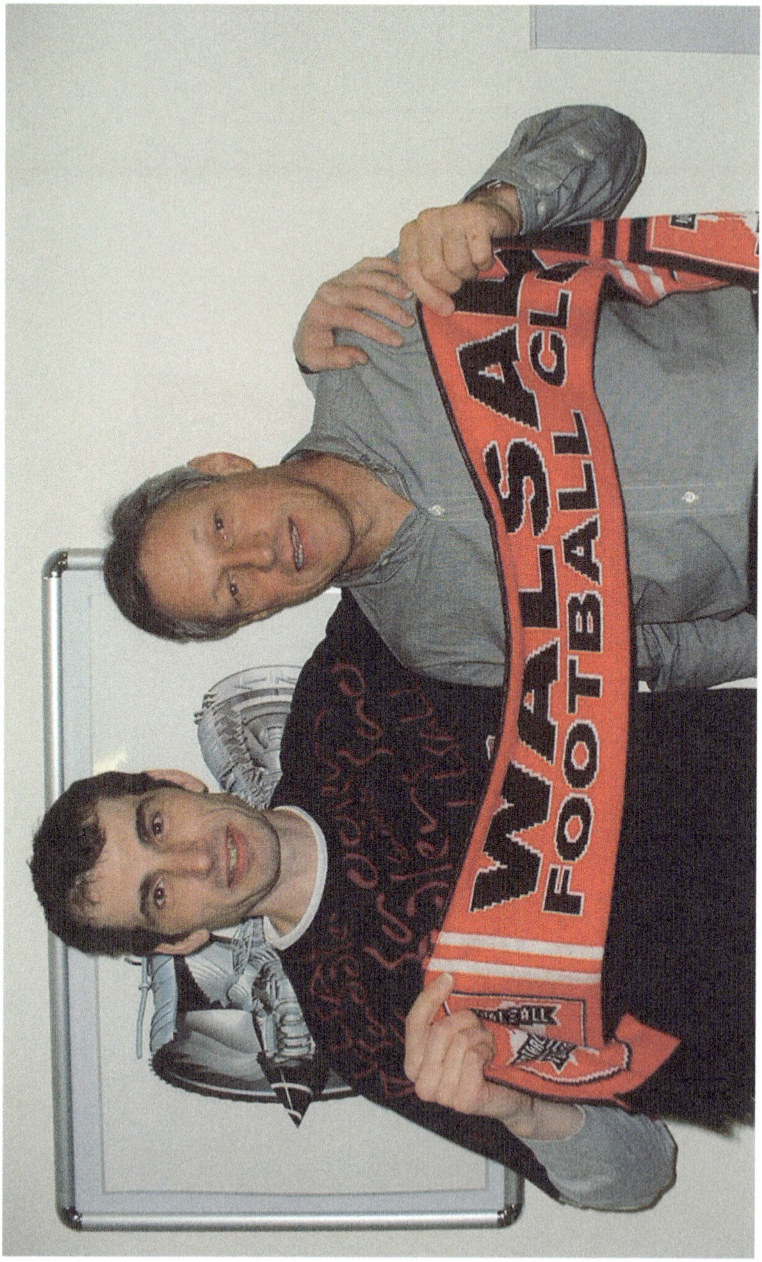
FOOTBALL

Allan Wells

Allan Wipper Wells is a former Scottish and British multi title winning athlete. He became Olympic Champion in the 100 metres at the 1980 games in Moscow. Within a fortnight he took on and beat America's best sprinters at an invitational meeting in Koblenz. In 1981 Wells was both the Golden Sprints and World Cup gold medalist. He is also a three time European Cup gold medalist among many of his other sprint successes.

Wells' big breakthrough came at the start of the 1978 season, when his times and victories began to improve, and he won the UK 100/200 Championships. British sprinters had made little impression on the international scene, and the sight of the Scot winning two gold medals (200 m, 4 x 100 m) and a silver (100 m) at the Commonwealth Games in Edmonton, Canada, was a surprise for British athletics fans.

This success continued in 1979, when he won the European Cup 200 metres in Turin, Italy, beating the new World record holder Pietro Mennea on his home ground; he also finished 3rd in the 100 metres.

In Moscow, a 28 year old Wells qualified for the final, with a new British record 10.11 seconds where he faced pre-race favourite Silvio Leonard of Cuba. By 60 metres the field were fading, and by 80 metres the race was between Leonard on the inside and Wells on the outside. Wells edged ahead, but Leonard drew even again. With seven metres to go Wells began an extreme lean which allowed his head and shoulder to cross the finish line 3 inches (76 mm) before Leonard's chest in a photo finish; both men were given a final time of 10.25. In doing so, Wells became the oldest Olympic 100 m champion at that time. He was also the last white male athlete to win the Olympic 100 metres title.

In 1982, in Brisbane, Queensland, Australia, Wells won two more Commonwealth titles in the 100 m, 200 m and a bronze medal in the relay. He shared the 200 m title with Mike McFarlane of England in a rare dead heat.

After his retirement he went on to become a coach for the British bobsleigh team. His wife Margot Wells was also a Scottish 100 m and 100 m hurdles champion, and they are now based in Guildford, Surrey where she is a fitness consultant and Allan is a systems engineer. Wells was also inducted alongside Eric Liddell and Wyndham Halswelle (two other former Scottish Athletic Olympic Champions) into the Scottish Sports Hall of Fame. Allan currently coaches the Bank of Scotland specialist sprint squad alongside another former Scottish sprinter, Ian Mackie. Wells' personal best for the 100 metres is 10.11, and for the 200 metres is 20.21, run at the Moscow 1980 Games and both are still Scottish records.

Shown here the scarf got a favourable invitation by Wells at Guildford University in their engineering department, although he had injured his shoulder earlier in the week on the golf course.

WALSALL FOOTBALL CLUB

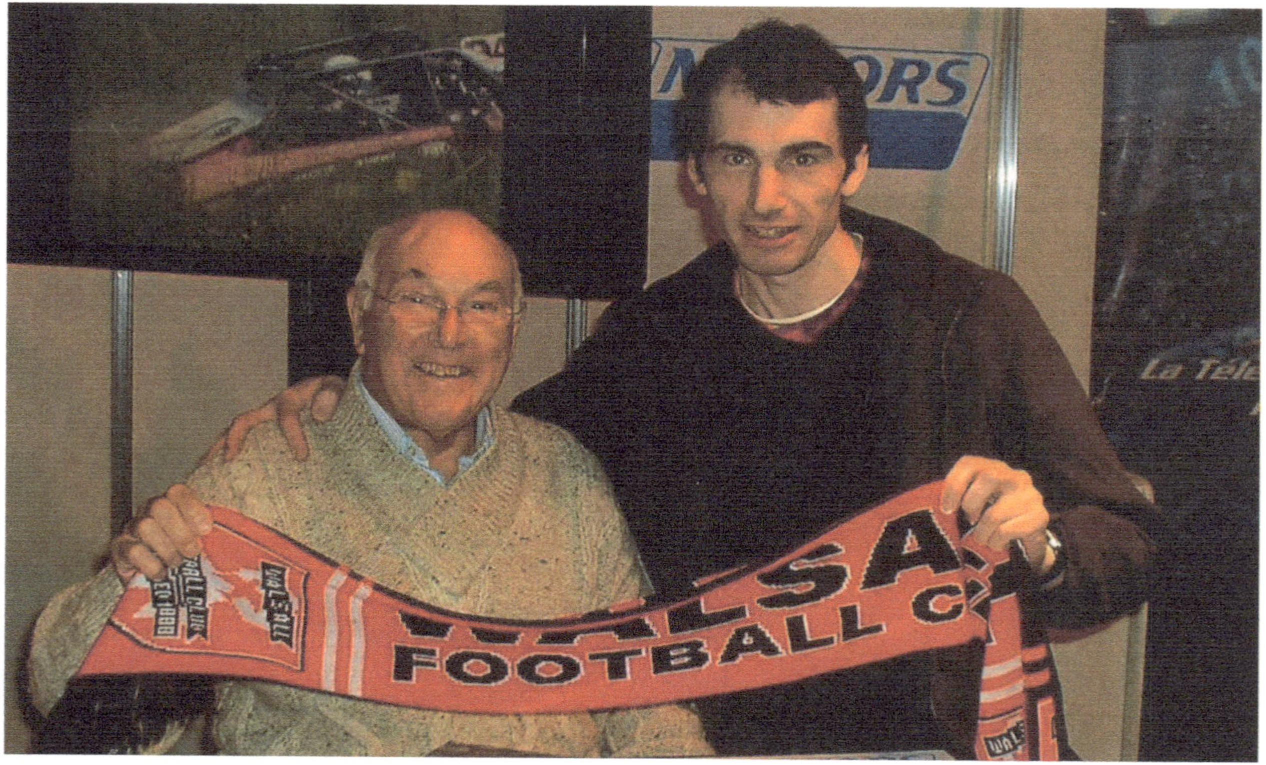
FOOTBALL

Murray Walker

Graeme Murray Walker is known throughout the country and motor racing circles for his distinctive, enthusiastic commentary style on the sport. Since 1978, British television commentary of the Formula 1 seasons has been used by other broadcasters right around the world, including Australia and Japan. He was an exponent of the commentator's curse, noting in an interview that he might say how well a driver was racing or that they would probably win the race, only to have them retire or crash out of the race shortly thereafter, hence his catch-phrase "...*Unless I'm very much mistaken...*" which might lead shortly after to a correction "...*And I am very much mistaken...*".

In his time Walker rarely criticised drivers and preferred to give the benefit of the doubt in attributing blame for incidents. One example of this was during the 1994 Australian Grand Prix where, following the controversial crash between Michael Schumacher and Walker's close friend Damon Hill which decided the World Drivers' Championship in the German's favour, Walker, unlike his fellow commentators at the time, most notably former 500cc Motorcycle World Champion Barry Sheene, declined to blame Schumacher outright for the crash.

His first regular work was on radio covering of the Isle of Man TT, initially alongside his father. After Graham's death in 1962, Murray took over the lead role. He commentated on motocross (initially for ITV) during the 1960s and rally cross in the 1970s and early 1980s. He occasionally commentated on motorcycle racing and rallying. Walker also covered the BTCC for the BBC between 1988 and 1997, and the Macao event for Hong Kong TV on nine occasions.

His Formula One coverage from 1980 to 1993 saw Walker strike up a surprisingly successful and extremely popular double act with 1976 World Champion James Hunt. Initially they did not get on, as Hunt's interests, personality and private life appeared to have little in common with Walker's. Murray and James were to work together for more than a decade at the BBC, until Hunt's sudden death from a heart attack the day after the 1993 Canadian Grand Prix. When in the commentary booth together, Walker would provide his typically animated descriptions of the action, with Hunt bringing in his expert knowledge and often opinionated nature, to his co-commentary role.

After Hunt died, former F1 driver Jonathan Palmer joined Walker in the commentary box until the end of 1996. The following year, the television rights for the UK coverage transferred to ITV, and Walker followed. His co-commentator from the 1997 season onwards until his retirement from commentating was another F1 driver Martin Brundle.

This appearance with Walker took place at the Autosport International show in Birmingham whilst Murray was promoting his new photographic autobiography.

WALSALL FOOTBALL CLUB

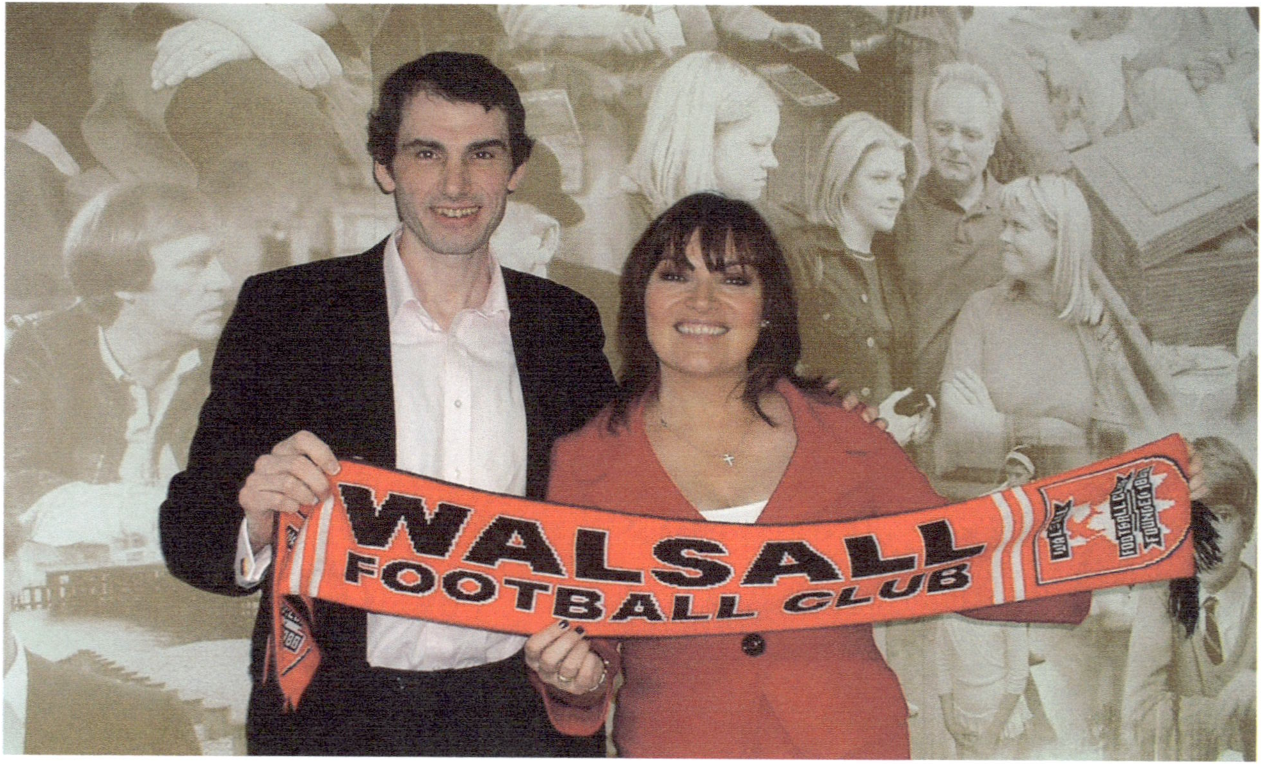
WALSALL
FOOTBALL CLUB

Lorraine Kelly

Lorraine Kelly was born in Gorbals, Glasgow in 1959. Her father, John, worked as a television repairman. She spent the first few years of her life in Glasgow before the family moved to East Kilbride where she attended Claremont High School. She turned down a university place to read English and Russian in favour of a job on the *East Kilbride News*, her local newspaper, and then joined BBC Scotland as a researcher in 1983. It was during this time that she moved to TV-am as an on-screen reporter covering Scottish news in 1984.

After five years in this role she went on to present TV-am's *Summer Sunday* programme with chief reporter Geoff Meade, and in February 1990 she became a main presenter of *Good Morning Britain* alongside Mike Morris.

She was heavily involved in launching GMTV in January 1993, and presented a range of programmes, including the main breakfast show with Eamonn Holmes. She presented her show *GMTV with Lorraine* which aired Monday to Thursday after GMTV, during an unbroken run from 1994 until late 2010. According to the *Sunday Mirror*, Kelly was banned from appearing in an advertising campaign for Asda because her boss, GMTV's managing director Clive Couch, feared that such a move would lead to more bad publicity for GMTV, which was fined £2 million by broadcasting regulator Ofcom in September for conning viewers with its premium-rate phone lines.

In September 2010, GMTV came to an end, and ITV Breakfast took over. *Lorraine* launched with a brand new look, alongside *Daybreak*, and airs every weekday during the final hour of the show. Each day the presenter gives a brief introduction describing what's coming up on the show, before discussing the main stories from the morning's newspapers with a male and female reviewer. On Fridays this is replaced by a showbiz update from Dan Wootton and a LA update from Ross King. In an eclectic show on Wednesdays we are treated to fashion from Mark Heyes and Thursdays feature money-saving advice from Martin Lewis. A summary of the day's news is shown at 09:00 from the *Daybreak* studio, presented by Ranvir Singh.

The chef who is appearing that week then cooks their dish for the day in "Lorraine's Kitchen", before the final guest's makes their appearance. The competition that runs on *Daybreak* also appears throughout the show. The programme was sponsored by Garnier, having been previously being backed by Actimel and Jergans Naturals.

In a recent survey she was voted the celebrity most people would like to buy a car from, as well as being described as 'TV's best loved sofa star' in another article published by the Daily Mail.

It was during a break at the end of her schedule that Lorraine Kelly took hold of the scarf after a dash by its owner through London's streets to be at the studios for the rendezvous, even though it was getting late.

WALSALL FOOTBALL CLUB

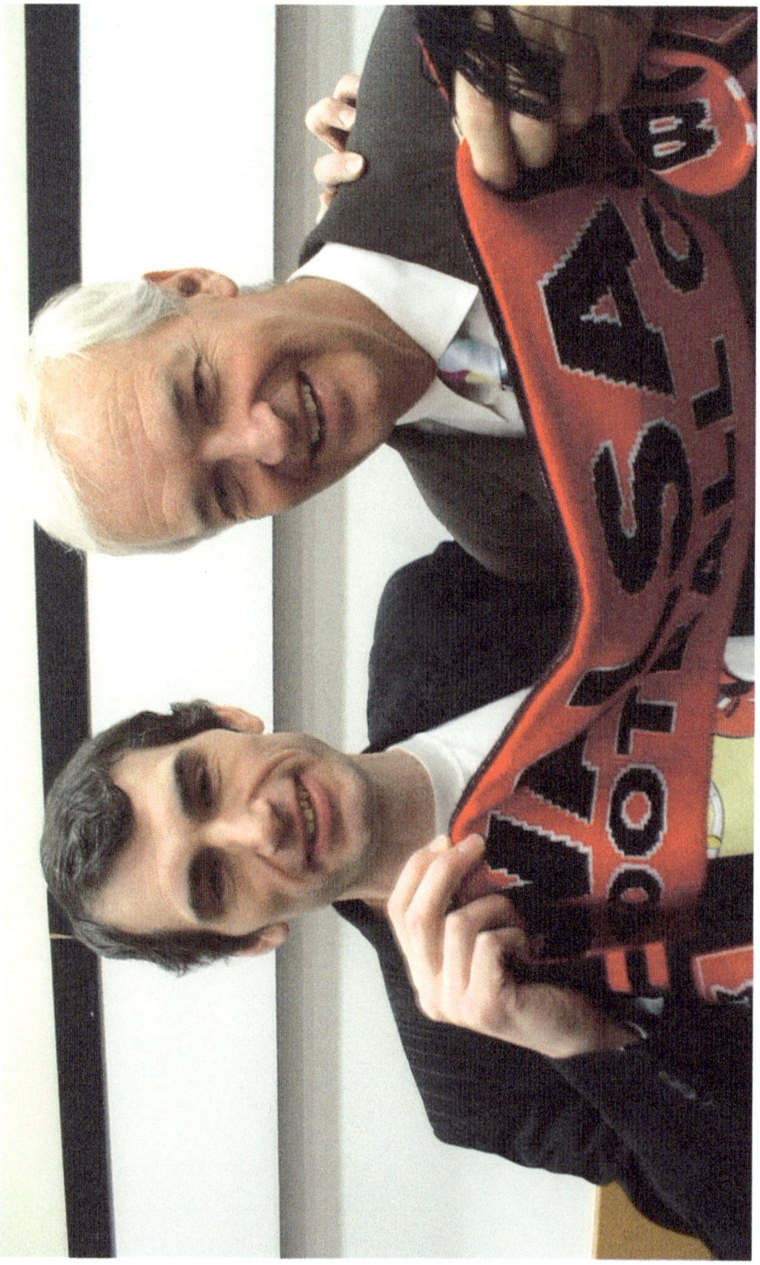

Jon Snow

Jon Snow is a journalist and presenter, currently employed by ITN. Perhaps he is best known for presenting Channel 4 News.

Snow was born in Ardingly, Sussex. The son of schoolmaster and Bishop of Whitby, George D'Oyly Snow, grandson of First World War general Thomas D'Oyly Snow (about whom he writes in his Foreword to Ronald Skirth's war memoir *The Reluctant Tommy.*) and cousin of retired BBC television news presenter Peter Snow.

In a varied career he has served as ITN's Washington correspondent and as their diplomatic editor before becoming the main presenter of Channel 4 News in 1989. In 1992 he was the main anchor for ITN's Election Night programme, broadcast on ITV; co- presenting the programme alongside Robin Day, Alastair Stewart and Julia Somerville. (Previously ITN's programme had typically been presented by Alastair Burnet, who left ITN in 1991. The 1992 election night programme was the only one hosted by Snow. He was replaced by Jonathan Dimbleby from 1997 onwards.) He has won several RTS Awards – two for reports from El Salvador, one for his reporting of the Kegworth air disaster and two as "Presenter of the Year"

In 2002 he returned to radio, presenting Jon Snow Reports on Oneword Radio, a weekly show and podcast. He also wrote regular articles for the Channel 4 News website and

'Snowmail' – a daily email newsletter on the big stories coming up on the evening edition of his news programme.

One memorable event recounted by Snow took place whilst he was working as a journalist in Uganda, when sitting next to President Idi Amin in the presidential jet. In his account he spoke of how whilst Amin appeared to be asleep he thought seriously about taking the despot's revolver and shooting him dead, but was worried about the consequences of firing a loose round in a jet.

In 1976, Snow rejected an approach by the British intelligence services to spy on his colleagues. At first he was asked to supply information about the Communist Party, but he was then asked to spy on certain "left-wing people" working in television. In return he would have received secret monthly, tax-free payments into his bank account, matching his then salary.

Known for his vast collection of colourful ties and socks he published an autobiography, called "Shooting History" which he was promoting in Coventry when he gave at a lecture at the University attended by the scarf which proved an enthusiastic listener in the audience.

WALSALL FOOTBALL CLUB

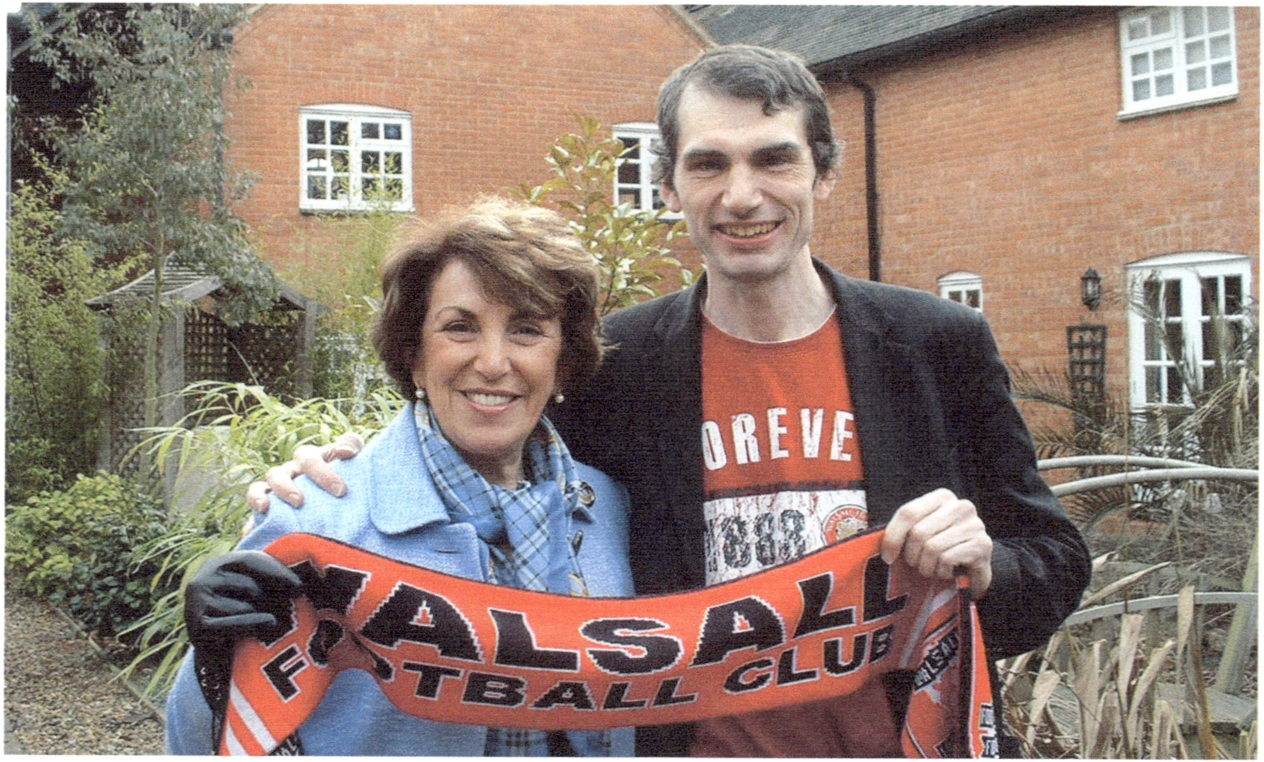

Edwina Currie

Edwina Currie was born in south Liverpool, her family being Orthodox Jews and has identified herself as Jewish, although she has stated,: "I find religious mumbo jumbo hard to swallow in any faith." She went to the Liverpool Institute High School for Girls in Blackburne House, in the Canning area of Liverpool, where she was Head Girl and her father served as caretaker. At St Anne's College, Oxford University she gained a degree in Philosophy, Politics and Economics being taught by Gabriele Taylor; before going on to gain a masters in economic history from the London School of Economics.

From 1975 until 1986, she was a Birmingham City Councillor for Northfield. In 1983, she stood for parliament as a Conservative Party candidate, and was duly elected as the member for South Derbyshire. Frequently outspoken, she was described as "a virtually permanent fixture on the nation's TV screen saying something outrageous about just about anything" and "the most outspoken and sexually interested woman of her political generation."

In September 1986 she became a Junior Health Minister. It was a post she held until December 1988 when she was forced to resign after issuing her now infamous warning about salmonella in British eggs. The statement that "most of the egg production in this country, sadly, is now affected with salmonella" sparked outrage among farmers and egg producers, and caused egg sales in the country to rapidly decline. Although the statement was widely interpreted as referring to "most eggs produced", in fact it related to the egg production *flock*; there was indeed evidence that a mid-1980s regulation change had allowed salmonella to get a hold in flocks.

Since losing her seat in 1997, Currie has maintained a presence in the media. For five years she was at the helm of an eponymous phone-in show on BBC Radio Five Live, *Late Night Currie*. In 2002 she moved to HTV, presenting the television programme *Currie Night* for a year. Since then, she has appeared in a string of reality television programmes, such as *Wife Swap* in which she and her second husband John swapped places with John McCririck and his wife, Jenny. She made an appearance in the reality cooking show *Hell's Kitchen* with celebrity chef Gordon Ramsay, and *Celebrity Stars in Their Eyes*, both in 2006. That same year she was interviewed about the rise of Thatcherism in the BBC TV documentary series *Tory! Tory! Tory!*. She triumphed on *Celebrity Mastermind*, specialising in the life of Marie Curie. Victory also came her way on *All Star Family Fortunes* in 2009. She followed this up an appearance on Channel 4's *Come Dine with Me* the same year when she finished third.

Recently Edwina took part in a series of *Strictly Come Dancing* partnering Vincent Simone, but was the first dancer to be eliminated from the competition.

Now living in Reigate the scarf was given a cordial invite where she graciously managed a quick welcome before leaving for an appearance on *Loose Woman*.

WALSALL FOOTBALL CLUB

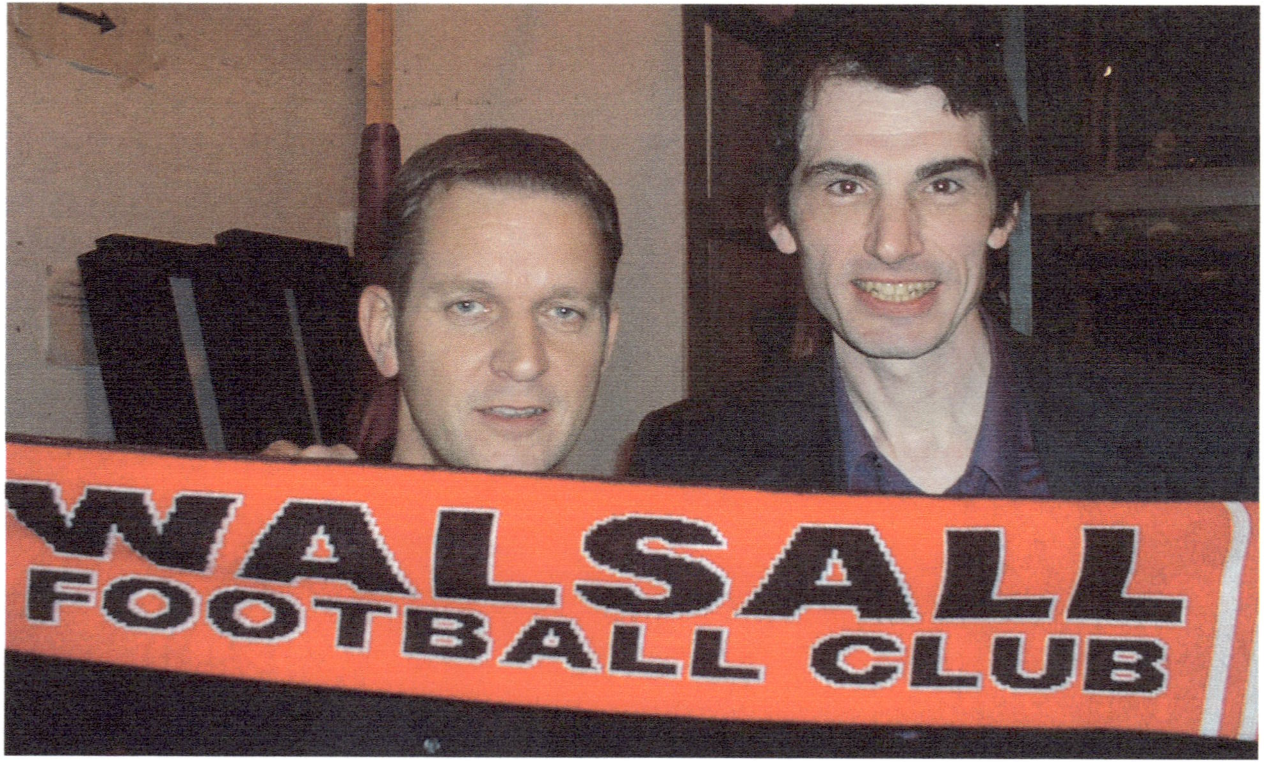
WALSALL
FOOTBALL CLUB

Jeremy Kyle

Jeremy Kyle has had a varied career in radio and television, but is perhaps best known for his British daytime television chat show on ITV, *The Jeremy Kyle Show*. Kyle is also the host of an American talk show of the same name.

After working for a series of local radio stations he joined BRMB in Birmingham, presenting shows such as *Late & Live* and *Jezza's Jukebox*.

In 2000 Kyle moved to the Century FM network, taking this format with him. The show was called *Jezza's Confessions*. He won a Sony Award for *Late & Live* and the year after started broadcasting for Virgin Radio, presenting *Jezza's Virgin Confessions* every weekday. He left Virgin Radio to present the *Confessions* show on London's Capital FM. *Capital Confessions* came to an end the following year to make way for *The Jeremy Kyle Show*, which ran into 2005.

It was around this time that he moved this format to ITV, with a programme also entitled *The Jeremy Kyle Show*. Here Kyle has reached his widest audience to date. The often aggressive manner he uses with guests has been the source of both popularity and criticism. Seemingly unafraid of reprisal from his guests, and in the belief that speaking one's mind is better than holding your peace. Guests sometimes take offence at Kyle's comments, one guest even attempted to throw a chair at him, whilst another threw an envelope at the back of his head. He has attempted to justify this criticism by claiming that he only wants to help them. Claims have been made by him on air that his show was watched by 1.8 million viewers, a very high figure for a daytime chat show.

As well as his television work Kyle has written a column for *Pick Me Up*, a women's weekly magazine published by IPC. In his column, titled *Jeremy Kyle Says...*, Kyle adopts a frank style in responding to readers' problems which, unsurprisingly perhaps, closely resembles the approach he takes on The Jeremy Kyle Show.

Kyle wrote his first book, 'I'm Only Being Honest', about Britain's social problems and his views on how to solve them including recounts of his past and personal life.

At the start of 2011 he fronted the ITV1 show *High Stakes*, which represented a new direction for him. Billed as a game of "knowledge, risk, and tension," the show involved participants answering questions and stepping on the correct six squares on a grid in order to avoid trap numbers.

Kyle is a keen supporter of West Ham United but showed no qualms in holding the famed Walsall banner backstage after it was forced to endure a dual recording of his show at Granada studio's in Manchester.

WALSALL FOOTBALL CLUB

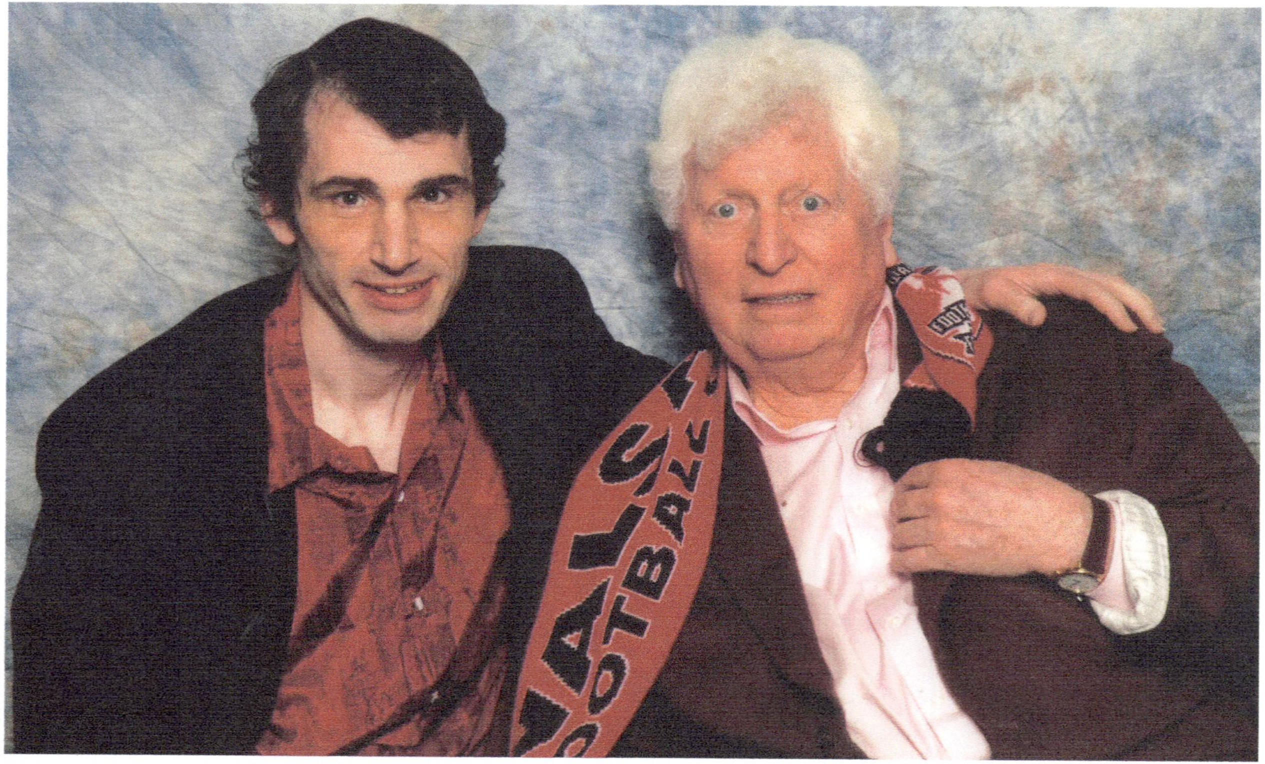

Tom Baker

A fine English actor, Tom Baker. is perhaps best known for his role as the fourth incarnation of the Doctor in the science fiction television series *Doctor Who*, which he played from 1974 to 1981.

Baker was born in Scotland Road, Liverpool, in 1934. His mother, Mary Jane was a cleaner, and his father, John Stewart Baker, was a sailor who was rarely at home.

His early work was part of Laurence Olivier's National Theatre company and he got his first big film break in 1971 with the role of Rasputin in the film *Nicholas and Alexandra* (after Olivier recommended him for the part). He also appeared in Pier Paolo Pasolini's film version of Geoffrey Chaucer's *The Canterbury Tales* as the younger husband of the Wife of Bath.

As everyone knows, his finest hour came in 1974, when Baker took over the role of the Doctor from Jon Pertwee in the BBC TV series. Bill Slater, who at the time was corporation Head of Serials, recommended him to the producer Barry Letts after he had directed him in *Play of the Month*. Impressed by Baker upon meeting him, Letts was convinced he was right for the part after seeing his performance in *The Golden Voyage of Sinbad*. Baker was working on a construction site at the time, as acting jobs were scarce. Initially he was dubbed "Boiler Suit Tom" by the media because he had been supplied for a press conference with some old studio set clothes to replace his modest garments.

After he had left *Doctor Who*, Baker portrayed Sherlock Holmes in a four part BBC1 miniseries version of *The Hound of the Baskervilles*; in the U.S., this production was telecast on A&E. He also made an appearance in *Blackadder II*, in the episode "Potato", as the sea captain 'Redbeard Rum'. Much later, he played Puddleglum, a 'marsh-wiggle', in the 1990 BBC adaptation of C.S. Lewis' *The Silver Chair*.

During the third series of the British game show *Cluedo*, Baker was cast as Professor Plum, a 'man with a degree in suspicion'. He also starred in the series *Strange*, as a blind priest who possessed knowledge of the Devil. Previously, he had appeared as a guest on the quiz show *Have I Got News for You* and was subsequently described by presenter Angus Deayton as the funniest guest in the series' history. A particular highlight was when Baker gave an anecdotal account of how, whilst entering a recording studio in Wales, he was accosted by a member of the public who told Baker: 'I will never forgive you, nor will my wife, for what you did to our grammar schools.' Baker responded with: 'What are you talking about, you daft bugger?' to which the stranger replied: 'I'm so sorry. For a moment I thought you were Shirley Williams.'

It is perhaps fitting that the Doctor known for his long flowing scarf should choose to wear this one rather than just hold it at an event held in Barking.

WALSALL FOOTBALL CLUB

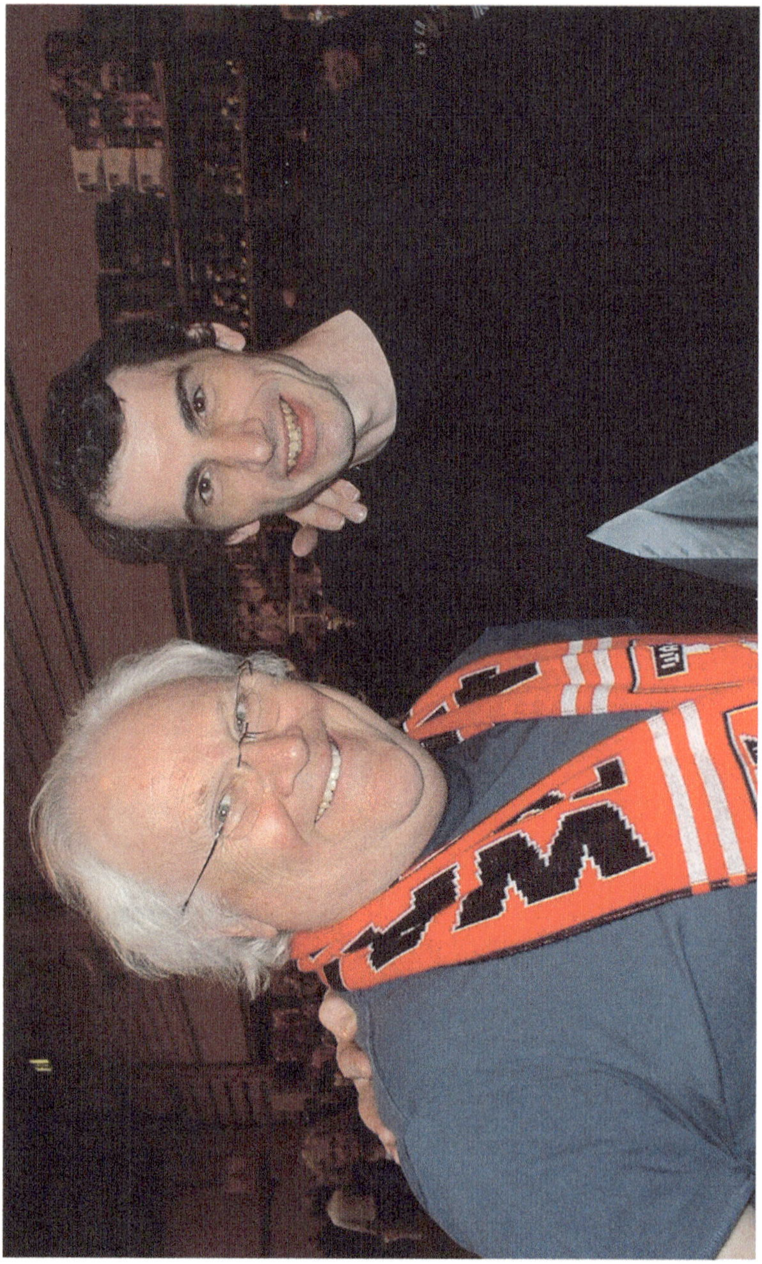

Colin Baker

In the mid-seventies he was best known as Paul Merroney in *The Brothers*, but Colin Baker also portrayed the 6th incarnation (1984-86) of The Doctor in the long-running *Doctor Who*.

Born in London in the 1940's, he moved north to Rochdale with his family early on in his life. He was educated at St Bede's College, Manchester, and originally studied to become a solicitor. At the age of 23, he decided to change profession and enrolled at the London Academy of Music and Dramatic Art (LAMDA), where he studied alongside the likes of David Suchet.

One of Baker's first acting jobs however, was in a supporting role of a BBC adaptation of Jean-Paul Sartre's trilogy *The Roads to Freedom*. In 1972, Colin played Anatole Kuragin in a BBC serial adaptation of *War and Peace*. His most prominent role during this period saw a sinister performance as the villainous Paul Merroney.

Baker's first appearance as the Doctor occurred at the final minutes of *The Caves of Androzani*, where he delivered his first few lines. The closing title sequence for episode four features Baker's face instead of Peter Davison, and credits him as the Doctor before Davison's own credit. This was the first (and, to date, only) time that the new lead received top billing in the final story of an outgoing Doctor. Baker then made his first full story debut the following week in *The Twin Dilemma*. It was the first time since 1966, and only the second time in the series' history, that a new leading actor's debut story was shown before the conclusion of the previous lead's season.

Since leaving *Doctor Who* Baker has spent much of his time on the stage with appearances throughout the country in plays as diverse as Peter Nichols' *Privates on Parade*, Ira Levine's *Deathtrap*, Ray Cooney's *Run for Your Wife* and Ariel Dorfman's *Death and the Maiden*. For many years he has been a pantomime stalwart. In 2000 he appeared in *Snow White and the Seven Dwarfs* alongside actress Louise Jameson who had previously played the Fourth Doctor's companion Leela. In 2003 he starred in the Carl Rosa Opera Company's production of operetta *H.M.S. Pinafore*, directed by Timothy West. In 2008, he toured with ex-wife Liza Goddard in *She Stoops to Conquer*.

More recently Baker has been seen on our screens in the 12th series of *I'm a Celebrity...Get Me out of Here!* He finished in 8th place out of 12 celebrities, losing out to Eric Bristow.

After the death of his son Jack in 1984, Baker became active in fighting Sudden Infant Death Syndrome. He raised funds for the Foundation for the Study of Infant Deaths and was a Trustee from 1989 and their Chairman from 1997 and 2005.

A frequent attendee at shows around the country he met the scarf at Birmingham and keenly embraced the project, chatting freely about his interest in the game.

WALSALL FOOTBALL CLUB

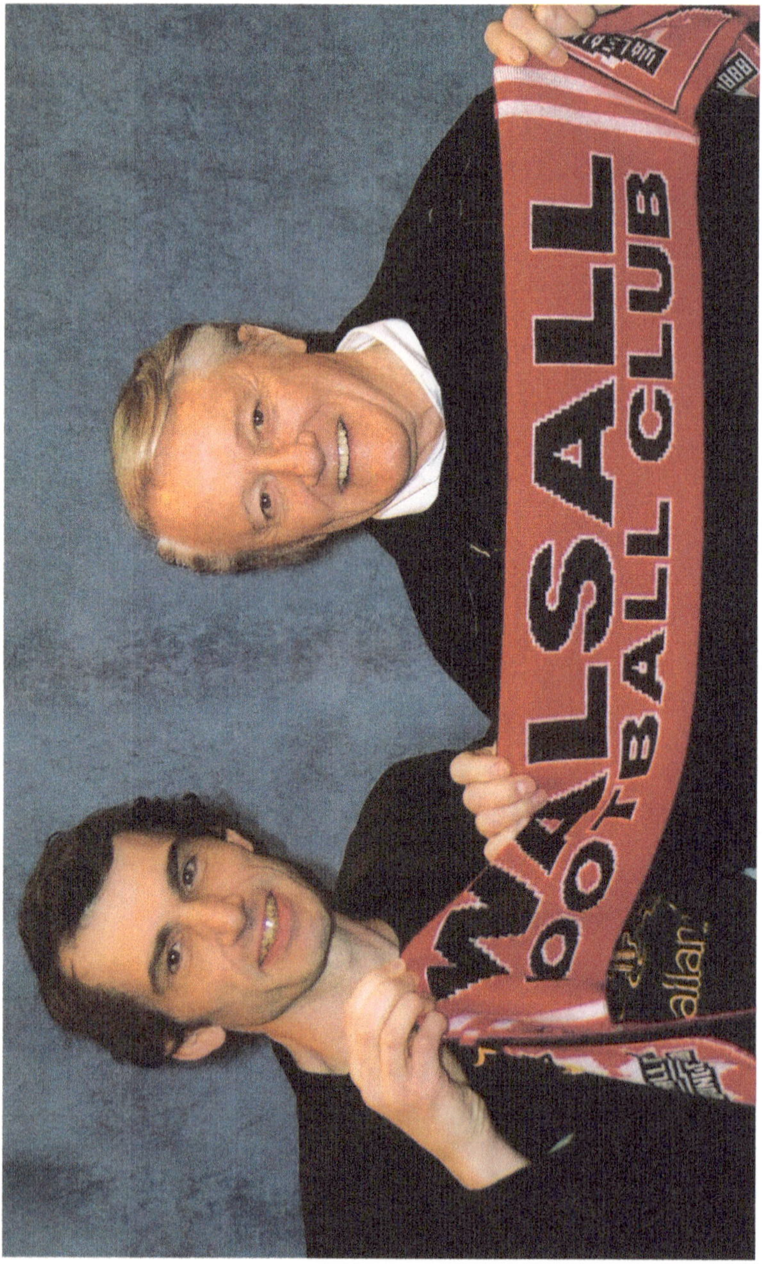
WALSALL

Robert Vaughn

Vaughn made his television debut in November 21, 1955 on the "Black Friday" episode of the American TV series *Medic*, the first of more than two hundred episodic roles played by him up to the middle of 2000.

Widely known for his U.S. television series roles including the suave spy Napoleon Solo in the 1960s *The Man from U.N.C.L.E.* and wealthy detective Harry Rule in the 1970s in *The Protectors*. In film, he portrayed one of the title characters in *The Magnificent Seven*, Major Paul Krueger in *The Bridge at Remagen*, and the voice of Proteus IV, the computer in *Demon Seed*.

A native to New York City both his parents were performers: Marcella Frances, a stage actress, and Gerald Walter Vaughn, a radio actor. His ancestry includes Irish, French, and German.

Vaughn's first notable appearance was in *The Young Philadelphians* (1959) for which he was nominated for an Academy Award for Best Supporting Actor and a Golden Globe Award for Best Supporting Actor – Motion Picture. Next he appeared as gunman Lee in *The Magnificent Seven* (1960), a role he essentially reprised 20 years later in *Battle Beyond the Stars*.

Vaughn starred in *The Lieutenant* as Captain Raymond Rambridge alongside Gary Lockwood, the Marine second lieutenant at Camp Pendleton. His dissatisfaction with the somewhat diminished aspect of the character led him to request an expanded role. During the conference, his name came up in a telephone call and he ended up being offered a series of his own – as Napoleon Solo, title character in a series originally to be called *Solo*, but which became *The Man from U.N.C.L.E.*

Vaughn continued to act, in television and in mostly B movies. He starred in two seasons of the British detective series *The Protectors* in the early 1970s.

In 2004, after a string of guest roles on series such as *Law & Order*, in which he had a recurring role during season eight, Vaughn experienced a resurgence. He began co-starring in the British series *Hustle*, made for BBC One, which was also broadcast in the United States on the cable network AMC

Recently Vaughn played Milton Fanshaw in the long-running British soap opera *Coronation Street*, as a new love interest for the character Sylvia Goodwin.

Slightly bemused by the appearance of the scarf in this photo-shoot he agreed to hold it after learning the reason for its presence, at a show in Northampton.

WALSALL FOOTBALL CLUB

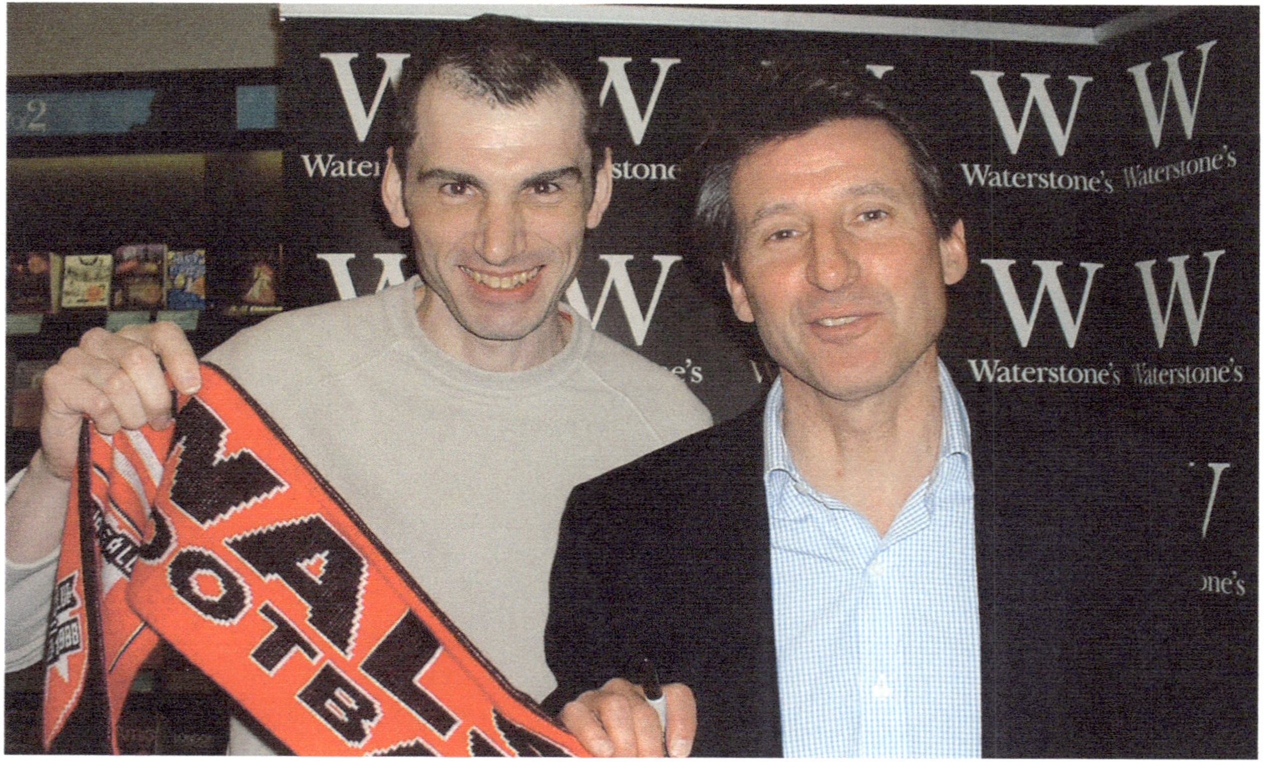
Waterstone's
Waterstone's
Waterstone's
Waterstone's

Sebastian Coe

Often known as just plain Seb Coe, Baron Coe CH KBE, is familiar to many of a certain age as a middle-distance runner. During his career Coe won four Olympic medals, including the 1500 metres gold medal at the Olympic Games in 1980 and 1984, as well as an 800 metre gold at the European Championships in Stuttgart. He set eight outdoor and three indoor world records in middle-distance track events – including, in 1979, setting three world records in the space of 41 days – and the world record he set in the 800 metres in 1981 remained unbroken until 1997. Coe's rivalries with fellow Britons Steve Ovett and Steve Cram dominated middle-distance racing for much of the 1980s.

He was injured in May 1987 after winning an 800m for his club, Haringey, and was out for the entire season. The following year he missed out on selection for the British Olympic Games team, when he failed to qualify from the heats of the 1500m at the Trials in Birmingham. The *Daily Mirror* ran a campaign and the president of the International Olympic Committee, Juan Antonio Samaranch, unsuccessfully tried to have the rules changed in Coe's favour. Both of these measures failed and Coe lost out to Peter Elliott.

Coe was elected as Member of Parliament for Falmouth and Camborne in 1992, for the Conservative Party, but lost his seat in the 1997 general election. He returned to politics for a short time as William Hague's chief of staff, having accepted the offer of a Life Peerage on 16 May 2000. During this time he tried his hand at a marathon, running a time of 2 hours and 58 minutes in London.

When London announced its bid to hold the 2012 Olympics, Coe became an ambassador for the effort and a member of the board of the bid company. With the May 2004 resignation of Chairman Barbara Cassani, Coe became the chairman for the latter phase of the bid. As Coe was a well-known personality in Olympic sport, it was felt he was better suited to the political schmoozing needed to secure the IOC's backing, Coe's presentation at the critical IOC meeting was viewed by commentators as being particularly effective, and the bid won the IOC's blessing on 6 July 2005.

After his work in delivering the London 2012 Games, Coe was presented with an Olympic Order. In the 2013 New Year Honours, Coe was appointed to the Order of the Companions of Honour for services to the London 2012 Olympic and Paralympic Games.

Coe has also received three separate awards at the BBC Sports Personality of the Year ceremony: The main individual award in 1979, a "Special Gold Award" in 2005 and the "Lifetime Achievement Award" in 2012.

Seb Coe proved a difficult subject to catch with the scarf, but after two attempts he finally met up with it at Leadenhall market in London at a signing held there for his motivational book, "The Winning Mind"

WALSALL FOOTBALL CLUB

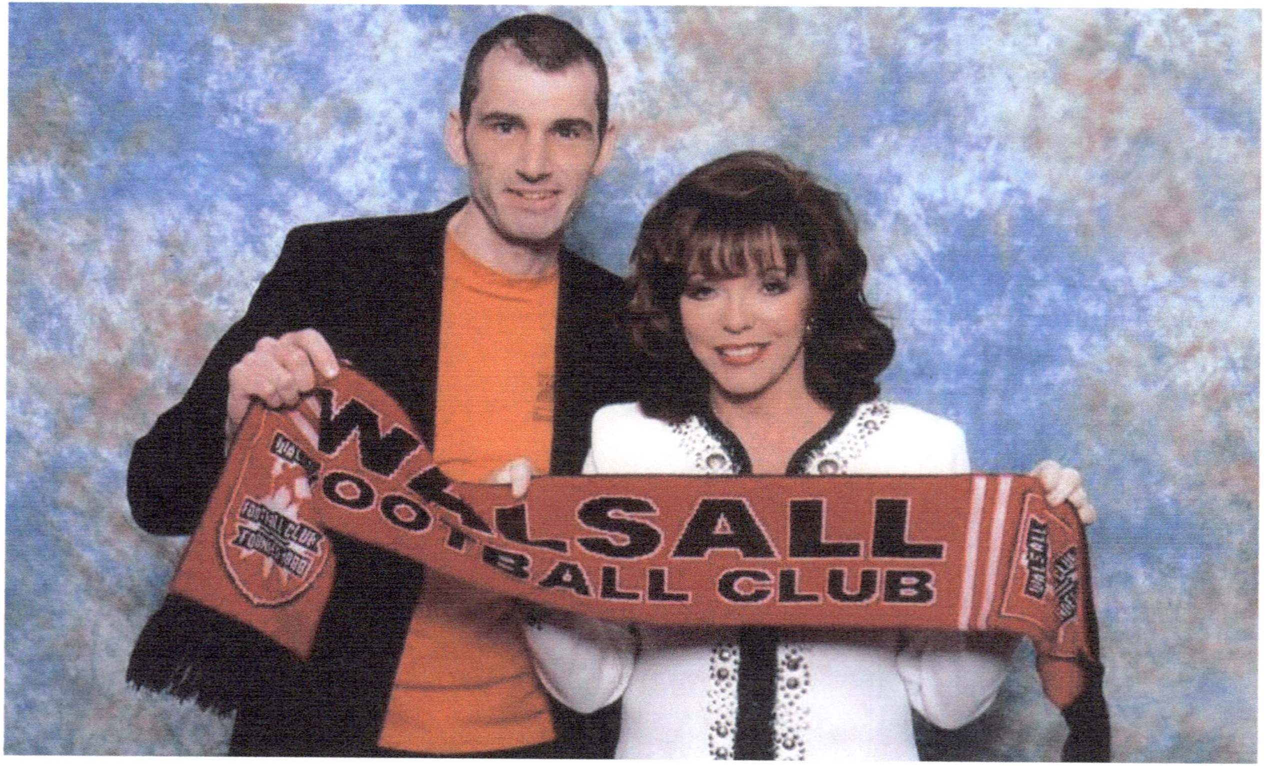
WALSALL
FOOTBALL CLUB

Joan Collins

Joan Collins has had a variety of careers including actress, author and columnist. Born in Paddington and brought up in Maida Vale, Collins grew up during the Second World War. After making her stage debut in *A Doll's House* at the age of 9, she was trained as an actress at the Royal Academy of Dramatic Art (RADA) in London. After eighteen months at the drama school, she was signed to an exclusive contract by the Rank Organisation and appeared in various British films.

At the age of 22, Collins headed to Hollywood and landed sultry roles in several popular films, including *The Girl in the Red Velvet Swing* (1955) and *Rally 'Round the Flag, Boys!* (1958). While she continued to make films in the US and the UK throughout the 1960s, her career languished in the 1970s, where she appeared in a number of horror flicks. Near the end of the decade, she starred in two films based on best-selling novels by her younger sister Jackie Collins: *The Stud* and its sequel *The Bitch*. Returning to her theatrical roots, she played the title role in the 1980 British revival of *The Last of Mrs. Cheyney* and later had a lead role in the 1990 revival of Noël Coward's *Private Lives*. In 1981, Collins landed Alexis Carrington Colby, the role for which she is perhaps best known, in the long-running 1980s television soap opera *Dynasty*.

By the time the soap opera had been cancelled, near the end of the decade, Collins followed in her sister's footsteps and published her first novel *Prime Time* which became a bestseller in spite of critical pans. Despite a protracted legal battle with Random House in 1996, she has since published many books: fictional, non-fictional and autobiographical. Flamboyant in her personal life and in roles she pursues, Collins continues to act in theatre, film and television in a career that has spanned more than 60 years.

In early 2006, Collins toured the United Kingdom in *An Evening with Joan Collins*, a one-woman show in which she detailed the highs and lows of her roller coaster career and life, directed by her husband Percy Gibson. Later on in that year she reunited with her *Dynasty* co-stars for the non-fiction special *Dynasty Reunion: Catfights and Caviar*. Hot on the heels of this success, she began a tour of North America in the play *Legends!* with former *Dynasty* star Linda Evans, which concluded in May 2007 after a 30-week run.

Collins has been married five times, to actor Maxwell Reed, actor and film composer Anthony Newley, Ron Kass, former president of Apple Records and Swedish singer Peter Holm. In 2002 Collins married theatrical company manager Percy Gibson, 32 years her junior. The pair appeared as contestants on the Christmas Day edition of the ITV game show *All Star Mr. & Mrs*.

During a brief visit to this country she appeared at the Hilton Metropole near Birmingham's NEC when she held the scarf in elegant white gloves before commenting on the rather small photograph she had done of it.

WALSALL FOOTBALL CLUB

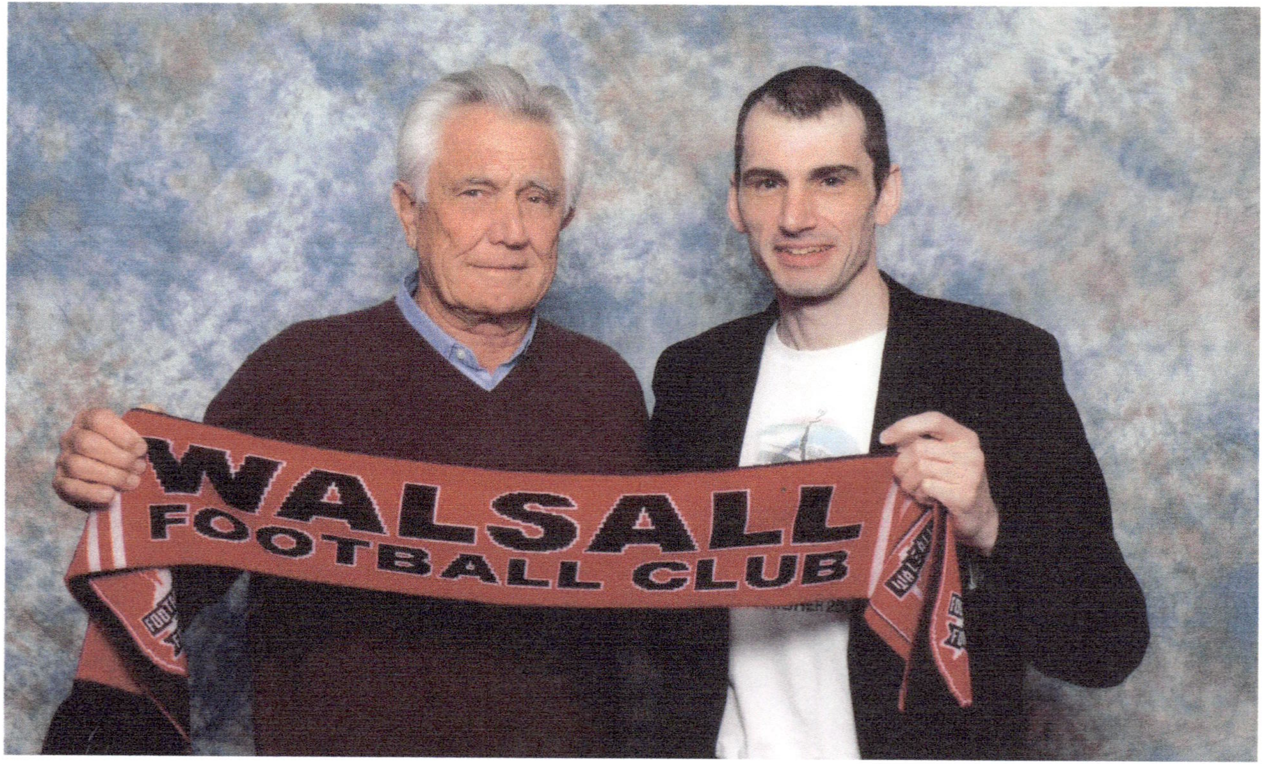
WALSALL
FOOTBALL CLUB

George Lazenby

George Lazenby was born in Goulburn, New South Wales, at the Ovada Private Hospital, to railway worker George Edward Lazenby and his wife Sheila, who worked at Fosseys.

When Lazenby was about 13 he moved with his family to Queanbeyan, where his father ran a store. He worked as a car salesman and mechanic, before serving in the Australian Army. Moving to London in 1963 he became a used car salesman in Finchley, then sold new cars in Park Lane. He was spotted by a talent scout who persuaded him to become a model, and was soon earning £25,000 a year. It was during this period in time when he became known for advertising Big Fry Chocolate.

In 1968, after Sean Connery quit the role of James Bond, producer Albert R. Broccoli first met Lazenby when getting their hair cut at the same barber. He later saw him in the Big Fry commercial and felt he could be a possible Bond, calling him in for a screen test.

Dressed for the part and sporting several sartorial Bond elements such as a Rolex Submariner wristwatch and a Savile Row suit (ordered, but uncollected, by Connery), Broccoli offered him an audition. The position was consolidated when Lazenby accidentally punched a professional wrestler, who was acting as stunt coordinator, in the face, impressing Broccoli with his ability to display aggression. Lazenby won the role portraying James Bond in the film *On Her Majesty's Secret*

Service based mainly on a screen-test fight scene, the strength of his interviews, fight skills and audition footage.

However, in November 1969, prior to the release of the film, Lazenby announced that he no longer wished to play the role of James Bond due to his conflict with the film's producers and quit after only one outing.

In 1973, Lazenby was set to work in Hong Kong with Bruce Lee. A planned meeting with Lee and Raymond Chow to discuss a movie project for the Golden Harvest film *Game of Death* collapsed after Lee's sudden death, although Lazenby would still go on to make three of the four films he signed to do with Lee in Hong Kong, *The Shrine of Ultimate Bliss*, *The Man from Hong Kong* and *A Queen's Ransom*. Lazenby was only featured with archive footage.

In spite of all this, he has continued to portray James Bond several times over the years in numerous parodies and unofficial 007 roles, most notably the 1983 television movie *The Return of the Man from U.N.C.L.E.* and an episode of *The New Alfred Hitchcock Presents*, entitled "Diamonds Aren't Forever". In 2012 Lazenby made a guest appearance on the Canadian sketch comedy series *This Hour Has 22 Minutes*, spoofing the 007 series in a skit called *Help, I've Skyfallen and I Can't Get Up*.

Traveling the world talking about Bond he came to the Midlands where he met up with the scarf in an airport hotel and was intrigued to know just who the Saddlers were.

WALSALL FOOTBALL CLUB

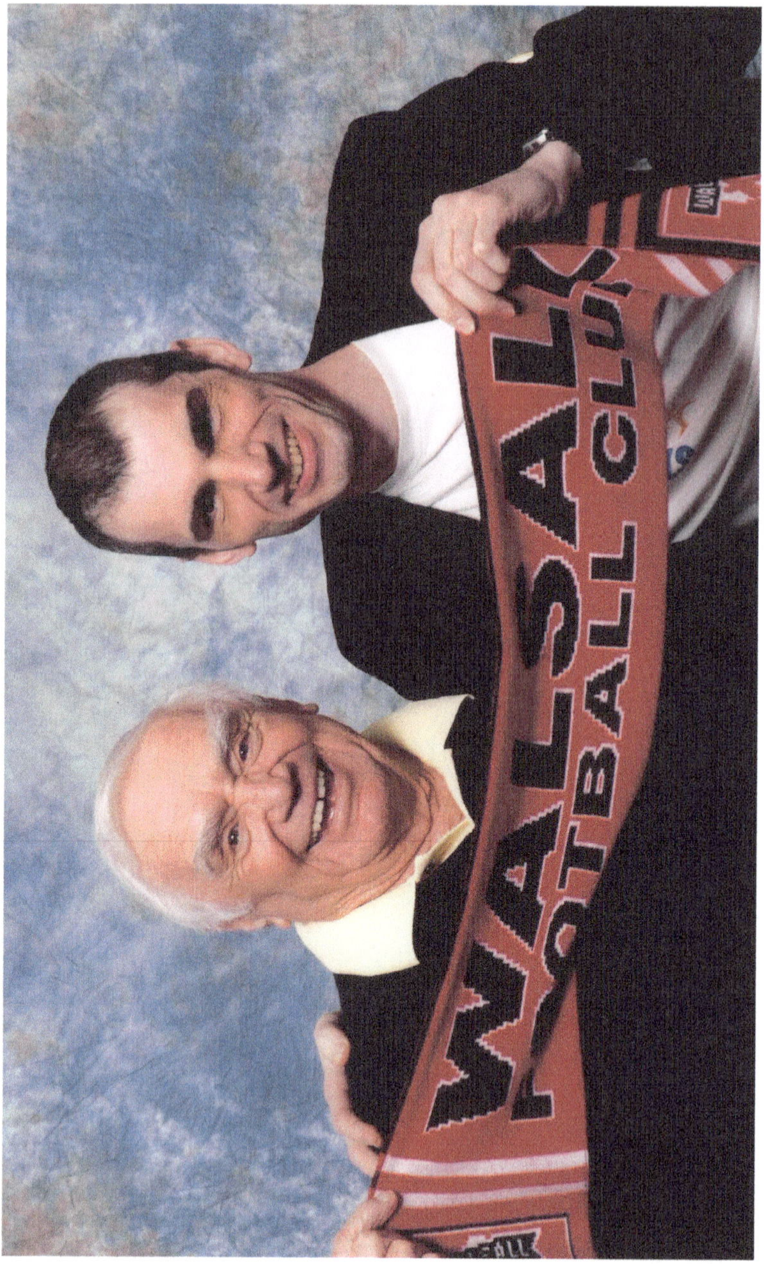

Ernest Borgnine

American film and television actor, Ermes Effron Borgnino's career has spanned more than six decades. He was an unconventional lead in many films of the 1950s, and made many appearances on television.

Having changed his name to Borgnine he moved to Los Angeles, in 1951 where he eventually received his big break in *From Here to Eternity*, playing the sadistic Sergeant "Fatso" Judson, who beats a stockade prisoner in his charge, Angelo Maggio (played by Frank Sinatra). Borgnine built a reputation as a dependable character actor and played villains in early films, including movies like *Johnny Guitar*, *Vera Cruz* and *Bad Day at Black Rock*.

Yet, arguably his greatest moment came in 1955, playing a warmhearted butcher in *Marty*, the film version of the television play of the same name, which gained him an Academy Award for Best Actor over the likes of Frank Sinatra, James Dean (who had died by the time of the ceremony), and former Best Actor winners Spencer Tracy and James Cagney.

From then on his film career flourished through the next three decades and was to include roles in *The Flight of the Phoenix*, *The Dirty Dozen*, *Ice Station Zebra*, *The Poseidon Adventure*, *Convoy* and *Escape from New York*.

Borgnine returned to a new contract with Universal Studios in 1983, for a co-starring role opposite Jan-Michael Vincent, on *Airwolf*. After he was approached by producer Donald P.

Bellisario, who had been impressed by Borgnine's guest role as a wrestler in an episode of *Magnum, P.I.* the previous year, he immediately agreed. He played Dominic Santini, a helicopter pilot, in the series which became an instant hit.

Starting in 1999, Borgnine provided his voice talent to the animated sitcom *SpongeBob SquarePants* as the elderly superhero Mermaid Man (where he was paired up with his *McHale's Navy* co-star Tim Conway as the voice of Mermaid Man's sidekick Barnacle Boy). He expressed affection for this role, in no small part for its popularity among children. Borgnine also appeared as himself in *The Simpsons* episode "Boy-Scoutz 'n the Hood", in addition to a number of television commercials. In 2000, he was the executive producer of *Hoover*, in which he was the only credited actor.

In 2009, at age 92, he starred as Frank, the main character of *Another Harvest Moon*, directed by Greg Swartz and also starring Piper Laurie and Anne Meara. On October 2, 2010, Borgnine appeared again as himself in a sketch on *Saturday Night Live*.

It was late on in his life that Borgnine was introduced to the scarf at a function Birmingham.

After his death, on July 11, 2012, Nickelodeon re-aired all of the episodes in which Mermaid Man appeared in memoriam.

WALSALL FOOTBALL CLUB

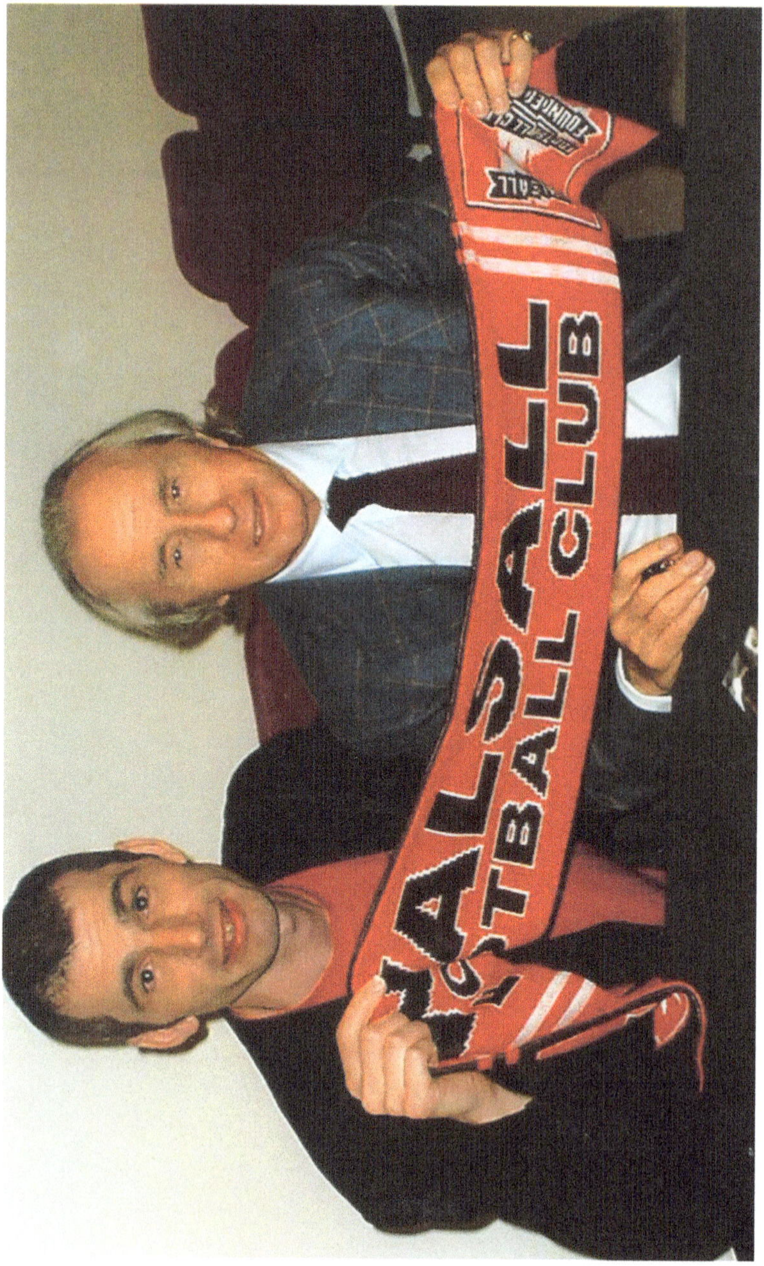

Sir Jackie Stewart

Sir John Young Stewart – "Jackie" as he became known – is a Scottish former racing driver. Nicknamed the "Flying Scot", he competed in Formula One between 1965 and 1973, winning three World Drivers' Championships.

He started his career driving for Tyrell in Formula Three. His debut, in the wet at Snetterton was dominant, taking an astounding 25 second lead in just two laps before coasting home to a win on a 44 second cushion. Within days, he was offered a Formula One ride with Cooper, but declined, preferring to gain experience under Tyrrell; he failed to win just two races (one to clutch failure, one to a spin) in becoming F3 champion.

Like Nigel Mansell years later, Stewart participated on the North American circuit completing a full season in Can-Am, driving a Carl Haas sponsored Lola T260-Chevrolet, and again in 1973. During the 1971 Can-Am series, Stewart was the only driver able to challenge the McLarens driven by Dennis Hulme and Peter Revson. Stewart won 2 races; at Mont Treblant and Mid Ohio. Stewart finished 3rd in the 1971 Can-Am Drivers Championship.

Stewart covered NASCAR races and the Indianapolis 500 on American television during the 1970s and early 1980s, and has also worked on Australian and Canadian TV coverage. He is well known in the United States as a colour commentator (pundit) of racing television broadcasts, and as a spokesman for Ford, where his Scottish accent has made him a distinctive presence.

For two years in the late 1990's Stewart returned to Formula One, with Stewart Grand Prix, as a team owner in partnership with his son, Paul. As the works Ford team, their first race was the 1997 Australian Grand Prix. The only success of their first year came at the rain-affected Monaco Grand Prix where Rubens Barrichello finished an impressive second. Reliability was low however, with a likely 2nd place at the Nürburgring among several potential results lost. 1998 was even less competitive, with no podiums and few points. Ford acquired Cosworth that same year and they risked designing and building a brand-new engine for the next season. It paid off. The SF3 was consistently competitive throughout the season. The team won one race at the European Grand Prix at the Nürburgring with Johnny Herbert, albeit somewhat luckily, while Barrichello took three 3rd places, pole in France, and briefly led his home race at Interlagos. The team was later bought by Ford and became Jaguar Racing in 2000 – it has since morphed into Red Bull Racing.

In 2009 he was ranked fifth of the fifty greatest Formula One drivers of all time by journalist Kevin Eason who wrote: "He has not only emerged as a great driver, but one of the greatest figures of motor racing."

It was on a cold night in Milton Keynes during a promotion of his book "Winning Is Not Enough" that he most graciously contributed his face to the project.

WALSALL FOOTBALL CLUB

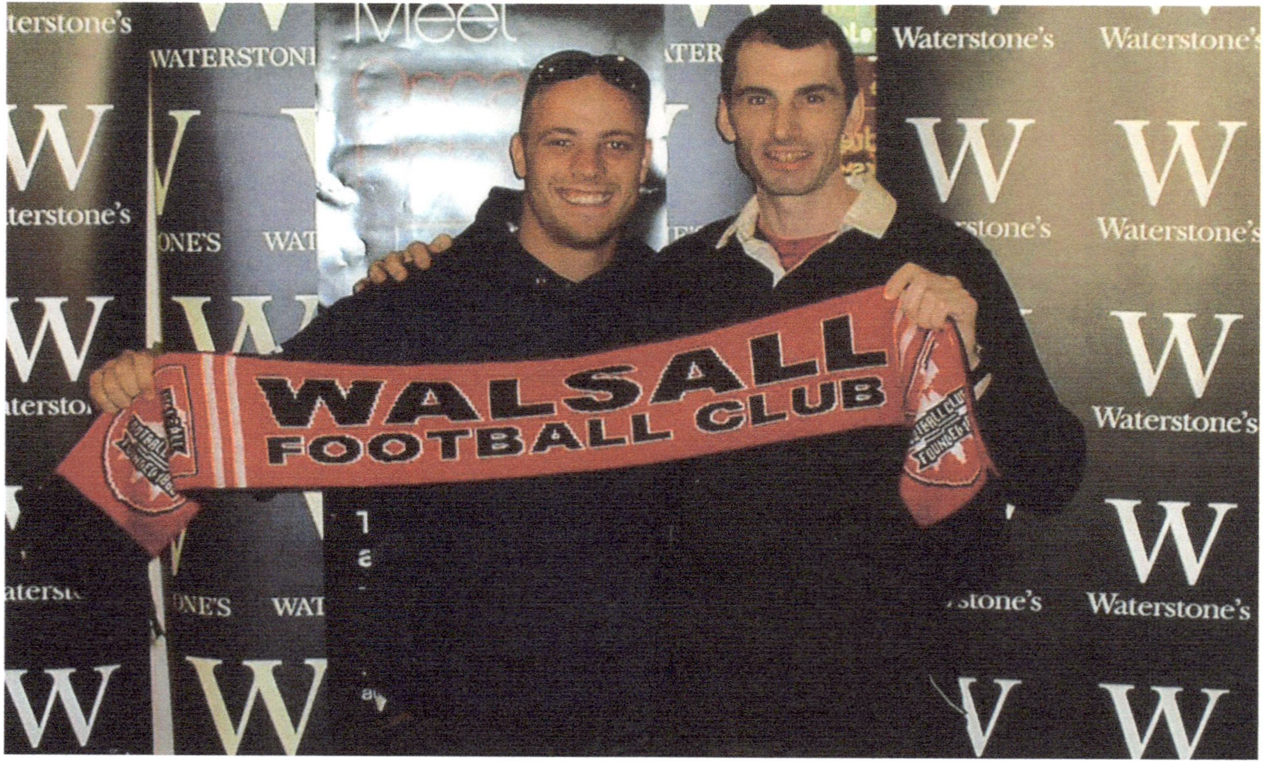
Waterstone's
WATERSTONE'S
Meet
WALSALL
FOOTBALL CLUB

Oscar Pistorius

Oscar Pistorius is a South African sprint runner, multiple Paralympic medallist and record holder.

Pistorius was born with fibular hemimelia (congenital absence of the fibula) in both legs. When he was 11 months old, his legs were amputated halfway between his knees and ankles. Pistorius has been the subject of criticism because of claims that his artificial limbs give him an advantage over runners with natural ankles and feet. He runs with J-shaped carbon-fibre prosthetics called the "Flex-Foot Cheetah" developed by biomedical engineer Van Phillips and manufactured by Össur.

Even though in major championships he competes in T44 (single below knee amputees) events, he is actually classified in T43 (double below knee amputee). In 2007, Pistorius took part in his first international competitions for able-bodied athletes. However, his cutting-edge prostheses gave rise to claims that he had an unfair advantage over able-bodied runners. The International Association of Athletics Federations initially ruled him ineligible for competitions conducted under its rules, but on 16 May 2008 the court ruled that since he was slower out of the blocks than an able-bodied athlete, there was insufficient evidence that he had an overall net advantage over able-bodied athletes.

At the 2011 World Championships in Athletics, he participated in the 400 metres sprint and the 4 × 400 metres relay. As part of South Africa's silver medal winning relay team, he became the first amputee to win an able-bodied world track medal although he was not selected for the final. At the 2012 Olympics in London, Pistorius became the first double leg amputee to participate in the Olympics when he entered the men's 400 metres race and was part of South Africa's 4 × 400 metres relay team. He also took part in the 2012 Paralympics. He won gold medals in the men's 400 metre race in a Paralympic record time of 46.68 seconds and in the 4 × 100 metres relay in a world record time of 41.78 seconds. He also took silver in the 200 metres race, having set a world record of 21.30 seconds in the semifinal.

Sadly all these events were overshadowed when on 14 February 2013; one police spokesman reportedly stated Reeva Steenkamp, Pistorius's girlfriend, had been shot and killed at Pistorius's Pretoria gated community home. On 22 February, in summarizing the three-day bail hearing, Magistrate Nair confirmed that Pistorius would be charged with premeditated murder but that he had "heard [an] extensive and thorough argument" that Steenkamp's death was not part of a premeditated murder. On 21 October 2014, Pistorius received a prison sentence of a maximum of five years for culpable homicide and a concurrent three year suspended prison sentence for the separate reckless endangerment conviction.

In a trip to Manchester to promote his book "Blade Runner" Oscar gladly showed his support for the scarf in being pictured with it.

WALSALL FOOTBALL CLUB

BBC Birmingham

Kay Alexander

Born in Surrey, the daughter of a doctor and an aeronautical engineer, Kay was educated at Frensham Heights School in Farnham, Surrey, and graduated in English from the University of Birmingham, just a stone's throw from Pebble Mill, the BBC's former regional centre.

She began her career in London working as a BBC radio reporter on programmes such as You & Yours, Woman's Hour and Checkpoint but after about a year moved to Pebble Mill, from where the immensely popular programmes Pebble Mill at One and Saturday Night at The Mill were networked.

Her chance to sit before the microphone on Midlands Today came about two years later while Tom Coyne was on holiday and she was gradually asked to do more for the programme.

Among her proudest and most memorable achievements was presenting three series of the nationally networked medical programme *Lifefile*.

And she presented a star-studded concert to raise funds for leukaemia research at Symphony Hall, Birmingham featuring the great Spanish tenor José Carreras.

In 1976, the first International Women's Year, Kay flew the flag by highlighting women's often unrecognised achievements in what, 36 years ago, were regarded by many as traditionally the domain of men, such as – to name just four – driving a traction engine, taking charge of a coach and sitting behind the wheel of a racing car and driving a loco on the Severn Valley Railway.

Alexander was until 2012 Chairman of the Birmingham Assay Office (the first woman to hold this position) and is a former Director of the Birmingham Hippodrome and a Patron of Acorns Children's Hospice.

Alexander arguably remains one of the Midlands' most popular and recognisable television faces, and prior to presenting her last news bulletin she welcomed the scarf to the *Midlands Today* studio at the Mailbox just before 30th October 2012, and the next evening appeared on air for the last time to receive her colleagues' congratulations.

WALSALL FOOTBALL CLUB

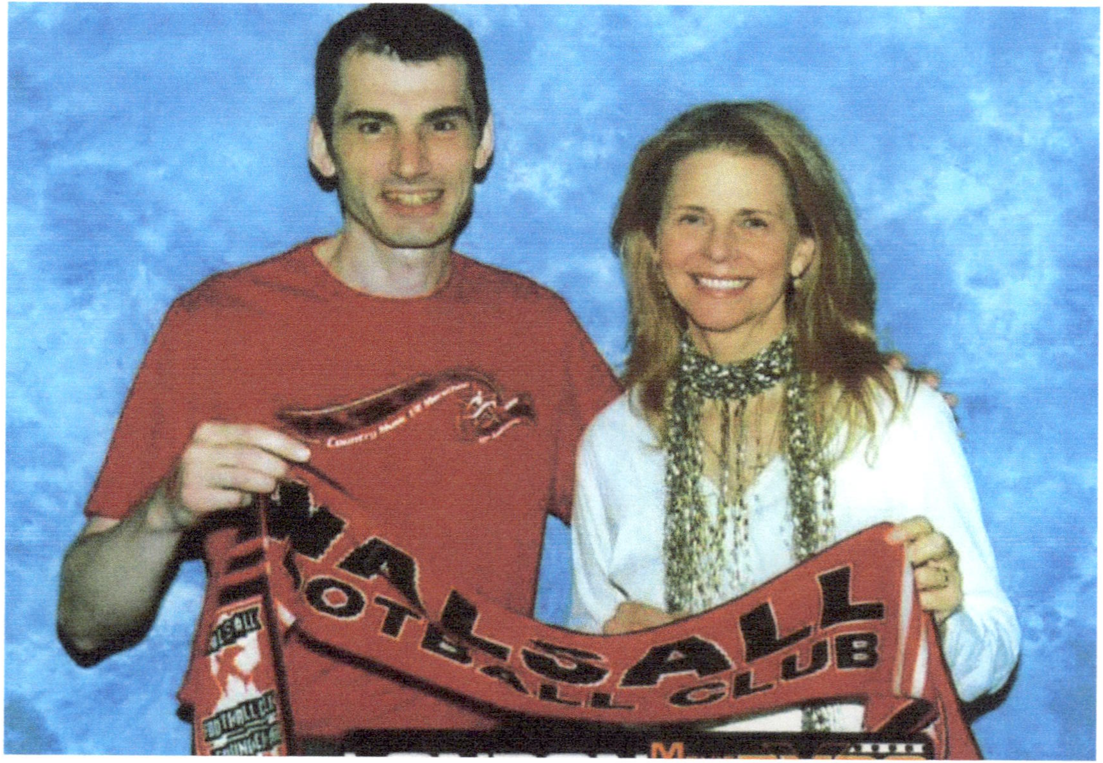
WALSALL

Lindsay Wagner

An American actress who is perhaps best known for her portrayal of Jaime Sommers in the popular television series *The Bionic Woman* (for which she won an Emmy Award), though she has maintained a lengthy career in a variety of other film and television productions since.

Lindsay Wagner worked as a model in Los Angeles, and gained some television experience by appearing as a hostess in *Playboy After Dark*. In 1971, she signed a contract with Universal Studios and worked as a contract player in various Universal productions. Her prime-time network television debut was in the series *Adam-12*, and she went on to appear in a dozen other Universal shows including *Owen Marshall: Counselor at Law*, *The F.B.I.*, *Sarge*, and *Night Gallery*. From 1971-75, she appeared in five episodes of Universal's *Marcus Welby, M.D.*, and two episodes of *The Rockford Files*. At around this time, Wagner branched into film roles when Universal cast her in *Two People* (Wagner's first feature film and lead role). She also starred in the film *The Paper Chase* (for 20th Century Fox) the same year.

In 1975, arranged under an extended contract with Universal Studios, Wagner played the role of Jaime Sommers, a former tennis professional who was the childhood sweetheart of *Six Million Dollar Man*, Steve Austin (played by Lee Majors). In the series a two-part episode called "The Bionic Woman", Jaime was critically injured in a skydiving accident and, at Steve's request due to his love for her; she was equipped with bionic implants similar to his own (with the exception of his bionic eye, as Jaime was equipped with a bionic ear instead). Jaime's body rejected her new bionics which ultimately led to her death.

This was intended to be Wagner's last role under her Universal contract, but public response to the character was so overwhelming that Jaime was "brought back to life" (it was discovered that Jaime hadn't really died but had been put into cryogenic suspension until she could be cured). She next appeared in a two-part episode of *The Six Million Dollar Man* entitled "The Return of the Bionic Woman", and soon after in her own spin-off series, *The Bionic Woman*, which debuted the following year.

Wagner continued to act, predominantly in television mini-series and made-for-TV movies. In 1983, she also appeared in an episode of Lee Majors' series, *The Fall Guy*.

In 1987, Wagner wrote a series of books with Robert M. Klein about using acupressure to achieve results akin to a surgical facelift.

More recently, Wagner has given seminars and workshops for her self-help therapy, "Quiet the Mind and Open the Heart", which promotes spirituality and meditation.

Seen here at the MCM Expo in London Wagner looks her radiant best and had to be called back for the picture, but did so without complaint, sparing her time only too readily for our scarf.

WALSALL FOOTBALL CLUB

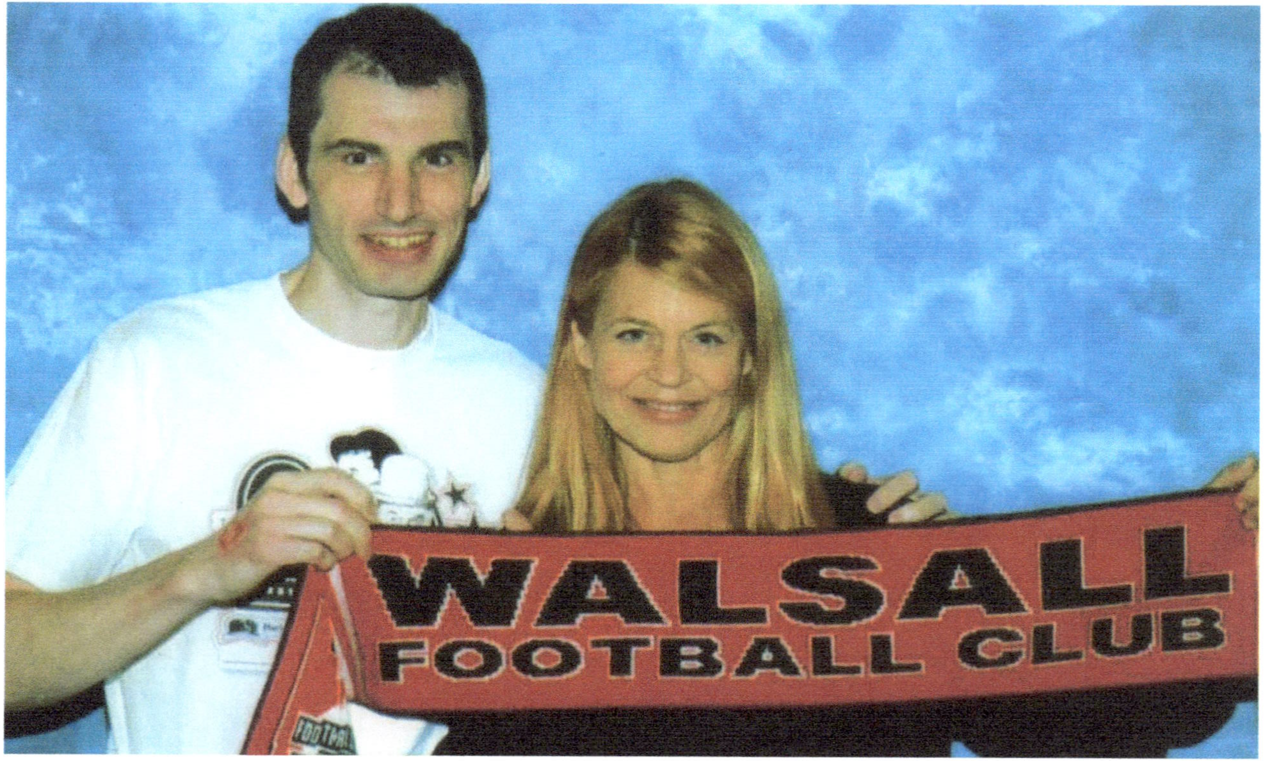
WALSALL
FOOTBALL CLUB

Linda Hamilton

Linda Hamilton is known to most for her portrayal of Sarah Connor in *The Terminator* and its sequel *Terminator 2: Judgment Day*. She was born in Salisbury, Maryland. Her mother was a Mayflower descendant and her father, Carroll Stanford Hamilton, was a physician.

Hamilton's acting debut came first on television, followed by a major role as Lisa Rogers in the prime-time soap opera *Secrets of Midland Heights*. Her theatrical debut was in the thriller *TAG: The Assassination Game* and as a result, she was listed as one of twelve "Promising New Actors of 1982" in John Willis' Screen World. She also shared a starring role in the CBS made for TV movie *Country Gold*, with Loni Anderson and Earl Holliman.

From such success she went on to play the lead in *Children of the Corn*, based on the horror short story by Stephen King. The movie, which made $14 million at the box office, was panned by critics. Hamilton's next role was in *The Terminator*, co-starring Arnold Schwarzenegger and Michael Biehn, in 1984. The movie was an unexpectedly huge commercial and critical success. Following *The Terminator*, Hamilton starred in *Black Moon Rising*, an action thriller with Tommy Lee Jones. She then returned to television as a guest-star in the mystery series *Murder, She Wrote*, scoring favorable reviews. Linda's next move saw her playing opposite Ron Perlman in the TV series *Beauty and the Beast*. Her work was critically acclaimed, and she quite rightly received Emmy and Golden Globe nominations, as well as being shown around the world. She left the series in 1989 and it came to an end in 1990.

With *Terminator 2: Judgment Day*, the sequel to *The Terminator*, she returned with a smash at the box office, grossing over $500 million, more than any other film of 1991. However, it was not before she underwent intense physical training to emphasize the character's transformation from the first film. Her identical twin sister Leslie Hamilton Gearren was Linda's double in *Terminator 2*. Hamilton received two MTV Movie Awards for her role in the film, one for Best Female Performance and the other for Most Desirable Female. She reprised the character, Sarah Connor, for the theme park attraction *T2 3-D*.

Post Terminator she has gone on to appear on the television shows *Frasier* (season 4 episode "Odd Man Out" as Laura) and *According to Jim* and has done more TV movies, including *On the Line*, *Robots Rising*, *Rescuers: Stories of Courage: Two Couples*, *Point Last Seen*, and *The Color of Courage*.

A warm and likeable person, she furnished the scarf holder with a kiss on this occasion at the MCM expo in London due to it being his birthday.

WALSALL FOOTBALL CLUB

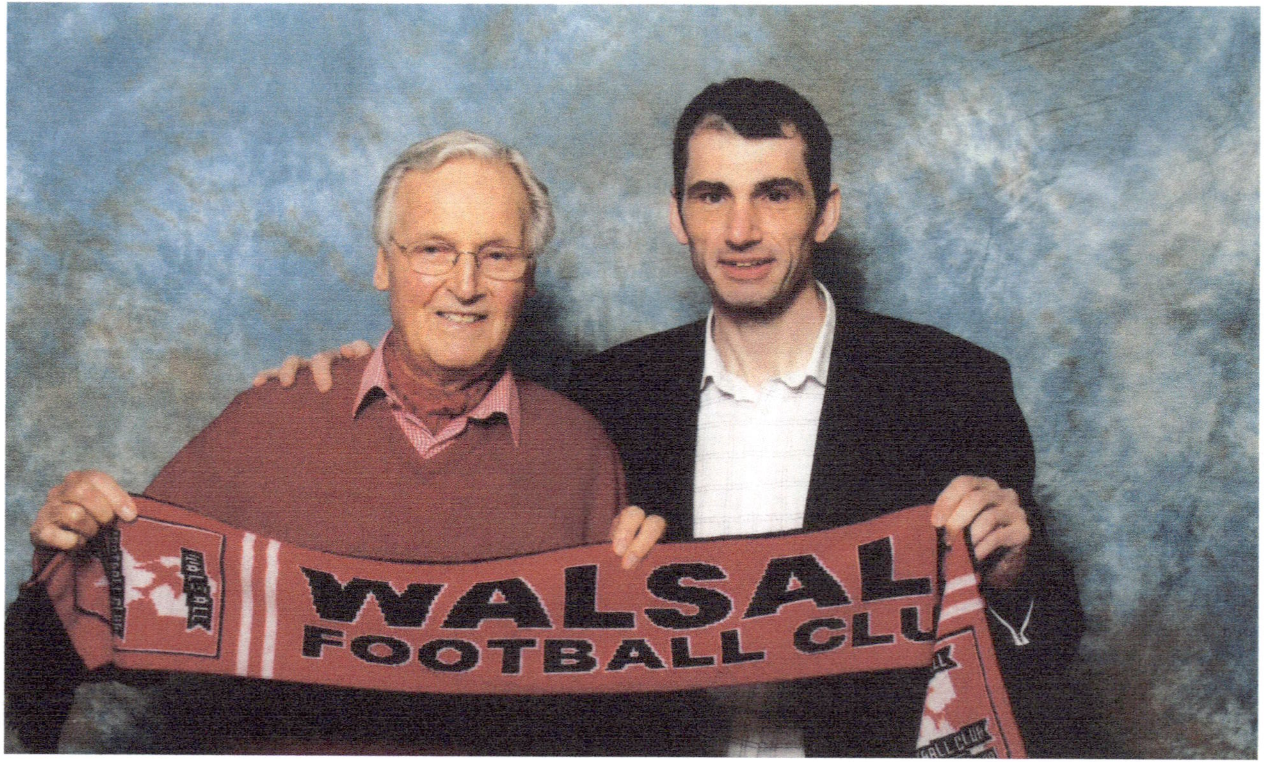
WALSAL
FOOTBALL CLU

Nicholas Parsons

At the end of World War II, Christopher Nicholas Parsons became a full time professional actor and gained parts in West End theatre productions. Parsons made his film debut in *Master of Bankdam* in 1947. He continued his stage career in West End theatre show and did two years in repertory at Bromley, Kent, and later Windsor, Maidstone and Hayes, as well as playing many supporting roles in British films in the 1950s and '60s. In 1952, he became a resident comedian at the Windmill Theatre, performing regular nights of stand-up comedy to packed houses. He starred in the West End show *Boeing-Boeing* for 15 months and continued to feature in West End productions throughout the 1970s.

Parsons became well known to TV audiences during the 1960s as the straight man to comedian Arthur Haynes. They had a successful season at The London Palladium as well as appearing on *The Ed Sullivan Show* in America in 1966. In the same year, the partnership broke up at Haynes request, allowing Parsons to return to the stage, before becoming a regular on *The Benny Hill Show* for five years. After Haynes' sudden death, Parsons appeared as a personality in his own right on television, including the long-running Anglia Television quiz show *Sale of the Century*, broadcast weekly from 1971 for almost a decade.

He was also the non-singing voice of Tex Tucker in the TV series *Four Feather Falls* at the suggestion of his then wife, actress and voiceover artiste Denise Bryer. During the late '60s he created and presented a satirical programme on Radio Four called *Listen to This Space*, which by the standards of its time was very avant garde, and he received the Radio Personality of the Year Award for his work on this programme in 1967. In the '50s and '60s he appeared in many supporting roles in British films. The big time truly beckoned when he portrayed "David Courtney" on the short-lived American sitcom *The Ugliest Girl in Town*.

Around this time he could also be found in the long-running BBC science fiction television series *Doctor Who* as the doomed Northumberland vicar Reverend Wainwright in the Seventh Doctor serial *The Curse of Fenric*. That same year he accepted a guest spot on *The New Statesman*, where he played the host of a daytime quiz show.

From 1988 to 1991, Parsons served as Rector of the University of St Andrews. Still active well into his eighties he became honorary Chairman of the International Quizzing Association (IQA), a body that organises the World and European Quizzing Championships in 2005.

He produced a book of memoirs in 2010 called *Nicholas Parsons: With Just a Touch of Hesitation, Repetition and Deviation*, and so it was during a book signing and promotion for this that the scarf caught up with him at the Thistle Hotel near to Heathrow.

WALSALL FOOTBALL CLUB

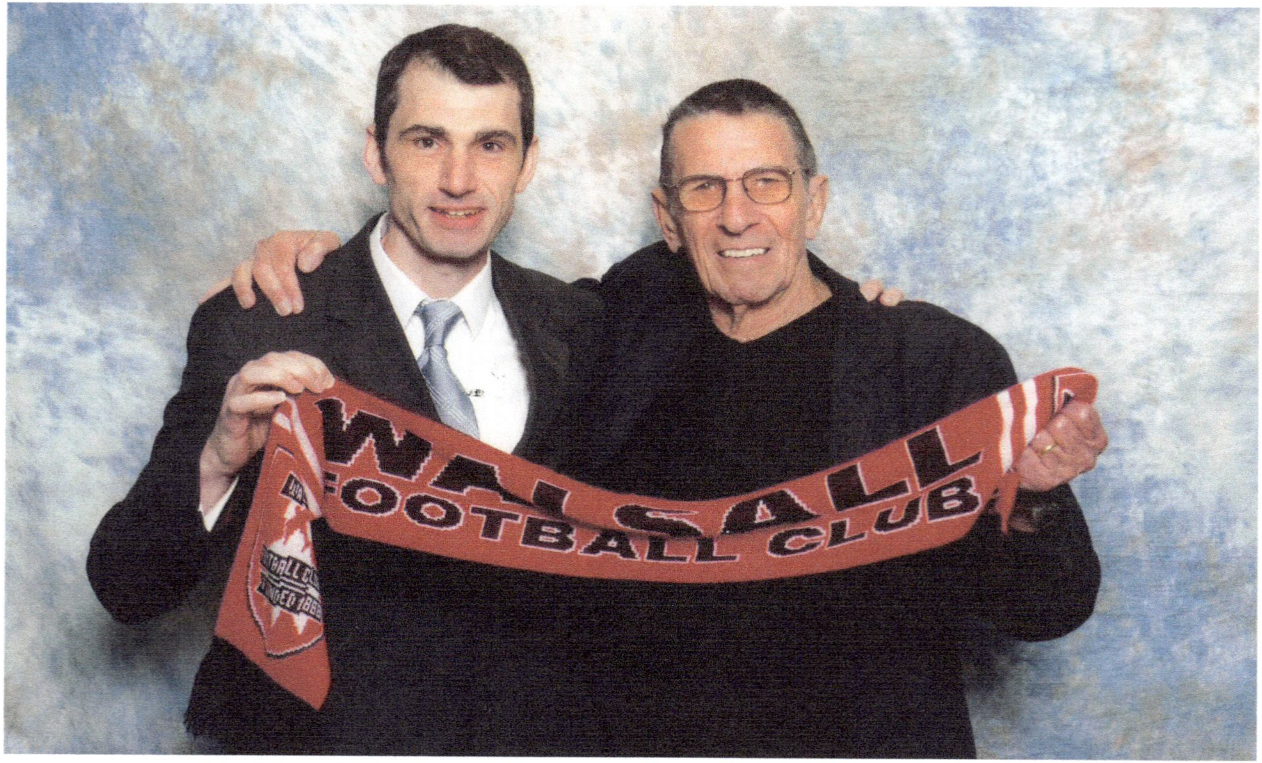
WALSALL
FOOTBALL CLUB

Leonard Nimoy

Nimoy began his career in his early twenties, teaching acting classes in Hollywood and making minor film and television appearances through the 1950s, as well as playing the title role in *Kid Monk Baroni*. In 1953, he served in the United States Army.

Undoubtedly his greatest prominence came from his role in the original *Star Trek* series. As the half-Vulcan, half-human Spock—a role he chose instead of one on the soap opera *Peyton Place*—he instantly became a star, and the press predicted that he would "have his choice of movies or television series." He formed a long-standing friendship with Shatner, who portrayed his commanding officer, saying of their relationship, "We were like brothers." *Star Trek: The Original Series* was broadcast from 1966 to 1969. He earned three Emmy nominations for his work on the iconic program that has defined American television science fiction, both for fans of science fiction, and beyond.

He went on to reprise the Spock character in *Star Trek: The Animated Series* and two episodes of *Star Trek: The Next Generation*. The six Star Trek movies feature the original *Star Trek* cast including Nimoy, who also directed two of the films. He played the elder Spock in the 2009 *Star Trek* movie, directed by J. J. Abrams.

Following on from success in *Star Trek*, Nimoy immediately joined the cast of the spy series *Mission: Impossible*, which was seeking a replacement for Martin Landau. Nimoy was cast in the role of Paris, an IMF agent who was an ex-magician and make-up expert 'The Great Paris'. He played the role during the fourth and fifth seasons of the show for three years.

Spock's Vulcan salute became a recognized symbol of the show and was identified with him. Nimoy created the sign himself from his childhood memories of the way *kohanim* (Jewish priests) held their hand when giving blessings. During an interview, he translated the Priestly Blessing which accompanied the sign and described it during a public lecture.

In April 2010, Leonard announced that he was retiring from playing the signature character of Star Trek's Spock, citing both his advanced age and the desire to give Zachary Quinto the opportunity to enjoy full media attention with the Spock character, *Kingdom Hearts: Birth by Sleep* was to be his final performance. However, in February the following year, he announced his definite plan to return to *Fringe* and reprise his role as William Bell.

During this period of retirement and resting Leonard Nimoy made a visit to Milton Keynes where amongst the crowds of fans and *Star Trek* cosplayers was a certain scarf waiting patiently in line for a turn with him.

"Live Long and Prosper Leonard!"

WALSALL FOOTBALL CLUB

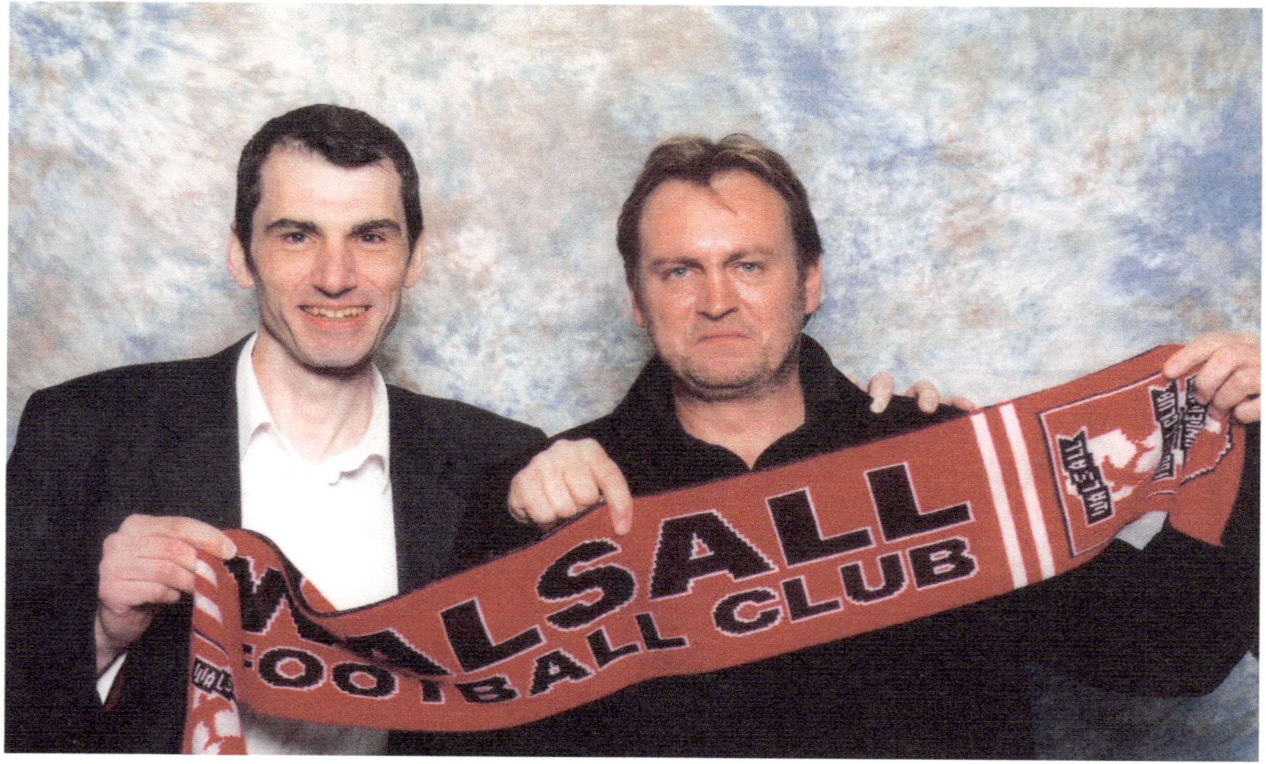
WALSALL
CLUB

Philip Glenister

In the early 1990s, Glenister appeared in various TV series including *Heartbeat*, *Dressing for Breakfast* and *Silent Witness*. He guest starred in *Sharpe's Justice* as Richard Sharpe's half-brother Matt Truman, as well as playing William Dobbin in the mini-series *Vanity Fair*.

At the close of the decade he co-starred as a mini-cab driver who aspires to be a rock star in the series *Roger Roger*. He went on to play factory boss Mack Mackintosh in the first three series of *Clocking Off*. In 2001, he appeared in two of the *Hornblower* TV films as Horatio's antagonist Gunner Hobbs.

Glenister played the photographer who took nude photos for a Women's Institute fundraising calendar in the feature film *Calendar Girls*. That same year, he appeared in the mini-series *State of Play*. The following year he could be seen taking on the role of a German commandant, Baron Heinrich Von Rheingarten, in another mini-series *Island at War* about the Occupation of the Channel Islands during World War II.

Of all these roles he is probably best known for his relatively recent role as DCI Gene Hunt in *Life On Mars*, in which he co-star's with John Simm as Sam Tyler, and its sequel *Ashes to Ashes* with Keeley Hawes as Alex Drake. Glenister also worked with Simm on *State of Play* and *Clocking Off*. Upon announcement of the film, he joked that he and Simm were contractually obliged to work with each other once a year.

After Gene Hunt be became the demon hunter Rupert Galvin in the ITV drama *Demons*. Using an American accent for the role, this received some criticism from reviewers. He decided against doing a second series, citing problems with the role and felt that he may have been miscast.

He was reunited with John Simm once more in the Sky TV mini-series *Mad Dogs* about a group of old friends whose holiday in Majorca takes an unexpected turn. After a successful reception, Glenister returned for a second run of the series a year later.

Outside of acting he is a patron of the charity Momentum in Kingston upon Thames, which aims to help children and the families of children undergoing treatment for cancer in Surrey

On the Paul O'Grady TV show recently, he claimed to be a fan of non-league football team Wealdstone. He is also a well known Arsenal fan and when asked to hold the Saddlers scarf in Milton Keynes he could be heard to scowl "Man City," under his breath.

WALSALL FOOTBALL CLUB

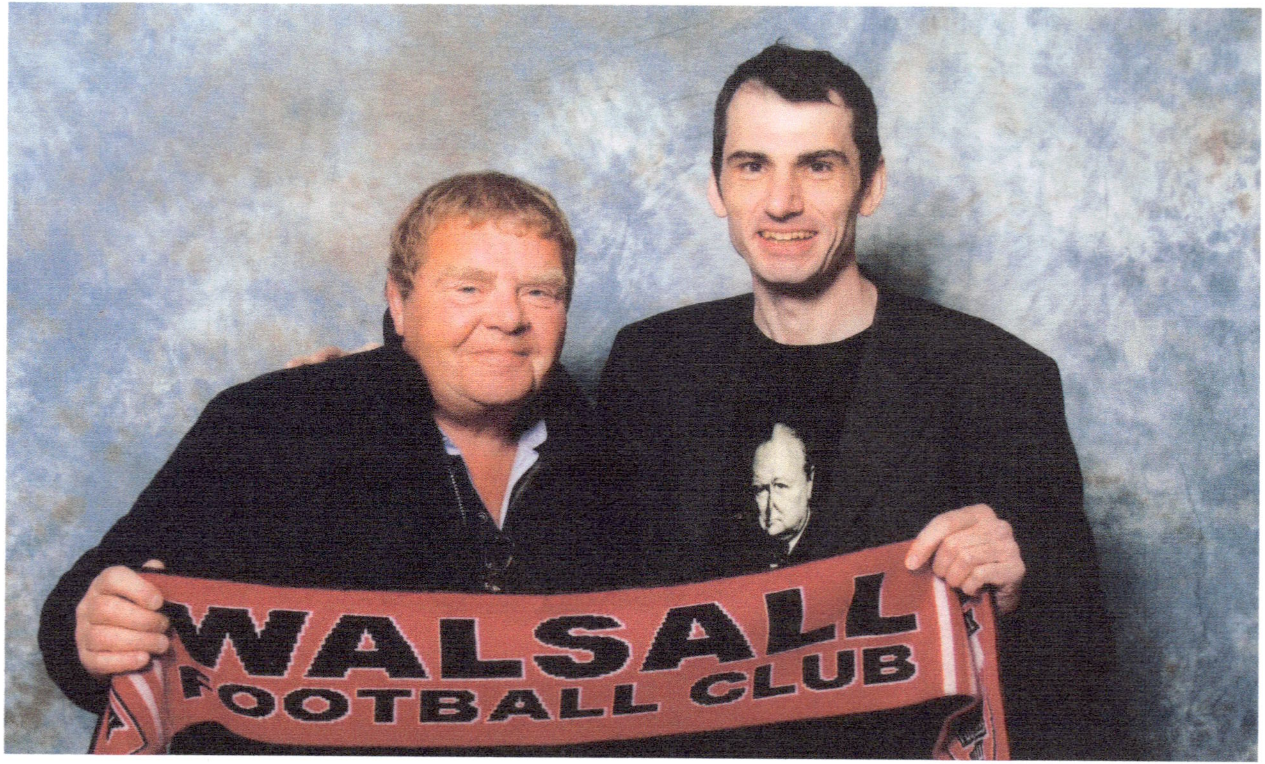
WALSALL
FOOTBALL CLUB

Geoffrey Hughes

Geoffrey Hughes first appeared on television in the 1960s, in series including *Z-Cars* and *The Likely Lads*, and was the voice of Paul McCartney in the film *Yellow Submarine*. Although usually cast in supporting roles, the 17-and-a-half stone Hughes invested them with a distinctive character which captured the hearts of television audiences. Meanwhile, his self-effacing but professional approach to acting meant that over nearly 50 years in the business he barely had a day's unemployment.

As everyone knows it was as the soft-hearted petty criminal turned binman Eddie Yeats, a role he played from 1974 to 1983 that cemented his popularity with the public. In fact, the part was not his first on *Coronation Street:* in 1965 he had appeared in three episodes as Eric Fairbrother, the bricklayer who beats up professional grumpy old man Albert Tatlock (Jack Howarth). For this he expected some abusive letters. "All I got," he recalled, "were two saying I should have killed him."

But it was as Eddie that Hughes became a household name. His character, an ex-Borstal boy, was introduced as Minnie Caldwell's lodger, newly paroled from prison, and provided a figure of comic relief in succession to his cellmate Ged Stone (played by Kenneth Cope).

He also appeared in several films, including *Smashing Time* (1967); *Till Death Us Do Part* (1965); *The Bofors Gun* (1968);

The Virgin Soldiers (1969); *Adolf Hitler: My Part in His Downfall* (1972); and *Carry on at Your Convenience* (1971).

Away from acting, Hughes retreated to Lilford Park, his 240-acre farm in the Nene valley, Northamptonshire, where he kept a small flock of sheep and renovated many of the old buildings, turning one into a craft centre which was run by his wife, Sue.

In 1996, during his spell as the beer-swilling Onslow in *Keeping Up Appearances*, Hughes was diagnosed with prostate cancer. He had major surgery and appeared to make a full recovery: within six weeks of the operation he was touring Australia in Alan Ayckbourn's play *Bedroom Farce*.

It was around this time that he put in some personal appearances around the country and the scarf caught up with him at Earl's Court in London for this shot.

In subsequent years he appeared in two short comedy films in aid of Macmillan Cancer Support, *Expresso* and *Waiting in Rhyme* (2009). In August 2010, however, he learned that the cancer had returned and he succumbed to the disease on July 27 2012. A loveable and warm hearted man he will truly be missed by his legion of fans.

WALSALL FOOTBALL CLUB

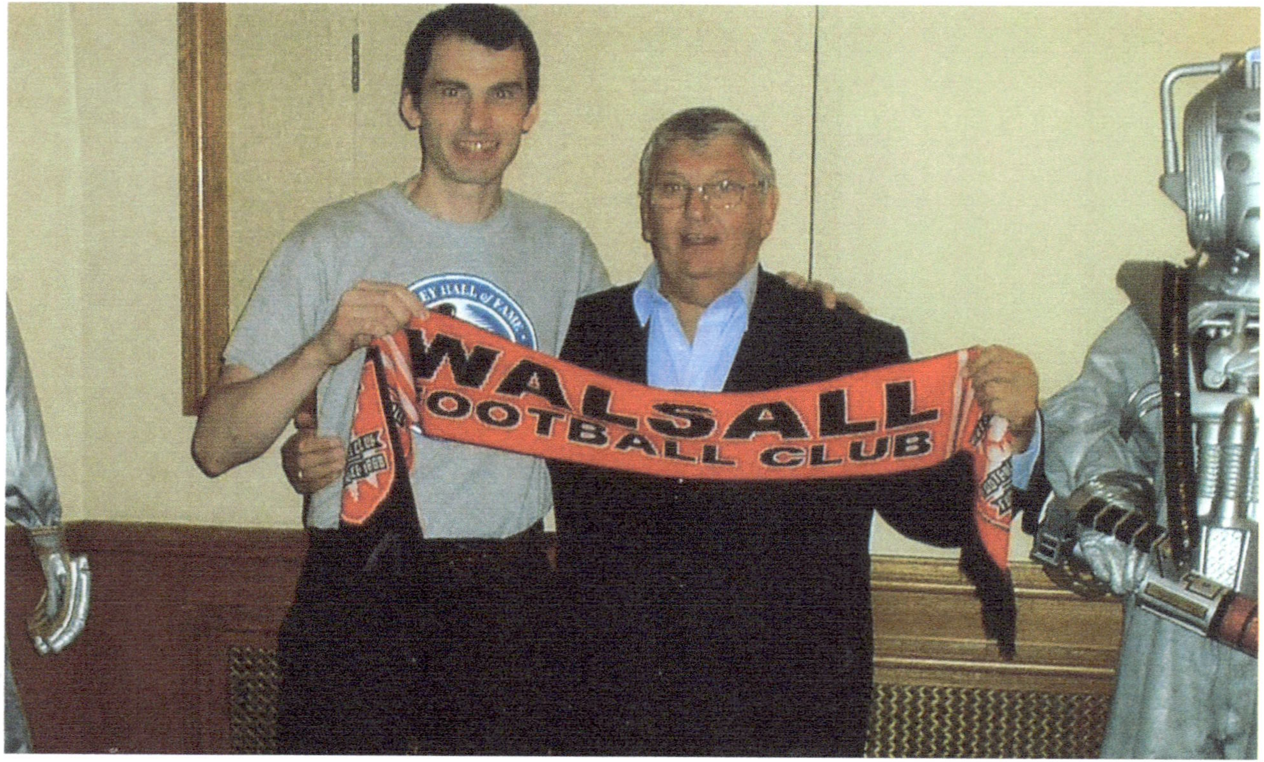
WALSALL
OOTBALL CLUB

Derek Martin

Derek Martin was born in Bow East London, where at the age of 15 his first job was as an apprentice to an Estate Agents and Surveyors, after this he worked in numerous jobs. Having found little fulfillment in any of these careers he joined the RAF at 18, becoming a 'snow drop' or RAF military police. He eventually left and for a time started a career in motor-racing, his ambition was to be world champion. During this period he fell foul of the law and found himself accused of receiving stolen goods, but was found not guilty. After this he decided to turn his hand to acting (after the strength of his recent performance).

His first job was as a walk on in a TV production. He caught the bug, left Smithfield and decided on the life of an actor. After a large number of small TV parts he then decided to become a stuntman and worked on many different techniques, including horses, car crashing, fencing, fights and arranging action scenes.

During his career as a stuntman he sustained a broken collar bone doing a horse fall in *Elizabeth R*. Three weeks after this accident he was back in the studio shooting another scene with his arm still in a sling.

He moved into acting and received his first big break in 1977 playing a leading character in the controversial drama series *Law and Order*, this put his name and face onto our screens.

In 1978 he appeared as Detective Inspector Fred Pyle in *The Detective's Tale*, the first play in the BBC television series *Law and Order*. From 1981 – 82, he played Det. Insp. Berwick in two series of the BBC drama *The Chinese Detective*. Later that year he became the second actor to take on the role of R. D. Wingfield's fictional Detective Inspector Jack Frost, starring in a BBC radio adaptation of *A Touch of Frost*. In 1984 he appeared in an episode of *Minder* alongside Dennis Waterman and George Cole. He then starred in *Eldorado* as Alex Morris.

In addition he has made a raft of guest appearances in many television programmes including *Doctor Who* appearing in The Ambassadors of Death as an uncredited heavy, The Claws of Axos as an uncredited UNIT soldier and Image of the Fendahl as policeman David Mitchell, *The Sweeney* episode 'Messenger of the Gods' as the villain Spooner, *Upstairs, Downstairs*, *The Bill* and *Only Fools and Horses*. Martin also played himself in an episode of *Little Britain*.

Starting in late September 2000 he landed the role of Charlie Slater in *EastEnders*. This proved to be a long and successful decade until it was announced that Martin had been cut from the show along with five other actors.

It was through an appearance to mark his time on Doctor Who that Derek Martin joined the illustrious in supporting the Saddlers along with a Cyberman in the background.

WALSALL FOOTBALL CLUB

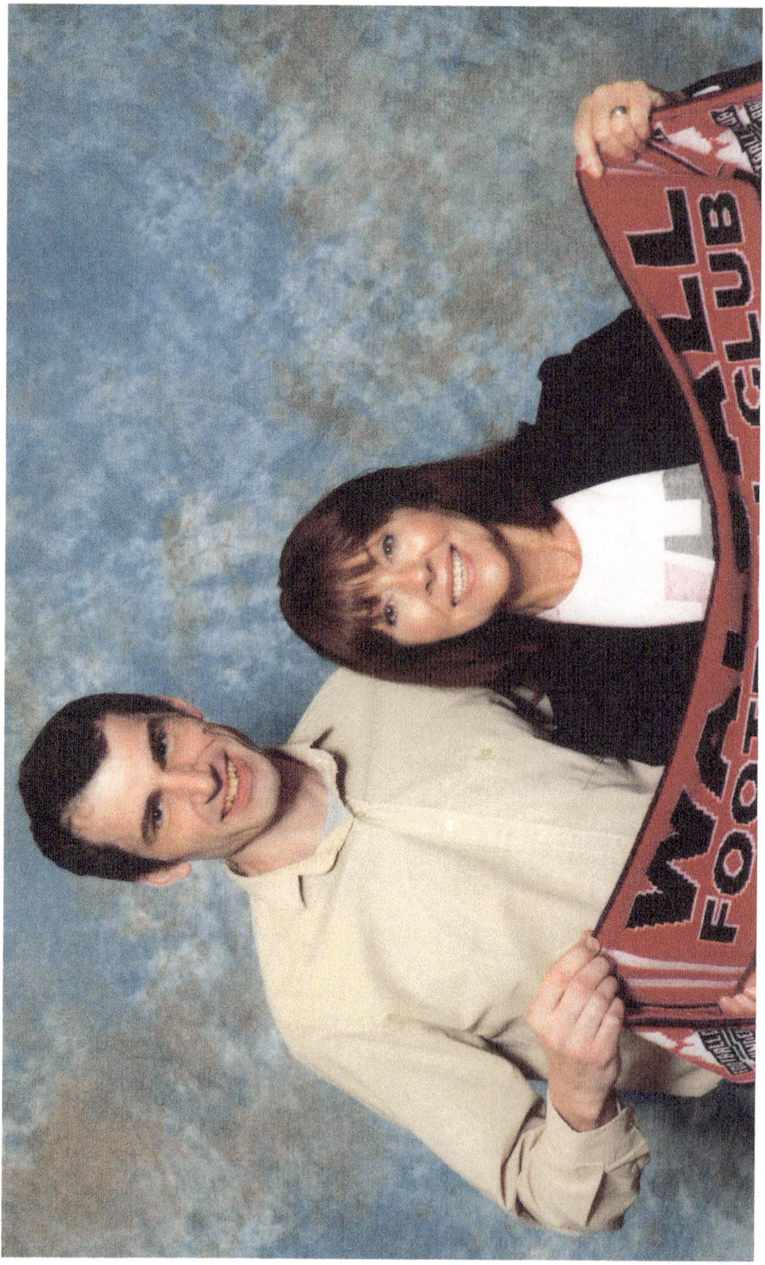

Elizabeth Sladen

After two years at drama school, Elisabeth Clara Heath-Sladen began work at the Liverpool Playhouse repertory company as an assistant stage manager. She eventually moved into weekly repertory work, traveling to various locations in England. Sladen and her future husband Brian Miller moved to Manchester, in 1966, spending three years there. They married two years later. She cropped up in numerous roles, most notably as Desdemona in *Othello*, her first appearance as a leading lady.

In around 1973, *Doctor Who* actress Katy Manning, who was playing the Third Doctor's assistant Jo Grant opposite Jon Pertwee, announced she was leaving the series; *Z-Cars* producer Ron Craddock gave Sladen an enthusiastic recommendation to Doctor Who supremo Barry Letts. She arrived at the audition not knowing it was for the new companion role, and was amazed at Letts's thoroughness. Upon being introduced to Pertwee for the first time she confessed to being a little intimidated at the time. As she chatted with Letts and Pertwee, each time she turned to look at one of them the other would signal a thumbs-up.

She stayed on *Doctor Who* for three-and-a-half seasons, alongside Pertwee as the Third Doctor and Tom Baker as the Fourth. She made further returns to the character of Sarah Jane Smith on several occasions.

The arrival of her first daughter Sadie in 1985 saw her go into semi-retirement, choosing her family before work commitments, but finding time for the occasional television appearance.

Upon the successful revival of *Doctor Who* in 2005, Sladen guest starred as Sarah Jane in "School Reunion", an episode of the 2006 series, along with David Tennant as the Tenth Doctor. Sladen worked herself into a lot of the characterisation as she had stated in an interview that she felt Sarah Jane was a bit of a cardboard cut-out one dimensional character as she stood.

Following her successful appearance in the series, Sladen later starred in *The Sarah Jane Adventures*, a *Doctor Who* spin-off focusing on Sarah Jane, produced by BBC Wales for CBBC and created by Russell T. Davies. A 60-minute special aired on New Year's Day 2007, with a 10-episode series commencing broadcast in September, and a second 12-episode series was broadcast. The programme won a Royal Television Society award for Best Children's Drama the year after.

Her final appearance in *Doctor Who* was a cameo in the concluding part of "The End of Time", Tennant's last episode as the Doctor before Matt Smith took over the mantle.

A frequent attendee of various shows nationally, it took two attempts to finally get this wonderful lady to pose with the scarf. Sadly Lizzie died early on 19 April 2011, after having been diagnosed with cancer two months earlier.

WALSALL FOOTBALL CLUB

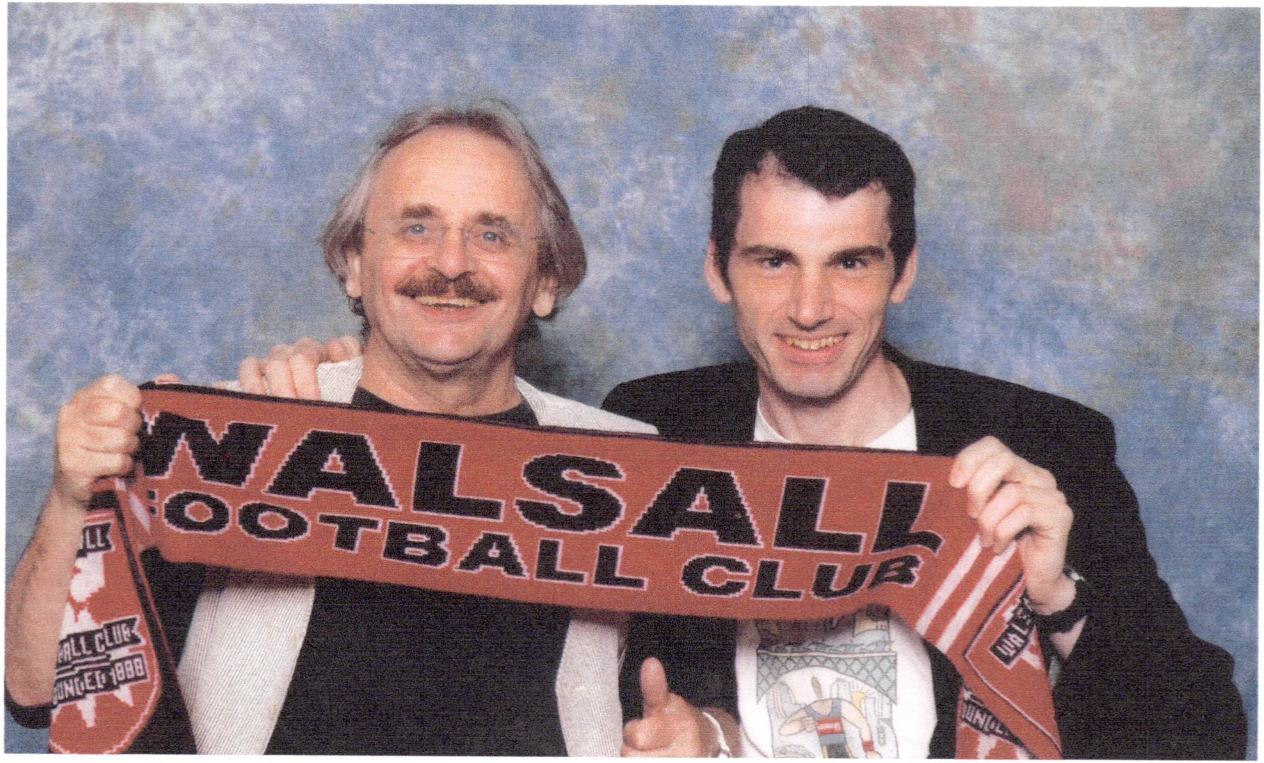
WALSALL
FOOTBALL CLUB

Sylvester McCoy

Born Percy James Patrick Kent-Smith on 20 August 1943, Sylvester McCoy is a Scottish actor. As a comic act and busker he appeared regularly on stage and in BBC Children's television during the 1970s and 80s, before going on to play the seventh incarnation of the Doctor.

Notable television appearances before he gained the role of the Doctor included roles in *Vision On* (where he played Pepe/Epep, a character who lived in the mirror), an O-Man in *Jigsaw* and *Tiswas*. He also could be seen in *Eureka*, often suffering from the inventions of Wilf Lunn. McCoy also portrayed, in one-man shows on the stage, two famous movie comedians: Stan Laurel and Buster Keaton. He played a more serious role as Henry "Birdie" Bowers in the 1985 television serial about Scott's last Antarctic expedition, *The Last Place on Earth*.

McCoy became the Seventh Doctor after taking over the lead role in *Doctor Who* from previous Timelord Colin Baker. He remained on the series until it ended in 1989. As Colin Baker had declined the invitation to film the regeneration scene, McCoy briefly wore a wig and appeared as him in the iconic scene. He played the Doctor in the charity special *Dimensions in Time*, and again in 1996, appearing in the beginning of the *Doctor Who* television movie starring Paul McGann as the Eighth Doctor. McCoy is thus acknowledged as the actor who, in a way, played the Doctor for a longer "period of time" than any other.

In the early 1990s, McCoy was hired for the role of Governor Swann in *Pirates of the Caribbean: The Curse of the Black Pearl* which Steven Spielberg was planning on directing, but Disney did not give permission for the film to be made. McCoy was the second choice to play the role of Bilbo Baggins in the Peter Jackson *The Lord of the Rings* film trilogy. In 1991, he fronted the *Doctor Who* video documentary release *The Hartnell Years* which showcased selected episodes of missing stories from the First Doctor's era and proved a great hit with fans.

On stage he has made appearances as the Sheriff of Nottingham in a musical version of Robin Hood that featured songs by British composer and lyricist Laurence Mark Wythe at the Broadway Theatre, Lewisham in London. He also appeared as the lawyer Dowling in a BBC Production of Henry Fielding's novel, *The History of Tom Jones, A Foundling*. In 2001 McCoy appeared in Paul Sellar's asylum comedy "The Dead Move Fast" at the Gilded Balloon as part of the Edinburgh Festival Fringe, playing the role of Doctor Mallinson.

Seen here is a seated Sylvester McCoy who attended a Big Finish event in Birmingham, after having sustained a fracture to his foot which necessitated the wearing of an air boot for the duration. Fortunately it had no effect on the scarf.

WALSALL FOOTBALL CLUB

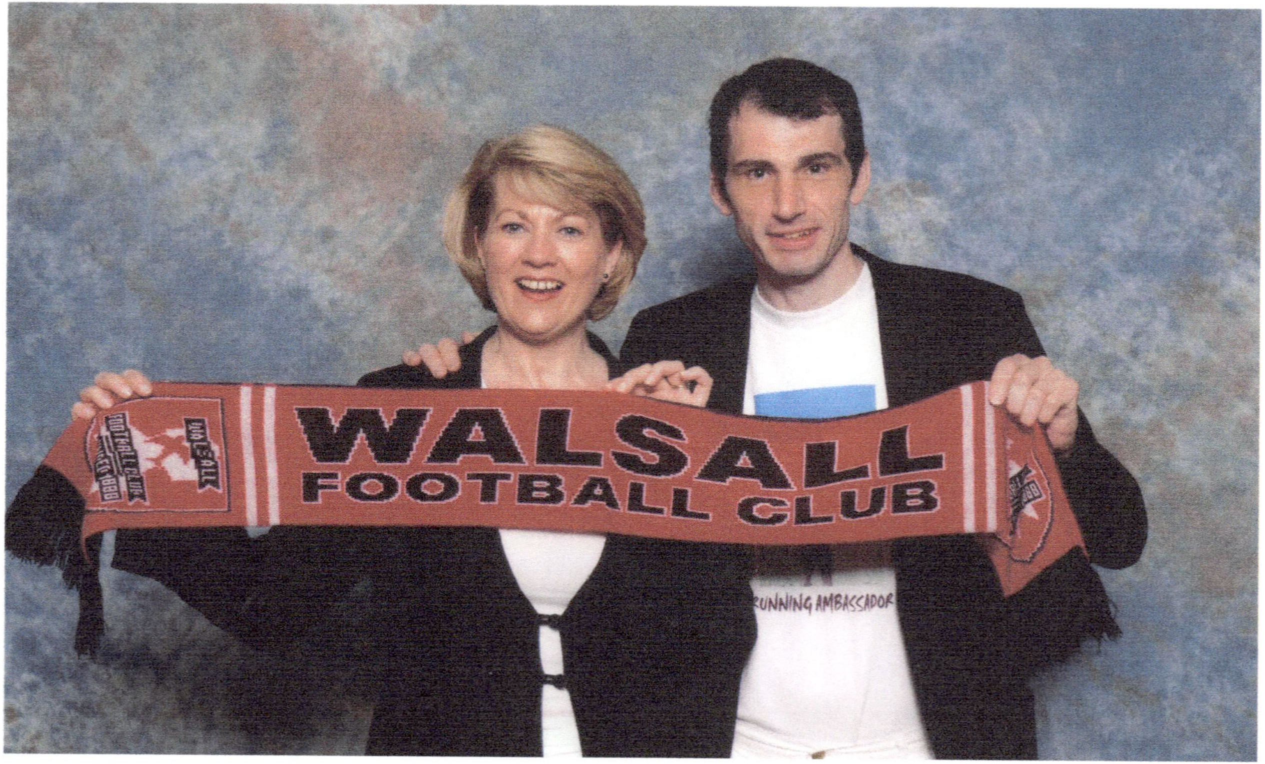

WALSALL
FOOTBALL CLUB
RUNNING AMBASSADOR

Tracey Childs

Tracey Childs is perhaps best known for playing Lynne Howard in the drama series *Howards' Way*, which ran for five years from 1985. Set around the river Hamble, it dealt with an aircraft designer who had become a boat builder, and whose daughter had an on-off-on affair with the character played by Anholt. The daughter was played by Childs, who became Anholt's real-life second wife after an affair that began while the series was still running.

Anholt died aged 61 after a period of illness caused by a brain tumour. Whilst Childs and Anholt were married they toured with Marc Sinden and Gemma Craven in Noël Coward's *Private Lives* throughout 1991 and into 1992. More recently, she has appeared in the light hearted drama Born and Bred based around the fictional village of Ormston in Lancashire during the 1950s, as Linda Cosgrove and as Patty Cornwell in *Hollyoaks*, the long running soap opera set in the fictional suburb of Chester.

Her first on-screen role was in the *Upstairs, Downstairs* episode, Wanted – a Good Home. She also appeared in *The Prime of Miss Jean Brodie* as Rose Stanley, *Sense and Sensibility*, *The Scarlet Pimpernel* and made an appearance in *Bergerac*, the episode "A Perfect Recapture". She appeared as Pompeiian citizen Caecilius's wife Metella in *The Fires of Pompeii*, in the fourth season of the BBC's re-launched Doctor Who. She also went on to voice the *Figurehead* in the Big Finish Productions audio version of Time Works, gaining a large following amongst Doctor Who fans.

She is a regular performer (and part of the original cast) of the international touring play *Seven Deadly Sins Four Deadly Sinners* and in November 2007, appeared at the Théâtre Princesse Grace, Monte Carlo, being directed by Marc Sinden, as part of his British Theatre Season, Monaco.

In 2008 Andrew Hall directed Edward Albee's "Who's Afraid of Virginia Woolf?" which included Matthew Kelly as George, and Childs as Martha, during a stint at The Garrick theatre in Lichfield. When the production was offered a run at The Trafalgar Studios the following spring, Andrew and Tracey joined forces to produce the transfer themselves. The show received rave reviews and enjoyed a sell-out season. Andrew and Tracey discovered they enjoyed producing and made a great team. So, a new producing partnership came into being. Haunting Julia at Riverside Studios was the first production under the Hall and Childs banner and they then took the show on tour. They currently have a slate of other projects in development. Tracey is now full time producing and is an outstanding new talent that truly excites in theatre circles.

An extremely friendly and approachable character she was keen to take hold of the scarf only too readily at Milton Keynes Doctor Whofest.

WALSALL FOOTBALL CLUB

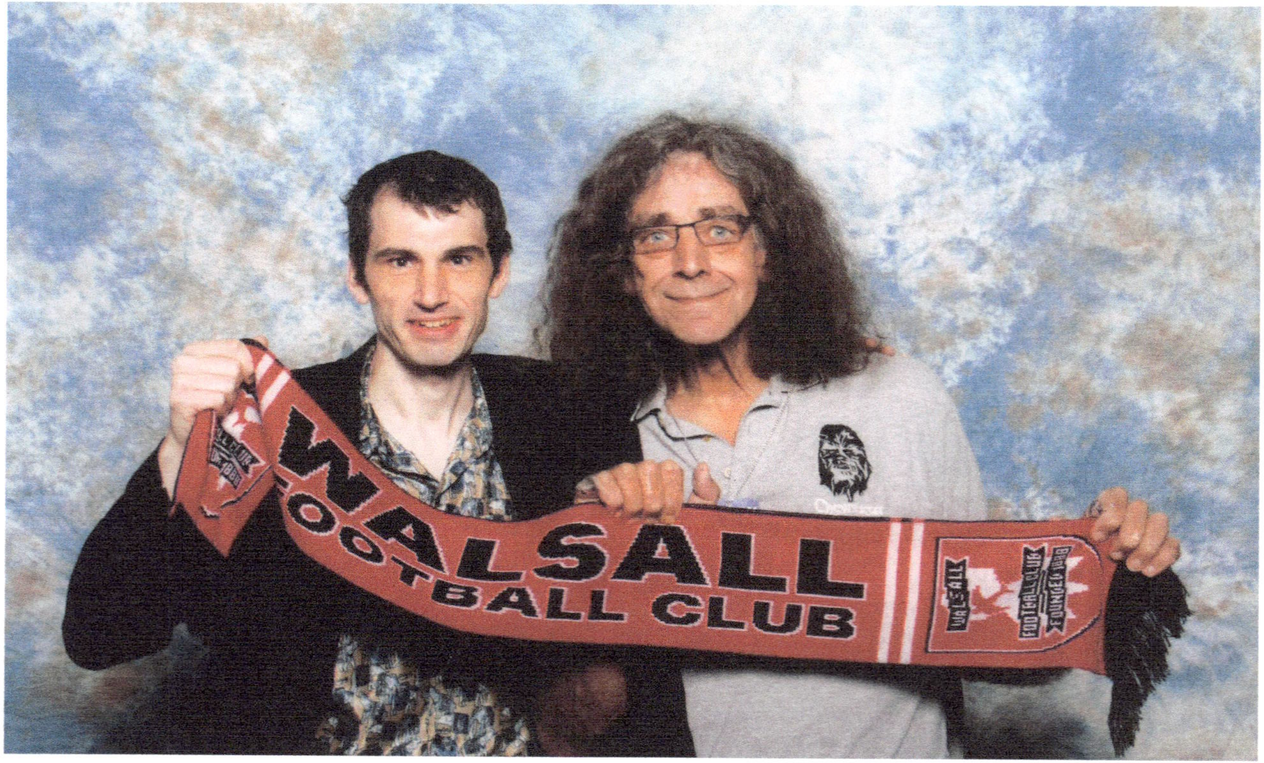
WALSALL
FOOTBALL CLUB

Peter Mayhew

He got his first acting job in 1976 when the producers of *Sinbad and the Eye of the Tiger* discovered Mayhew from a photograph in a newspaper article about men with large feet, and they instantly cast him in the role of the Minotaur.

When scouting talent for his first *Star Wars* film, producer George Lucas needed a tall actor who could fit the role of the beastly Chewbacca. He originally had in mind 6 feet 6 inches bodybuilder David Prowse, but he was instead cast to play Darth Vader. This led Lucas on a search which turned up Mayhew, who says that all he had to do to be cast in the role of Chewbacca was stand up. He reprised his signature role during *Star Wars Episode III: Revenge of the Sith*, which was released in cinemas on his birthday in 2005.

Mayhew has played the part of Chewbacca in four *Star Wars* films in total. The original Star Wars trilogy (*Star Wars Episode IV: A New Hope*, *Star Wars Episode V: The Empire Strikes Back*, and *Star Wars Episode VI: Return of the Jedi*) and *Star Wars Episode III: Revenge of the Sith*. He also played the role in the 1978 television film *The Star Wars Holiday Special*, as well as in an appearance on *The Muppet Show*. In addition, he recorded dialogue as Chewbacca for the animated show *The Clone Wars*, in the Season 3 final episode called *Wookiee Hunt*. Mayhew often can be seen donning his costume for commercials and also hospital appearances for sick children. Whilst getting into the part, he studied the movement of large animals at the zoo to come up with an authentic sense of movement for Chewbacca. When Mayhew grew ill in the shooting of *The Empire Strikes Back*, a similarly tall stand in was used, but the actor could not match Mayhew's studied movement style and the scenes had to be re-shot upon his recovery. Mayhew did not provide the voice of Chewbacca; that was created by the film's sound designer, Ben Burtt, by mixing together the growls of different animals.

Mayhew has made numerous appearances as Chewbacca outside the *Star Wars* films. He was honoured with a Lifetime Achievement Award at the MTV Film Awards 1997. In addition he has been honoured at the release of the new PlayStation Portable where he dressed as Chewbacca and held up the new PSP slim version. Mayhew also reprised his role in the Disney theme park attraction, *Star Tours: The Adventures Continue*.

He has made other media appearances without the Chewbacca costume. Mayhew appeared on NBC's *Identity*, where his identity was based on the fact that he played Chewbacca.

Amongst a varied film career, Mayhew has appeared in the horror film *Terror*, directed by Norman J. Warren. In the English version of *Dragon Ball GT: A Hero's Legacy*, he also voiced the character Susha. As well as being seated for this meeting with the scarf in London, Mayhew is probably one of the tallest to have the honour.

WALSALL FOOTBALL CLUB

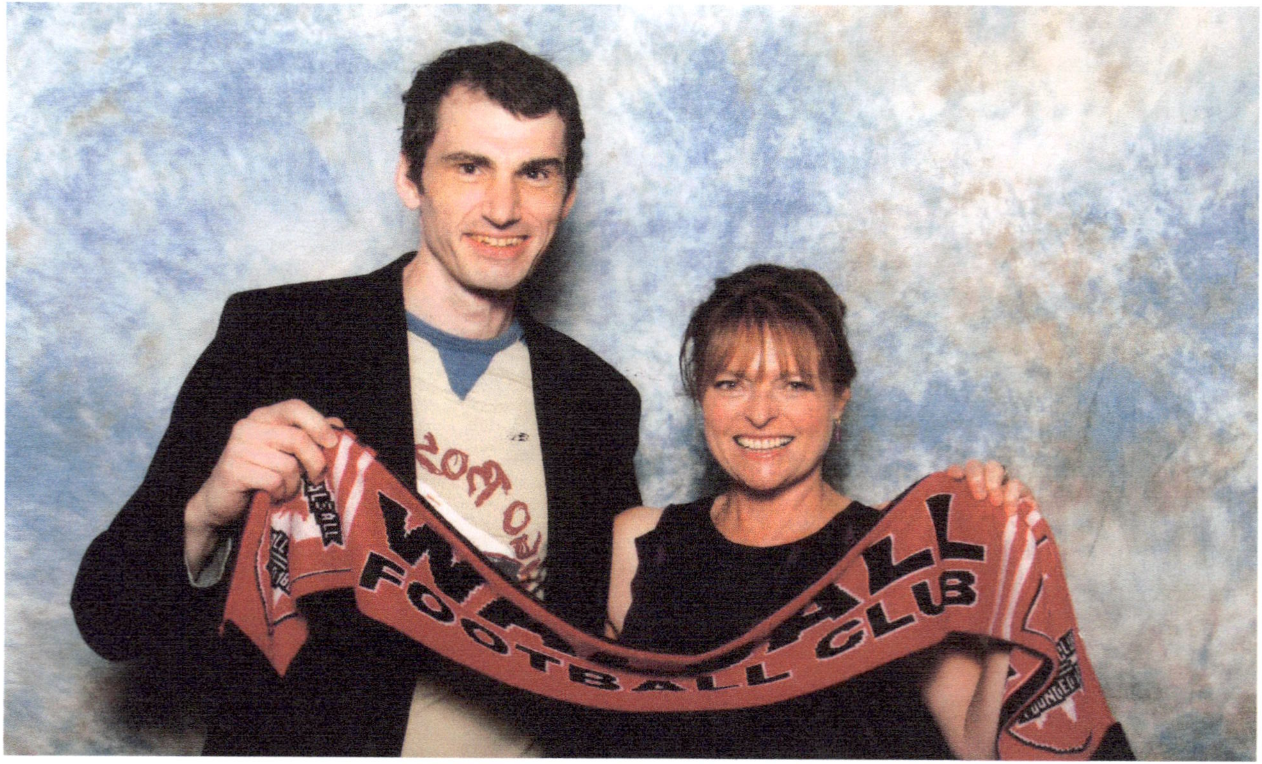
FOOTBALL CLUB

Janet Ellis

Janet trained as an actress before turning her talents to presenting. Her first screen credit was playing 'Susie, Marge's friend' in an episode of *The Sweeney*, but her big break was as Tika in the Doctor Who story *The Horns of Nimon* in 1979.

Three years later she went on to present *Jigsaw*, the children's puzzle series alongside Adrian Hedley, the animated Jig, Mr Nosey Bonk and a pre-Doctor Who Sylvester McCoy as one-half of the O-Men. it was this show which brought Janet to the attention of the *Blue Peter* production team, who were impressed by her presenting and acting skills.

But Janet's appearance on the show wasn't the first time that she had appeared on television with Simon Groom, Peter Duncan and Sarah Greene. They had all appeared on the 1982 *All-star Record Breakers* show, with Janet appearing in a chorus line of lovely lady presenters.

During her time on the show Janet impressed fellow presenters with her ability to learn the scripts and cope with last-minute changes. "Janet could learn the bible if she had to," remembers Mark Curry.

But it is for her pluck and courage during her free fall jumps with the RAF that Janet is best remembered, especially when she returned to her training after injuring her pelvis to break a record and become the first British woman to make a free fall parachute jump in 90 seconds.

Janet left *Blue Peter* to have her second child. Rumour has it that she was sacked because she wasn't married to the father, but in actual fact it was Janet's decision to leave. Contrary to popular myth the child was not in fact Sophie Ellis Bexter

She also returned to *Blue Peter* for The Quest and Christmas at the Club Blue Peter.

In recent years, Janet has returned to broadcasting. She's interviewed Tom Baker for *Loose Ends* and appeared in a regular guest spot on Channel Five's topical discussion show *The Wright Stuff*.

Ellis came back to our screens in 2000. She played a TV reporter in an episode of the first full series of *Waking the Dead* in 2001.

. Her first major presenting job since *Blue Peter* was the property show *Housebusters* between 2003 and 2005 on Five.

The scarf caught up with her in Earl's Court where she gamely held the scarf, before examining it closer to check to see if it did not have anything derogatory.- it would seem that caution is still a trait for a *Blue Peter* presenter.

WALSALL FOOTBALL CLUB

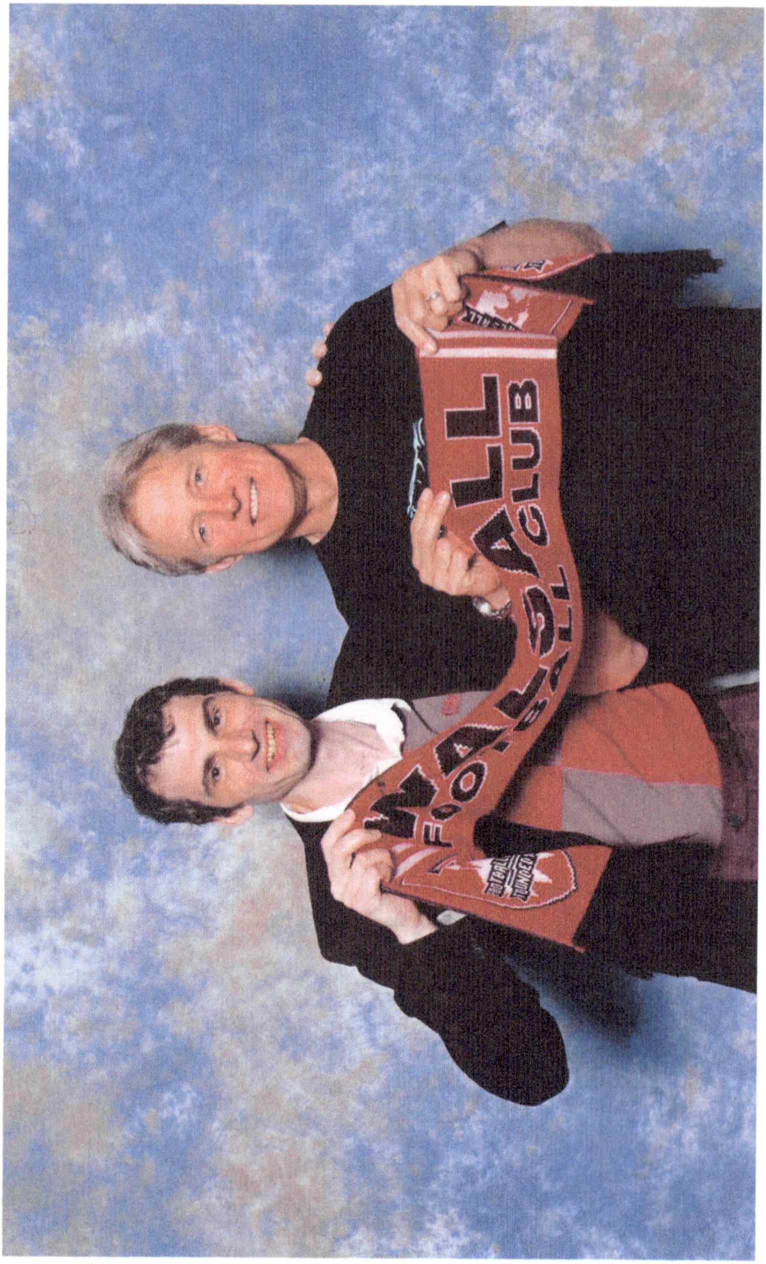

Bruce Boxleitner

Boxleitner was born in Elgin, Illinois, the son of a certified public accountant. He attended Prospect High School in Mount Prospect, Illinois, and the Goodman Theater School of Drama of the Art Institute of Chicago (later renamed The Theatre School at DePaul University).

Probably best known for his leading roles in the television series *How the West Was Won*, *Bring 'Em Back Alive*, *Scarecrow and Mrs. King* (with Kate Jackson), and *Babylon 5* (as John Sheridan in seasons 2–5). He also starred in *The Gambler* TV film series (as *Billy Montana*, alongside Kenny Rogers). In 2005, he co-starred as Captain Martin Duvall in *Young Blades*. He has also starred in several films within the *Babylon 5* universe, including *Babylon 5: In the Beginning*, *Babylon 5: Thirdspace*, *Babylon 5: A Call to Arms*, and the direct-to-DVD *Babylon 5: The Lost Tales* and on CHAOS – Glory Days episode.

He has made appearances in many other TV shows, such as *The Mary Tyler Moore Show*, *Gunsmoke*, *Judith Krantz's Till We Meet Again*, *Tales from the Crypt*, *Touched by an Angel*, *The Outer Limits* and *She Spies*. In 1982, he went on to play Chase Marshall in the TV film *Bare Essence*, with Genie Francis. He also was a member of the cast of *Heroes* for seasons three and four, playing New York Governor Robert Malden in three episodes. He could also be seen in the television series *Chuck* as the father of Devon Woodcomb.

He has also been in the made-for-television films *The Secret, Hope Ranch, Falling in Love with the Girl Next Door, Pandemic, The Bone Eater, Sharpshooter* and *Aces 'n Eights*.

Perhaps his most famous role was in the classic sci-fi film *Tron* – in which he played the title role) and *The Baltimore Bullet* with James Coburn. Later he cashed in on this by reprising his role in the *Tron* sequel *Tron: Legacy* and in the video game *Tron: Evolution* which was released alongside the film *Tron: Legacy*.

A little known fact is that during most of the 80's, Boxleitner appeared in advertisements for Estee Lauder's "Lauder for Men" fragrance.

Boxleitner was a guest-star on *NCIS* in the fall of 2010. He played Vice Admiral C. Clifford Chase, a high-ranking Navy official. Boxleitner also lends his voice to the animated version of his iconic character Tron in the animated series *Tron: Uprising*.

Seen here at the Olympia 2 hall during a film convention the scarf met up with him on another occasion in Birmingham when he recognised it after such a long period away.

WALSALL FOOTBALL CLUB

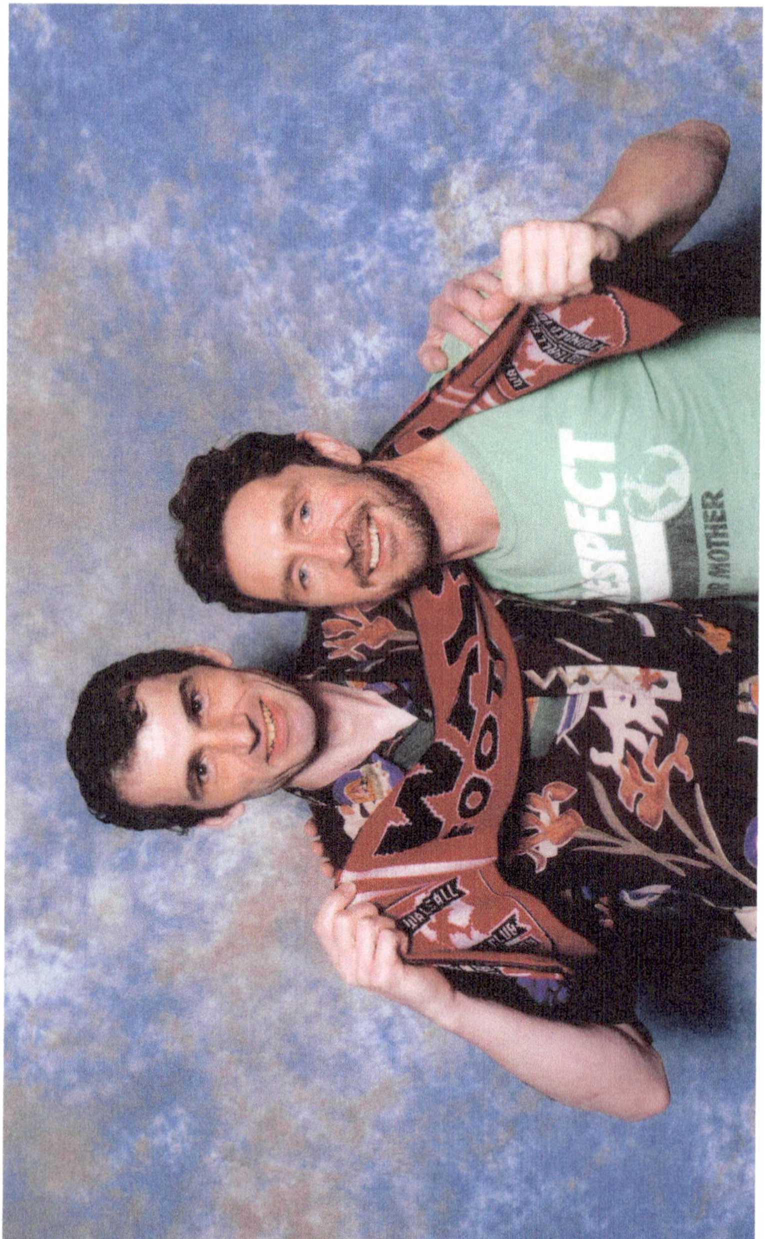

Paul McGann

McGann's breakthrough role was *Give us a Break* devised by Geoff McQueen who also created the long running ITV series, *The Bill*. McGann played a good snooker player who got into scrapes with Robert Lindsay, who took on the role as his manager.

Following on from this he scored his first major dramatic role as the infamous British deserter and criminal Percy Toplis in the 1986 BBC serial *The Monocled Mutineer*. The film was based on the book of the same name, which was written by William Alison and John Fairley.

Although McGann received praises for his dramatic performance, the drama was never re-broadcast on the BBC. This is because they came under fire from the Conservative Government due to the sensitivity of the subject matter of the Étaples Mutiny in 1917 at the "Bull Ring". The events that transpired remain hotly debated, and documents concerning the occurrences there will remain sealed until 2017. They claimed that the film was inaccurate and displayed a Left-wing bias.

Rather surprisingly after *Mutineer*, he sought a less controversial and more comedic role for his next project. In 1986, he was cast as the eponymous "I" in Bruce Robinson's cult film comedy, *Withnail and I*. He also starred as Anton Skrebensky in Ken Russell's adaptation of D.H. Lawrence's *The Rainbow*.

Perhaps his finest hour was when he played the eighth incarnation of the Doctor in the *Doctor Who* television film. The project was a joint venture between the BBC, Universal Studios and the Fox Broadcasting Network, with the option to appear as the Eighth Doctor in a new Doctor Who series, if Fox or Universal exercised their option. Thus, the television film was supposed to be a "back door pilot" in that, if it obtained respectable ratings, the new series would continue to be produced.

Since the years following his appearance as the Doctor, Paul McGann continued to diversify his acting portfolio with the television and film roles he accepted. In 1997 he appeared as a concerned father in the film *Fairytale: A True Story* and later that same year as Rob in *Downtime*, and then he took on the part as Capt. Greville in *The Dance of Shiva*.

Perhaps his most totemic role, since Doctor Who, came in 2002, when he appeared in the film adaptation of the third story from Anne Rice's The Vampire Chronicles, *Queen of the Damned*. Playing the part of David Talbot, a member of the secret organisation the Talamasca, this researches and investigates the supernatural. Talbot has appeared in many of Rice's novels and has become a central character over the years.

Tenth Planet Events hosted the first Big Finish Day in Barking with guests and Paul McGann enthusiastically hoisted the scarf, but I have a feeling he thought it was from another team also known as the Reds.

WALSALL FOOTBALL CLUB

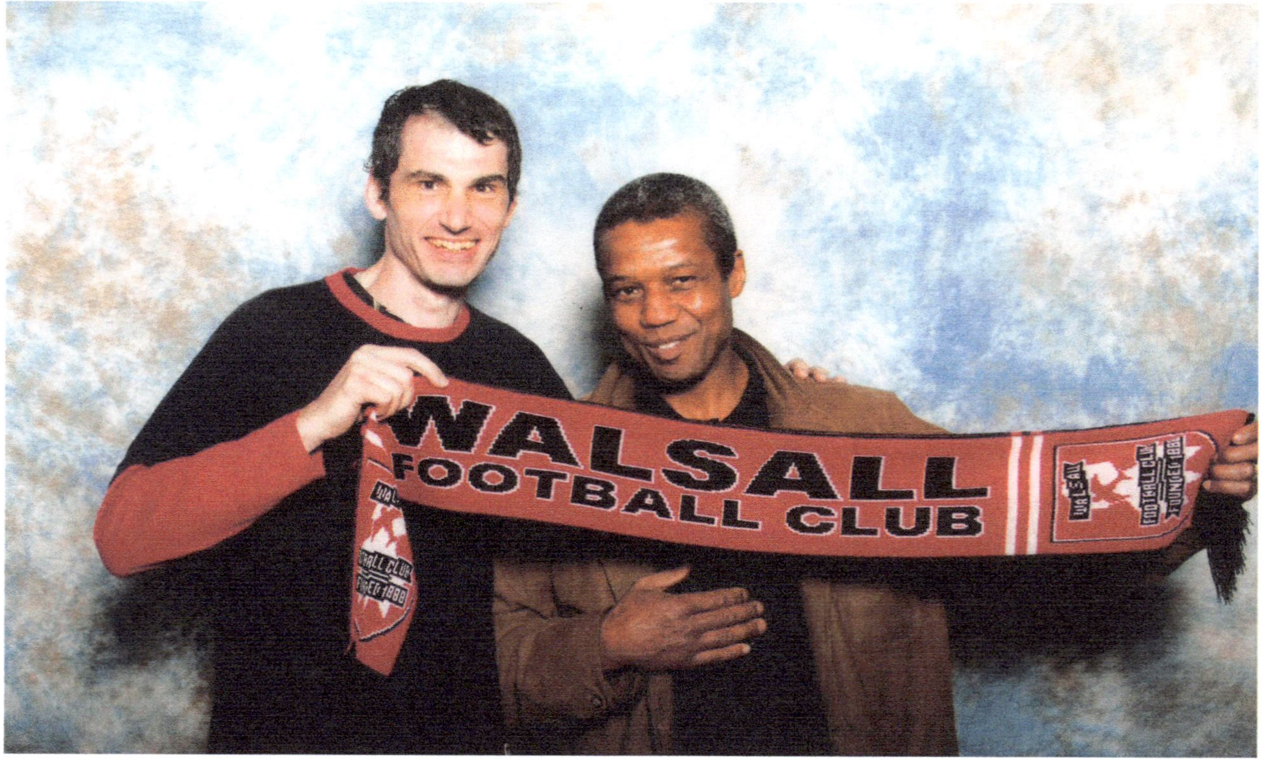
WALSALL
FOOTBALL CLUB

Hugh Quarshie

Hugh Quarshie lives in England but maintains close links with Ghana where he was born and spent the first years of his life. He studied politics, philosophy and economics at Oxford where he was president of the OU African Society and co-director of the Oxford and Cambridge Shakespeare Company.

After graduating he worked as a journalist, becoming sub-editor at West Africa Magazine. He helped produce the Channel 4 arts programme *Signals*, and co-produced *Othello* at the Greenwich Theatre. He wrote the play *The Prisoner of Hendon*. He has worked extensively in film, television and theatre. Some of his credits include *The Murder of Stephen Lawrence*, *A Respectable Trade*, *Star Wars: The Phantom Menace* and he has appeared with the Royal National Theatre and the RSC. Hugh Quarshie has made a special study of *Othello*. His paper *Second Thoughts about Othello* has been issued by the International Shakespeare Association (Occasional Paper No. 7). It was originally delivered by the author to inaugurate the 1998/99 Hudson Stroke Lectures on Race and Class in the Renaissance at the University of Alabama, Tusacaloosa.

He also appears in the hospital drama series *Holby City* as Ric Griffin. Quarshie has been nominated for several awards for his portrayal of Ric, and won "Favourite Male TV Star" at the 2008 Screen Nation Awards. He was nominated for the "Male Performance in TV" award at the 2006 Screen Nation

Awards and received a Mention in the same category the following year. In addition, he leads the cast of Michele Soavi's *The Church* as Father Gus and plays Aaron the Moor in the BBC Television Shakespeare *Titus Andronicus*.

Quarshie has narrated a number of television programmes, including the informative documentary *Mega Falls of Iguacu* about the Iguaçu Falls, and the TV adaptation of *Small Island*. In 2010 he lent his voice to the BBC Wildlife series *Great Rift: Africa's Wild Heart* to critical acclaim.

In September of that same year he appeared in an episode of *Who Do You Think You Are?*, tracing his Ghanaian and Dutch origins. The entry revealed that he traced his ancestry to Pieter Martinus Johannes Kamerling, a Dutch official on the Gold Coast, making him a distant relative to the late Antonie Kamerling, who was also an actor.

As a big fan of a certain London club, Quarshie easily got into the swing of holding the scarf at London's Olympia hall, but couldn't help but quip that he was "actually more of an Arsenal man, myself!"

WALSALL FOOTBALL CLUB

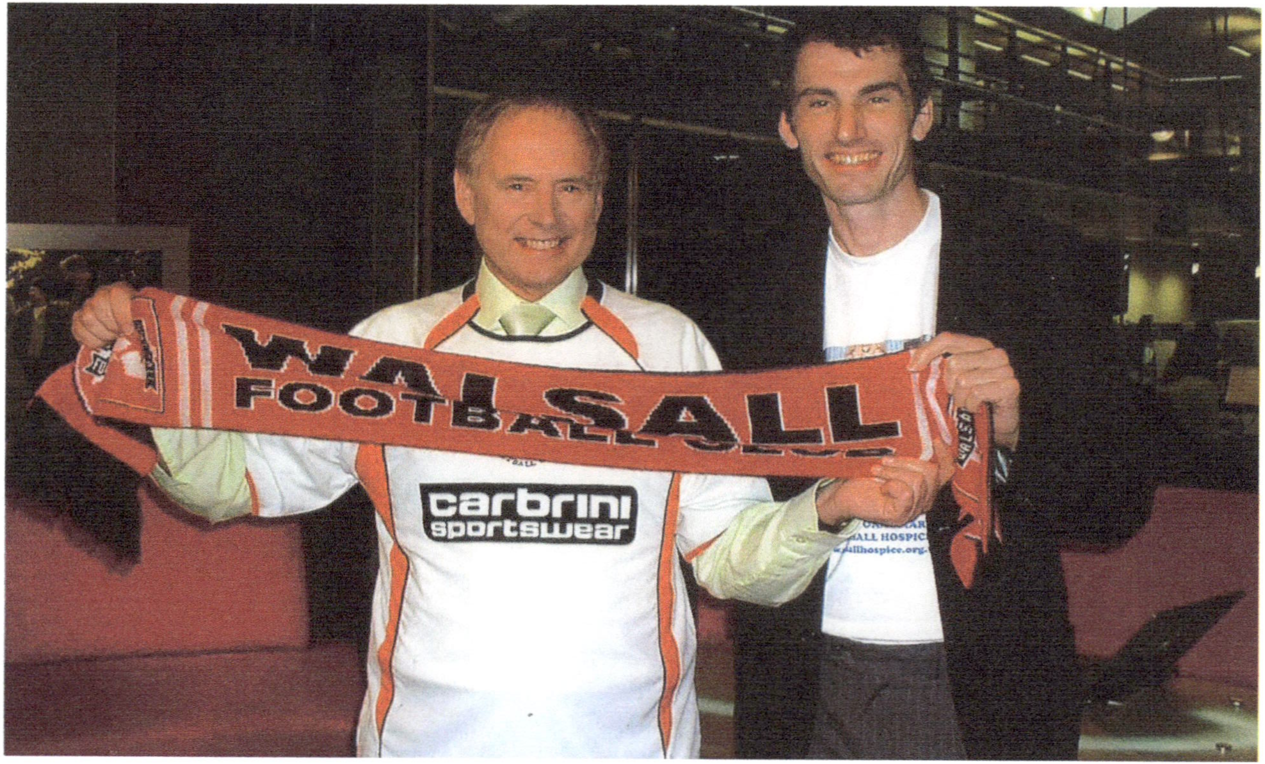
WALSALL
FOOTBALL
carbrini
sportswear

Nick Owen

Early on in his career, Owen's first job was as a graduate trainee on the *Doncaster Evening Post*. After two years he moved to a job at the *Birmingham Post*, where he reported local news. He started working for the BBC's local radio station Radio Birmingham in 1973, as a news producer and later as Sports Editor. His first live broadcast was an early morning news bulletin during the Les Ross show.

Five years later he joined what was ATV, where he worked as a sports reporter, commentator and presenter. He covered the European Football Championships in 1980 and commentated on the World Cup in Spain. As well as his sporting commitments, he became a news presenter at Central TV, teaming up with Anne Diamond.

His national break came through presenting *Good Morning Britain* on TV-am in 1983, the start of breakfast television in the UK, co-presenting it with Anne Diamond which he did for three years. He hosted a TV game show "Hitman" in the late 80s. He then became a presenter for ITV Sport after leaving TV-am presenting *Midweek Sports Special* and also playing a big part in ITV's coverage of the Olympic Games, Euro 88 and the following World Cup as well as the game show *Sporting Triangles*. From 1992 to 1996 he co-presented *Good Morning with Anne and Nick* on the BBC.

Currently the main presenter on *Midlands Today*, the BBC regional television news programme for the West Midlands.

He is well known for his awful jokes and puns, usually connected to light hearted stories. In the fictional world of Alan Partridge, he is friends with the chat show host.

On 17 October 2006, *Midlands Today*'s science and environment correspondent David Gregory helped launch an official MySpace page for Owen in an attempt to make a mark on the world's largest blogging community. During that evening's bulletin when the page was featured, the page received over 200 friend requests and a deluge of comments for the TV presenter. During the experiment, Owen received thousands of friend requests, emails and comments through the site, which closed in March 2007.

In 2006, he was awarded the Baird Medal by the Royal Television Society, Midlands, for his lifelong achievement in television.

Nick Owen, a self-confessed Luton Town football fan, became the Club Chairman when the Club 2020 consortium purchased the concern in 2008 following a period in administration. It would also go some way to explain why in meeting the scarf at the television studios in this picture he was insistent upon wearing one of the clubs shirts.

WALSALL FOOTBALL CLUB

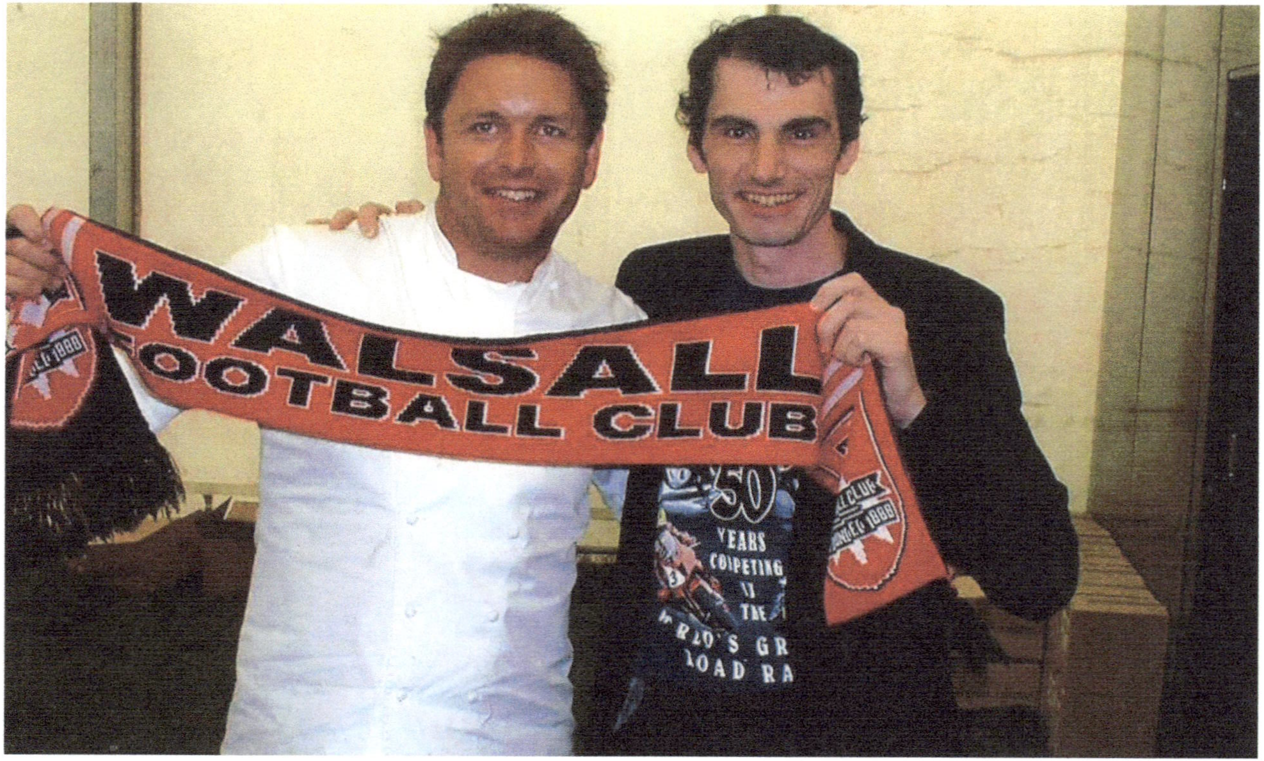
WALSALL
FOOTBALL CLUB

James Martin

Martin's families were farmers on the Castle Howard Estate and he helped his mother in the kitchen, which started his interest in cuisine. He attended Amotherby School in Malton and Malton School, the local comprehensive where he was a member of the school rugby and cricket teams, but did not enjoy academic subjects due to undiagnosed dyslexia.

He first started to appear on television in 1996 with varied programmes including *"James Martin: Yorkshire's Finest"* (set in various Yorkshire locations with an emphasis on the areas cuisine) but came to wider public attention on the BBC 2 programme *Ready Steady Cook*. In 2005 Martin was partnered with Camilla Dallerup for a stint on *Strictly Come Dancing*, a celebrity ballroom dancing TV show, coming fourth.

Martin co-presented BBC Food's *"Stately Suppers"* with Alistair Appleton, and then appeared on the Channel 4 programme *Richard & Judy*, where he would visit a member of the public in their own home who had been nominated to be cooked a 'comfort food' meal. He has been the presenter of the new version of the BBC 1 show *Saturday Kitchen*, which is made by Cactus TV, the company behind the "Richard & Judy" show for a number of years now.

In 2007 he starred in a BBC 2 series named *Sweet Baby James* (named in reference to the James Taylor song) in which he focused on desserts, puddings and cakes while visiting places from his culinary past that have inspired his recipes. Upcoming chef Will Torrent appeared as his assistant.

Martin appeared on *Blue Peter* that same year on *Can You Cook It?* being a celebrity judge choosing the new *Blue Peter* "Junior Chef".

In June and July that same year, he appeared co-hosting the 12 Yard series *The Great British Village Show* on BBC 1. He finished off what was a busy and packed schedule with a series on UKTV Food called *James Martin's Christmas Feasts*.

One of his other interests is his passion for performance cars, which led to him entering a vintage Maserati in the 2008 Mille Miglia. This was televised but unfortunately, he failed to complete the race. He also writes a motoring column for UK newspaper *The Mail on Sunday*. Martin once confessed in his column that he deliberately drove an electric Tesla Roadster in an erratic and careless manner that he startled two cyclists causing a "look of sheer terror as they tottered into the hedge".

A guest for many years at the Shrewsbury Festival, after giving a cooking demonstration he gladly donned the scarf.

WALSALL FOOTBALL CLUB

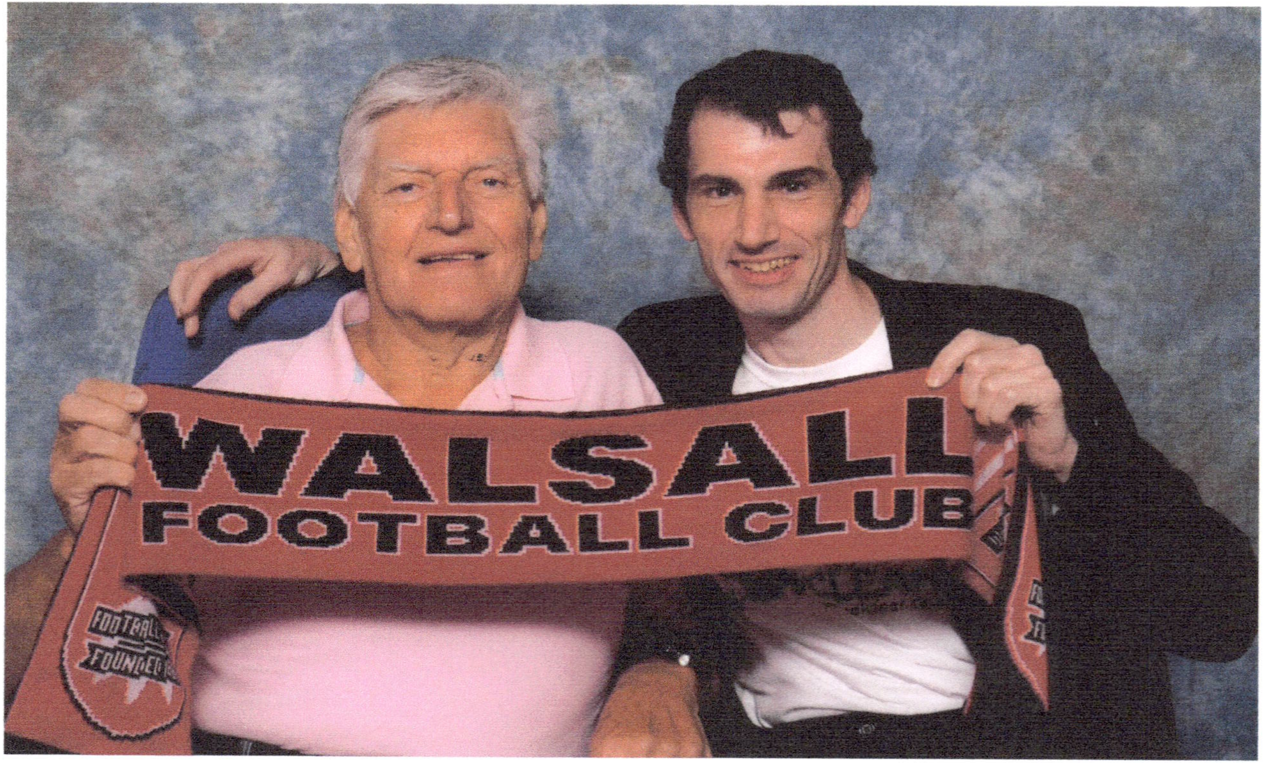
WALSALL
FOOTBALL CLUB

Dave Prowse

Dave Prowse first came to prominence when he won the British heavyweight weightlifting championship in 1962, a title he retained for the next two years. He also represented England in the weightlifting event at that years British Empire and Commonwealth Games in Perth, Western Australia.

Following on from such a successful career he was credited with helping train Christopher Reeve for the role of Superman in the 1978 film and its sequels after lobbying for the part himself. In a television interview, he related how his response to being told "We've found our Superman" was "Thank you very much." Then he was told that Reeve had been chosen and he was only to be a trainer. He also trained Cary Elwes for his role as Westley in *The Princess Bride*. Prowse is now the official leader of the 501st Legion, a fan group dedicated to *Star Wars* costuming.

Perhaps his best known role was portraying the physical form of Darth Vader in the original *Star Wars* trilogy. James Earl Jones, however, provided the voice for the character. Prowse spoke the dialogue during the making of the film, and didn't actually know Vader was Luke's father until he saw *The Empire Strikes Back* in the cinema. Though he was never going to be used as the voice of Darth Vader, he claims he was originally told that he would be seen and heard at the end of *Return of the Jedi* when Vader's mask was removed. This was not to be the case as actor Sebastian Shaw was brought in instead. Lucas claims he wanted a 'darker voice' (Lucas has stated that Darth Vader had to have a deep, reverberating voice) that Prowse could not provide and never intended to use Prowse's voice, which had a West Country accent. In the 2004 documentary, *Empire of Dreams*, actress Carrie Fisher, who played Princess Leia Organa in the original trilogy films, quipped that they nicknamed Prowse "Darth Farmer" because of his un-intimidating West Country accent. In the light saber battle scenes between Vader and Luke Skywalker (Mark Hamill), Prowse, who was not a skilled swordsman, was doubled by the scene's fight-choreographer, the stuntman and fencing coach Bob Anderson (who also taught the sword fighters in *The Princess Bride* and *Lord Of The Rings*).

Within the United Kingdom, Prowse is also well known as the Green Cross Code Man, a superhero invented to promote a British road safety campaign for children in 1975. As a result of his association with the campaign, which ran between 1971 and 1990, he received the MBE in 2000.

A frequent attendee at many film shows he took time out between surgery on his hip and foot to visit Newcastle Upon Tyne where he enquired as to the meaning of the Saddlers, before taking the challenge and holding it for the town.

WALSALL FOOTBALL CLUB

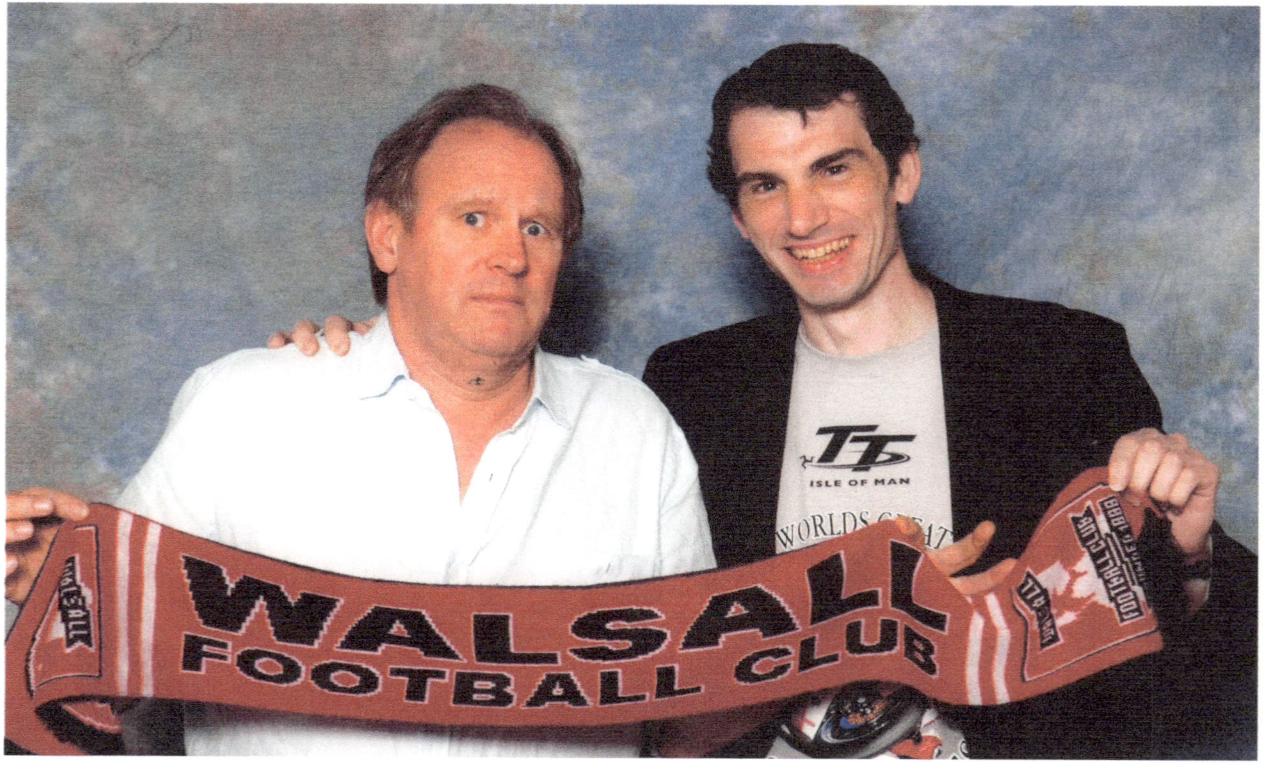
WALSALL
FOOTBALL CLUB
ISLE OF MAN

Peter Davison

Davison was born Peter Moffett in Streatham, London, son of an electrical engineer who was originally from Guyana.

His acting career received an early boost when he had a prominent role in the 13-segment TV miniseries *Love for Lydia* opposite a young Jeremy Irons. A year later, Davison's performance as the youthfully mischievous Tristan Farnon in *All Creatures Great and Small* made him a household name. Davison has said that he was mainly cast in the role because he looked as if he could be Robert Hardy's younger brother.

At the start of 1981, Davison had signed a contract to play Doctor Who for three years, succeeding Tom Baker and, at age 29, was at the time the youngest actor to have played the lead role, a record he retained for nearly thirty years until Matt Smith took on the role in 2009 beating Davison by three years.

Attracting such a high-profile actor as Davison was as much of a coup for the programme's producers as getting the role was for him, but he did not renew his contract because he feared being typecast. No lesser than a former Doctor, Patrick Troughton had recommended to him that he leave the role after three years, and Davison followed his advice. As the Fifth Doctor he encountered many of the Doctor's best-known adversaries, including the Daleks (in *Resurrection of the Daleks*) and the Cybermen (in *Earthshock*). However, Peter Davison has since stated that he also felt too young for the role (all the previous actors had been over 40), and if given the chance at the role now he would have made a better Doctor. In 1982, Davison had lent his name to two series of short stories published by Arrow. The two were *Peter Davison's Book of Alien Monsters* and *Peter Davison's Book of Aliens* which both featured a photograph of him on the cover.

After Davison left *Doctor Who*, he did not work on another popular series until 1986, when he played Dr Stephen Daker, the ingenuous hero of *A Very Peculiar Practice*, written by Andrew Davies. The surreal comedy-drama was revived several years later as *A Very Polish Practice*. Davison also played the lead in *Campion*, a series based on the period whodunnits of Margery Allingham. This, and the opportunity to play Tristan Farnon again in 1985 and 1990, kept Davison busy until the early 1990s, when he gradually faded from the public eye.

He made a triumphal return in *At Home with the Braithwaites* in 2000, a drama about a family of dysfunctional lottery winners that finally broke the mould of the genial types he ended up playing, with the distinctly flawed and unlikeable David Braithwaite.

Here again, in Newcastle, Davison amused the crowds by pulling faces and generally clowning around whilst holding onto the scarf.

WALSALL FOOTBALL CLUB

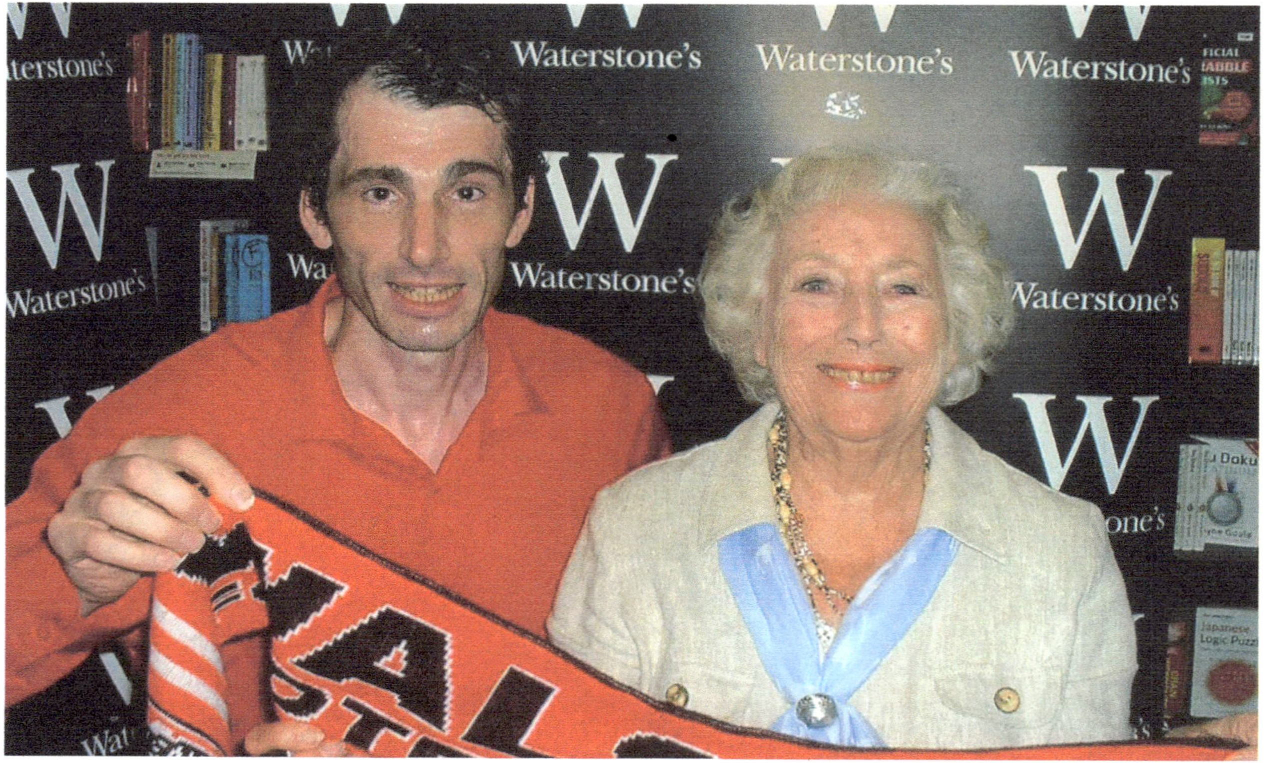
Waterstone's

Dame Vera Lynn

Vera Lynn was the most popular singer of World War II-era Britain, known during and after the war as the Forces' Sweetheart. The nickname was an apt one, for Lynn helped raise morale during the war effort by virtue of a down-to-earth quality that reminded servicemen of those they had left behind at home. Lynn had her own British Broadcasting Corporation (BBC) radio program, and her popularity was phenomenal. Welsh-born comedian and *Goon Show* star Harry Secombe was once quoted in London's *Independent* newspaper as saying, "Churchill didn't beat the Nazis. Vera sang them to death."

In 1941 she married musician Harry Lewis. The relationship got off to an unpromising start. "I don't think I thought much of him at first. He wooed me with chewing gum," Lynn told London's *Guardian* newspaper. But the marriage lasted 58 years, until Lewis's death in the late 1990s. For much of the singer's career, Lewis served as her manager

Lynn's popularity easily survived the wartime years. After peace came, she and Lewis had a daughter, Virginia, but Lynn soon returned to performing. She toured all over the British Commonwealth and appeared in a Las Vegas cabaret and on radio in the United States as a guest on the *Big Show* program hosted by actress Tallulah Bankhead. She gave eight command performances for the British royal family, and her most successful single recording came, not during the war, but in 1951 with

"Auf Wiederseh'n Sweetheart," a song ironically enough with a German theme. That recording brought Lynn to the top of the charts in the United States, making her the first English performer to reach that level. Telling the *Courier-Mail* that "I don't live in the past even though I have never been allowed to forget it," she experimented with newer pop styles and had some success in the 1970s with a cover of Abba's "Thank You for the Music." But audiences mostly wanted to hear her wartime classics.

Many of her numerous honors in later life included elevation to the Order of the British Empire in 1959 and to the rank of Dame of the British Empire in 1975, as well as such novelties as the Show Business Personality Award from the Grand Order of Water Rats. She took tea with the Queen and celebrated her 80th birthday at a reception with Princess Margaret, and she sponsored an organization of London taxi drivers who gave free rides to veterans. In 2000, six decades after becoming the Forces' Sweetheart, Lynn came out on top in another nationwide British poll: she was named the Briton who best exemplified the spirit of the twentieth century.

A long term resident in Sussex she is now in the twilight of her life, and whilst promoting her book *Some Sunny Day*, the scarf took the longest journey so far to Brighton, and after a speedy dash through the streets to get there finally met this wonderful lady who encompasses all that is British. It was one of the highest honours for the scarf and its keeper on a memorable day.

WALSALL FOOTBALL CLUB

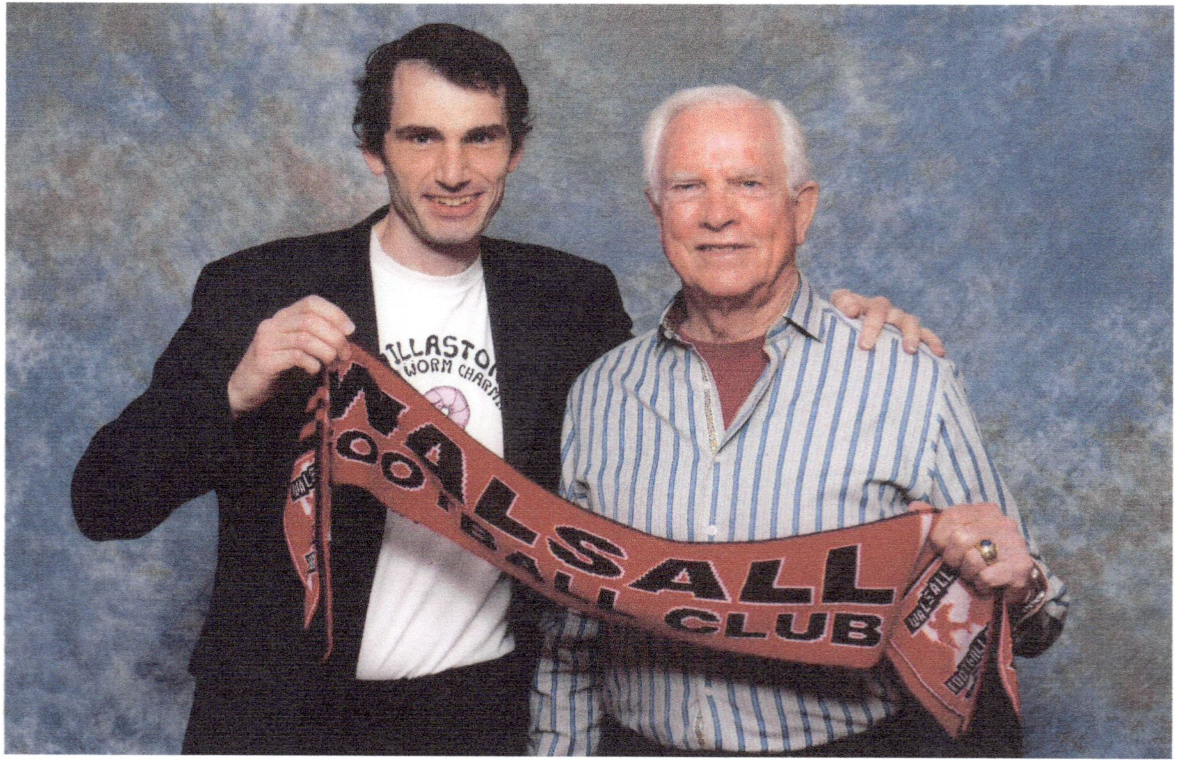
CLUB

Dave Scott

As an astronaut, Scott became the seventh person to walk on the Moon. He made his third space flight as spacecraft commander of Apollo 15 (July 26–August 7, 1971). His companions on the flight were Alfred M. Worden (command module pilot) and James B. Irwin (lunar module pilot).

Apollo 15 was the fourth successful manned lunar landing mission and the first to land near mountains instead of the relatively flat mare region where the previous 3 missions had landed. The landing site was between 2 mountains just north of Hadley Rille and Apennine Mountains which are located on the southeast edge of the Mare Imbrium (Sea of Rains). After landing, Scott and Irwin donned their pressure suits and Scott performed the first and only stand up EVA on the lunar surface. He stood on the engine cover and poked his head out the docking port on top of the lunar module and took panoramic photographs of the surrounding terrain from an elevated position and scouted the terrain they would be driving across the next day.

The lunar module, "Falcon," remained on the lunar surface for 66 hours and 54 minutes (setting a new record for lunar surface stay time) and Scott and Irwin logged 18 hours and 35 minutes each in extravehicular activities conducted during three separate excursions onto the lunar surface. Using "Rover-1" to transport themselves and their equipment along portions of Hadley Rille and the Apennine Mountains,

Scott and Irwin performed a selenological inspection and survey of the area and collected 180 pounds (82 kg) of lunar surface materials. They deployed an ALSEP package which involved the emplacement and activation of surface experiments, and their lunar surface activities were televised using a TV camera which was operated remotely by ground controllers stationed in the mission control center located at Houston, Texas.

Other Apollo 15 achievements include: largest payloads ever placed into earth and lunar orbits; first scientific instrument module bay flown and operated on an Apollo spacecraft; longest distance traversed on lunar surface; first use of a lunar surface navigation device (mounted on Rover-1); first sub satellite launched in lunar orbit; and first extravehicular (EVA) from a command module during transearth coast. Apollo 15 concluded with a Pacific Ocean splashdown and subsequent recovery by the USS *Okinawa*.

After the return of Apollo 15 to Earth, it was discovered that, without authority, Scott, with the knowledge of his crew, had taken 398 commemorative postal covers to the moon of which a hundred were then sold to a German stamp dealer. Following this the administration decided to make an example of Scott and his crew and none of them flew in space again.

At the Hotel Metropole in Birmingham Dave Scott joined other astronauts in hoisting the Walsall flag.

WALSALL FOOTBALL CLUB

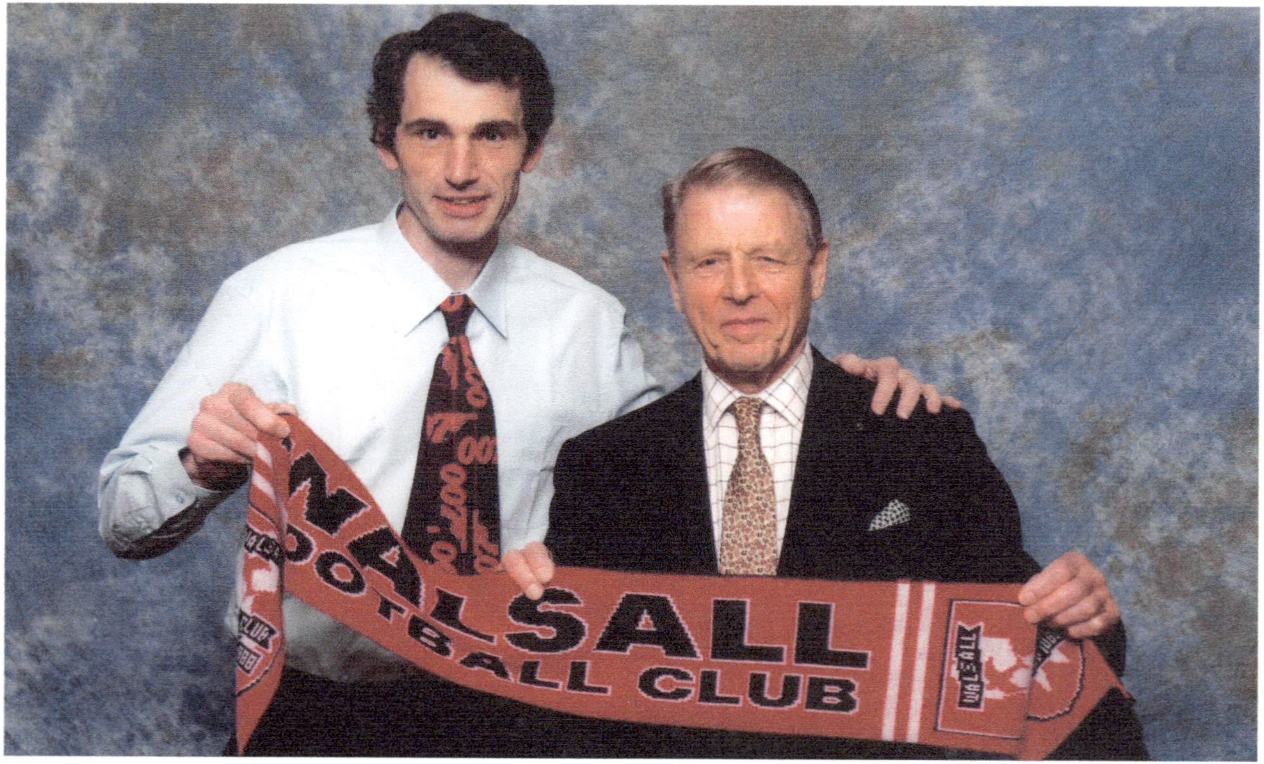
SALL
OTBALL CLUB

Edward Fox

The eldest son of agent Robin Fox and brother of James Fox, Edward Fox has quietly racked up a very impressive list of theatre, television and film credits, including nearly 40 on screen appearances since that first bit part.

Fox made his theatrical début in 1958, and his first film appearance was as an extra in *The Loneliness of the Long Distance Runner*. He also had a non-speaking part as a waiter in *This Sporting Life* the following year. Throughout the 1960s he worked mostly on stage, including a turn as *Hamlet*. In the late 1960s and early 1970s he established himself with roles in major British films including *Oh! What a Lovely War* (1969), *Battle of Britain* (1969) and *The Go-Between* (1970).

Even in bits he was noticeable, and he went on to hone his very English persona so as to suggest with equal conviction generosity, as in his beautiful performance as Trimingham in *The Go-Between*. He was more than capable of showing sympathetic cynicism; one only has to witness his performance as the world-battered Krogstad in *A Doll's House*, or bitterness, as the second-rate actor in *The Dresser*. He has perhaps the most *courteous* smile in films, but it doesn't always mean the same.

His acting ability also brought him to the attention of director Fred Zinnemann, who was looking for an actor who wasn't well-known and could be believable as the assassin in the film *The Day of the Jackal*. Harrow-educated Fox won the role, beating out other contenders such as Roger Moore and Michael Caine.

He has consolidated his reputation with regular appearances on stage in London's West End. He was seen in *Four Quartets*, a set of four poems by T. S. Eliot, accompanied by the keyboard music of Johann Sebastian Bach and performed by Christine Croshaw. He also put in an appearance as Harold Macmillan on stage in *Letter of Resignation*, and has done remarkable TV, including the indolent Harthouse in *Hard Times* and disreputable Uncle Giles in *A Dance to the Music of Time*.

In 1983's *Never Say Never Again* Edward Fox played M as a bureaucrat, contemptuous of Bond— and thus far removed from the relationship shared between previous actors who took on the part and Bond. Academic Jeremy Black notes that the contempt felt for the 00 section by Fox's M was reciprocated by Connery's Bond. Fox' incarnation is also notably younger than any of the previous incarnations.

As a tribute to his part in the 007 film and the role that he played the scarf made an appearance with a special tie to mark this association. An extremely polite well-mannered gentleman, Edward Fox enquired if the scarf was one from a school, and was keen on its origin.

WALSALL FOOTBALL CLUB

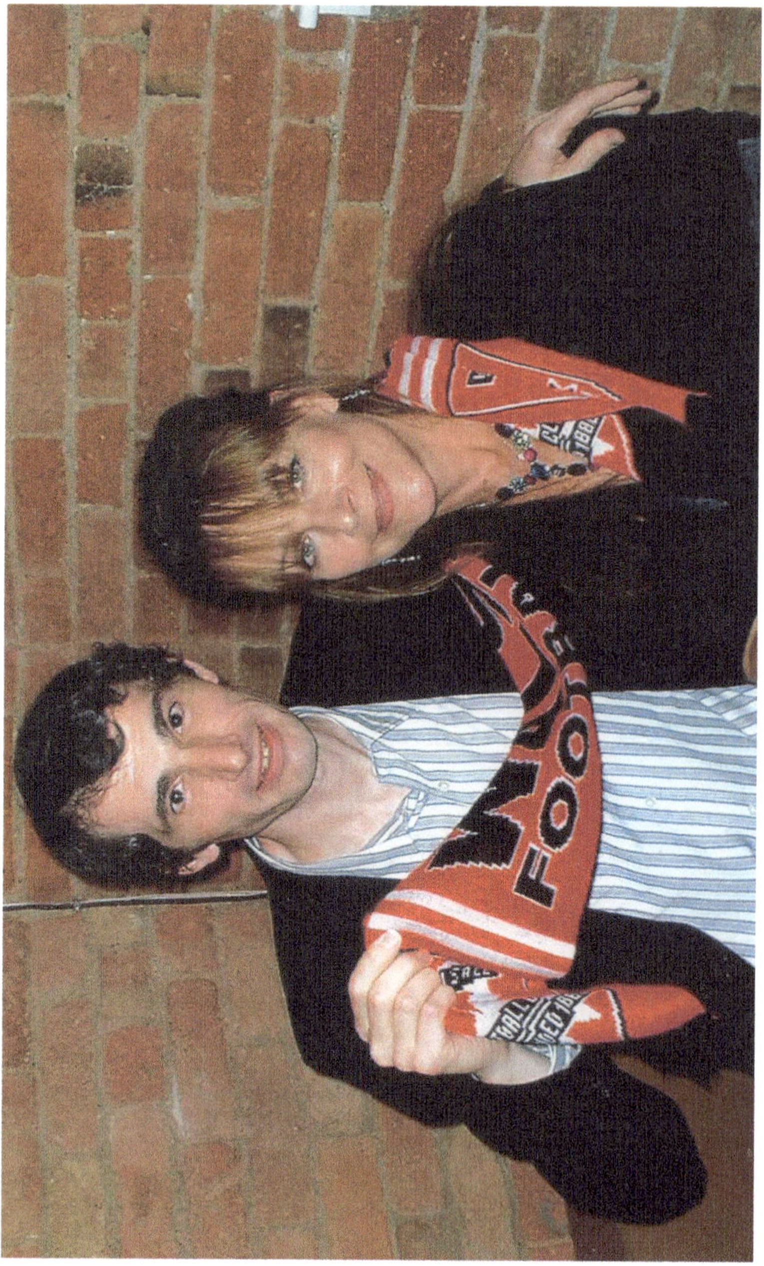

Mary Tamm

The daughter of Estonian refugees (her first language was Estonian), Mary Tamm was born on March 22 1950 in Bradford, where her father worked at a local mill. She was educated at Bradford Girls' Grammar School, went on to RADA and in 1971 joined Birmingham Rep.

Before landing her role in *Doctor Who*, Mary Tamm had appeared in a number of other television series, among them *The Donati Conspiracy*, *Coronation Street*, *Warship* and *Return of the Saint*.

Meanwhile, on the big screen, she had already been seen as Jon Voight's love interest, Sigi, alongside Maximilian Schell and Derek Jacobi in the film of Frederick Forsyth's tense thriller *The Odessa File*, and as Christina, the Finnish girlfriend of Terry Collier (James Bolam) in the 1976 comedy *The Likely Lads*.

She appeared in the 16th series of *Doctor Who*, in 1978-79, in the character of Romanadvoratrelundar – Romana for short, as a Time Lady who helped the Doctor (Tom Baker) in his quest to find "The Key to Time" — a quest set for him by The White Guardian of the Universe.

Initially Mary had been reluctant to take the part, assuming that she would be required to represent a stereotypical "damsel in distress". But she relented when it became clear that Romana, as a "female Time Lord", was conceived as something rather more substantial. "There was a bit of snobbery there," she later admitted. "In those days it was seen as a children's programme."

Having decided to leave *Doctor Who* after only one series, she appeared alongside Malcolm Stoddard in *The Assassination Run* and its sequel *The Treachery Game* (1981), both series for the BBC. In 1983 she played Blanche Ingram in a television adaptation of Jane Eyre, and the next year, also for the BBC, she starred opposite Ian Lavender in the comedy series *The Hello Goodbye Man*.

Her theatre credits include a dramatisation of Agatha Christie's *Cards on the Table*; *The Maintenance Man*; *Abigail's Party*; *Present Laughter*; and *Stage Struck*. In 2006 she took the lead role of Amanda in Noël Coward's *Private Lives*, which enjoyed a successful tour of the Far East.

In 2009 she published an autobiography, First Generation, and she was working on a second volume (to be called Second Generation) at the time of her death. It was during this period of promoting her book that the scarf met up with her twice – once in Derby at a *Doctor Who* event, and again a few weeks later at Borders in Birmingham.

Mary Tamm died of cancer on July 26 2012

WALSALL FOOTBALL CLUB

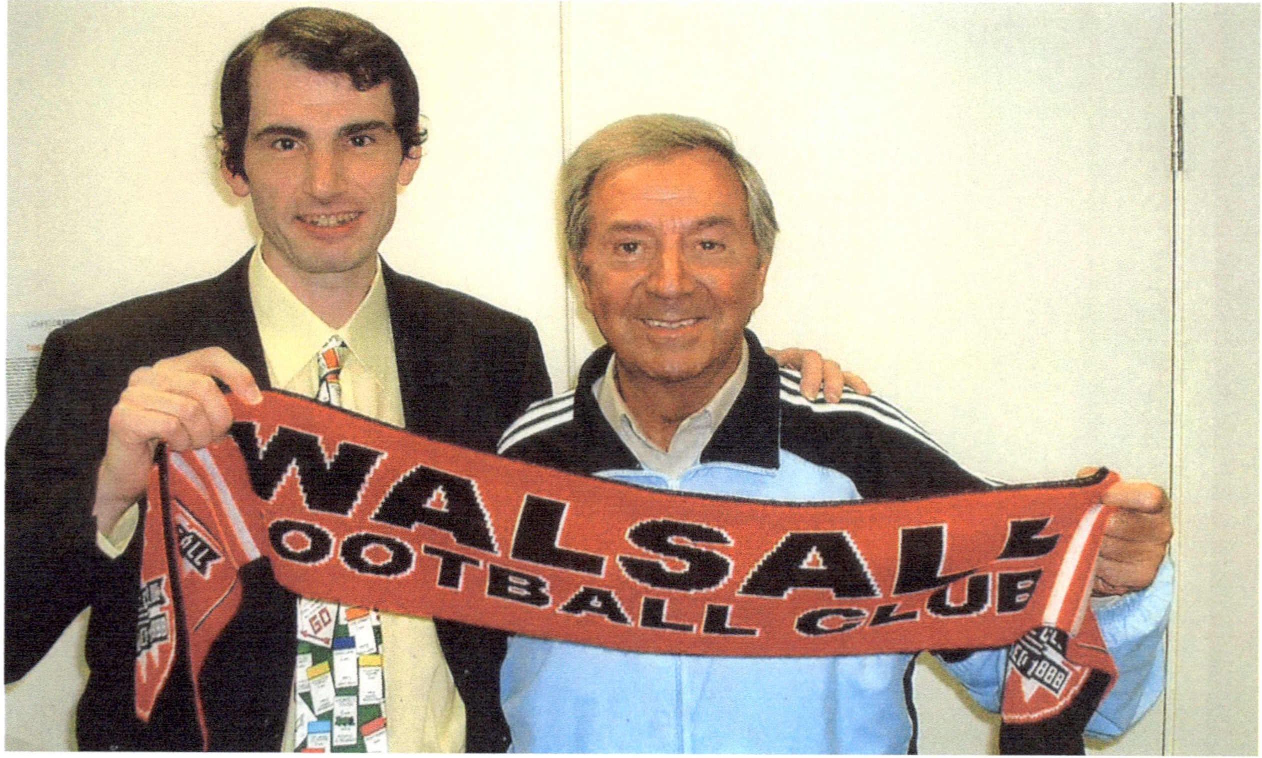
WALSALL
OOTBALL CLUB

Des O'Connor

Des O'Connor is one of Britain's best-loved and longest-serving all-round entertainers, who had a string of hit singles in the late '60s, including a number one single, "I Pretend," in 1968.

He was born in Stepney, East London, on January 12, 1932, and was evacuated to Northampton during the Second World War. Briefly a professional footballer with Northampton Town, he joined the Royal Air Force in order to complete his stint at national service. His first job on leaving the services was as a complaints clerk in a boot and shoe factory, but he followed his dream to work in show business and got a job as a Butlin's redcoat entertainer.

He appeared in variety theatres throughout the country before his break in television in the late '50s as a presenter for the ITV interlude *Spot the Tune*.

In 1963 he was given his own variety show called *The Des O Connor Show*. Four years on he began his recording career, and like his contemporary Ken Dodd, he recorded some comic novelties but it was with his romantic ballads that he gained chart success, firstly with the single 'Careless Hands' and the number one hit 'I Pretend.'

His highest-placed album was also entitled 'I Pretend', which reached number seven early in 1969 although throughout his career he recorded a total of 34 albums and sold over 15 million records.

One of his more popular television shows has been *Today with Des & Mel*, a daytime magazine/talk show with co-host Melanie Sykes which ran from 2002, and at the beginning of 2007 he took over the chairmanship of the daytime quiz favourite *Countdown*.

During his long and varied career he has notched up an impressive record at the London Palladium of 1,220 performances and appeared at sell-out concerts at the most prestigious venues throughout the world, including the MGM Grand Hotel – Las Vegas, the Opera House – Sydney, the Concert Hall – Auckland, the O'Keefe Centre – Toronto, and the Arts Centre – Ottawa. He holds a further title for hosting a mainstream television program every year between 1963 and 2007, which is longer than anyone else, globally.

Des was awarded a CBE by the Queen in her birthday honours list in June 2008 , and proudly collected his award at Buckingham Palace a few days after the release of his 34th album "Inspired" .

Perhaps not as highly rated as this honour, but still only witnessed by a select few, the scarf caught up with Des at the Lichfield Garrick theatre and took a tour backstage with him whilst he entertained his great friend Tony Christie.

WALSALL FOOTBALL CLUB

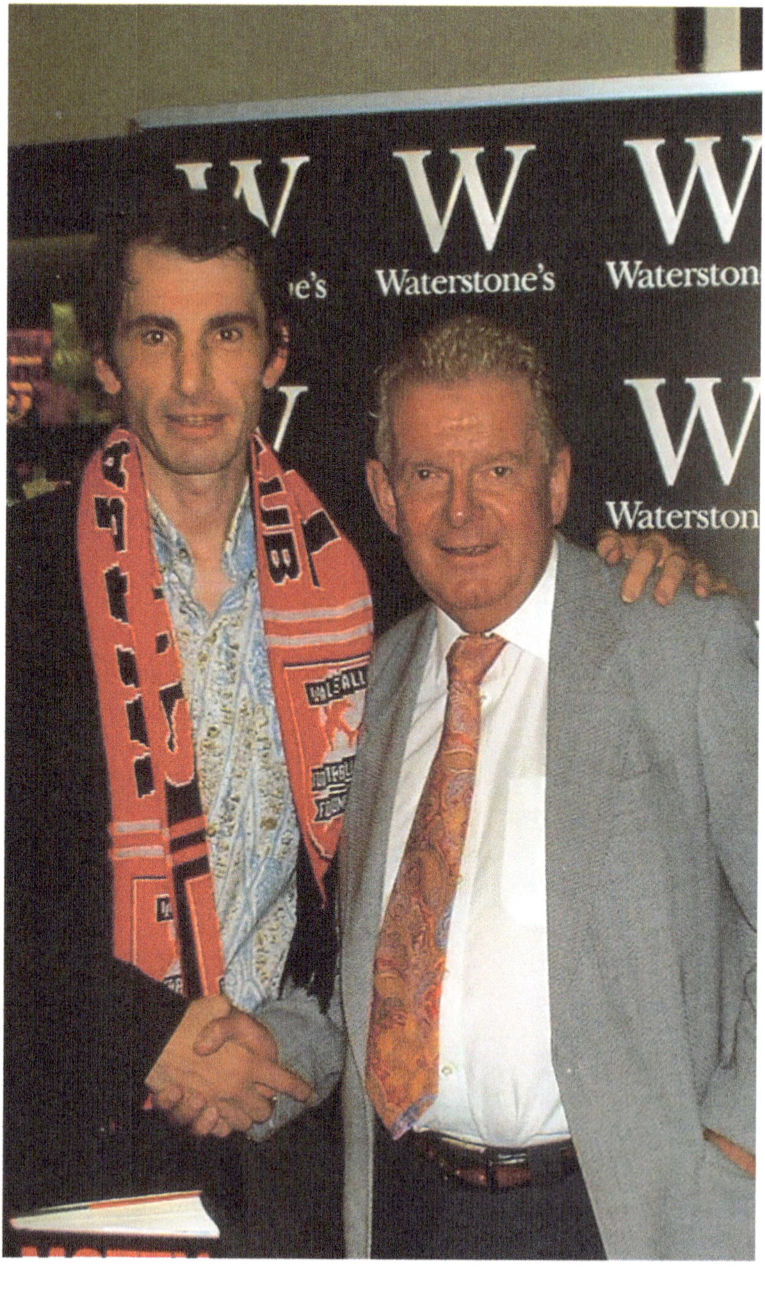

W
W
W
W
W
Waterstone's
Waterston
Waterston

John Motson

John Motson has been a member of the *Match of the Day* team for nearly 30 years and because of this he is regarded by many as the voice of football.

The son of a Methodist minister, 'Motty' joined the Barnet Press newspaper as a junior reporter at the age of 18.

He later moved to the Morning Telegraph in Sheffield where he first covered league football.

A short freelance spell with BBC Radio Sheffield was followed by a switch to network radio in 1968, where on Radio 2 (then BBC Radio's main sports station) he made his name as a sports presenter as well as a commentator on football, tennis and boxing.

At the age of 26, John became a junior member of the *Match of the Day* staff following the departure of Kenneth Wolstenholme, and soon became one of its key commentators.

Between 1979 and 1994, Motson was the BBC's TV commentator for 29 consecutive major cup finals – FA Cup, World Cup and European Championships.

He completed his 30th assignment at this level with the final of Euro '96 and subsequently covered the World Cup final in 1998 and 2002 and the final of Euro 2000.

Altogether, John has covered well over 1,000 matches for the BBC.

He has also researched and narrated over 30 football videos and written four books, including Motty's Diary – A Year in the Life of a Commentator, which was published in 1996.

John and his wife Anne have one son, Frederick, and away from football his interests are running, the cinema and reading thrillers.

In 1998 John was honoured with his own 'audience with' show on BBC One, *The Full Motty* and appears in 'mini' form on BBC Sport's website.

Following the BBC's loss of rights to cover live FA Cup football and the BBC's refusal to release Motson from his contract to join Setanta Sports, he announced his retirement from live television commentary. The Euro 2008 final was his last live television broadcast. He has continued to cover games for *Match of the Day* highlights.

Unfortunately, John Motson remains the only person who would not hold the scarf – instead it was furled around the owner in this shot at Leadenhall market for his book promotion.

WALSALL FOOTBALL CLUB

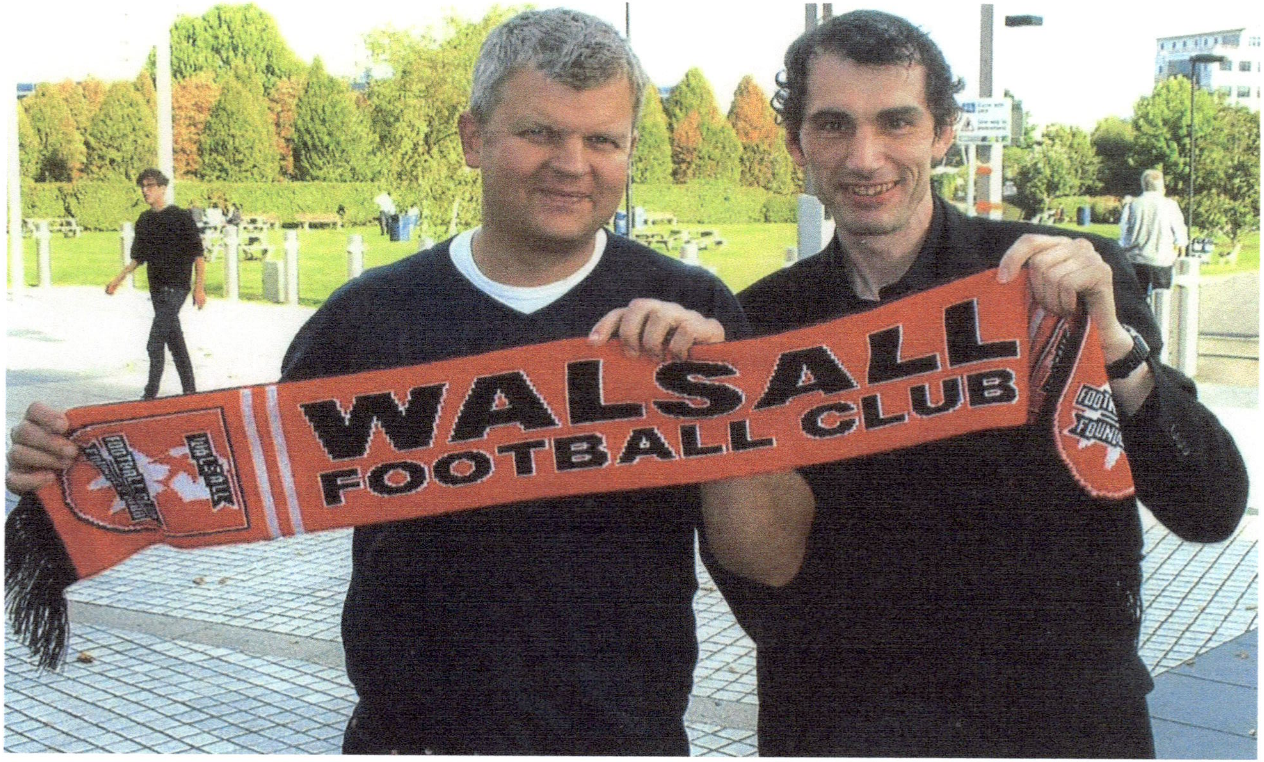
WALSALL
FOOTBALL CLUB

Adrian Chiles

Adrian was born in Birmingham in 1967 but was raised in Hagley, 11 miles west of the city.

His life has been occasionally enhanced, but more often than not blighted by West Bromwich Albion who he's followed doggedly since he was seven.

After graduating with a degree in English Literature from the University of London he broke his leg playing football, allowing him a good six months to loll around working out what to do with his life.

At this time the only interesting thing that happened to him was an invitation to be interviewed for a position with MI5. He doesn't know why they picked on him but he does know that, having interviewed him, the decision to reject him was certainly the correct one.

For want of anything better to do he enrolled on a journalism course in Cardiff which led to a three week stint on a work experience with the BBC in the Business Programmes department. Incredibly, they kept him on as a researcher and before long someone saw fit to give him a chance as a presenter. He started on Radio 4 presenting the *Financial World Tonight* and moved on to Radio Five Live for whom he worked for many years.

His work on radio led to him presenting BBC 2's new daily business show *Working Lunch*. He hung onto this spot for 13 years as well as hosting various other series, most notably the Apprentice spin-off *You're Fired!*

Adrian became the host of *Match of the Day 2* when the BBC won back the rights to the Premier League. He was also a member of the BBC's team at the 2006 World Cup and the European Championships two years later. In 2008 he hosted the daily morning coverage of the Beijing Olympics.

It was on a *One* show programme, that Adrian also broke the World Record for most number of kisses received in 60 seconds. With help from the production team he received a whopping 78 kisses.

In September 2010 he made his first appearance on *Daybreak*, ITV's new breakfast television programme. The show failed to capture a larger market share than its competitor BBC Breakfast, and just over a year later it was announced that Chiles would be axed from the show.

The scarf made a trip to see Chiles at White City in London, and he proved a good sport in holding the scarf of West Brom's neighbours and sometime rivals through the season's.

WALSALL FOOTBALL CLUB

The last word in books
WATERSTONE'S
The last word in books
ALSALL
BALL CLUB

Jo Brand

Long established for her stand-up comedy, Jo Brand is a leading light of the entertainment world. She regularly appears on panel shows and undertakes a range of challenges from *Question Time* to *Mock the Week*.

Jo began her career working in a Dr Barnardo's home for children in Kent after which she moved to London and trained as a psychiatric nurse – a subject which often features in her comedy.

As a nurse, Jo dealt with drug addicts, alcohol abuse and the clinically depressed on a daily basis. She quickly discovered that it was her sense of humour that kept her going.

Jo's first brush with television came in the 90s on *Saturday Live* before making it into mainstream viewing with her award-winning series *Through The Cakehole*.

Eventually, spurred on by a comedy agent, Jo took the brave step and started her stand-up career in London's alternative comedy clubs. It wasn't long before Jo became firmly established on the comedy circuit and has since gone on to become one of the most memorable British female comics ever.

Although Jo is predominantly thought of as a comedienne, she is in fact a diverse performer. Her more recent television appearances include the BBC's *QI*, *Mock the Week* and *Question Time*. She also made an unforgettable appearance on BBC One's *Let's Dance for Comic Relief*. More recently, Jo fronted a moving documentary about World War I nurse Vera Brittain.

On radio, she regularly guest hosts the Jonathan Ross Show on BBC Radio 2. Jo also narrated *Laughter & Tears*, a documentary tribute to Les Dawson.

Brand co-wrote and starred in the BBC Four sitcom *Getting On* alongside Joanna Scanlan and Vicki Pepperdine, for which she won the 2011 Best TV Comedy Actress BAFTA award. The series was directed by Peter Capaldi and is a gritty and realistic satire on the current state of the NHS, set in a geriatric ward.

Brand has written a number of commercially successful books including *Sorting Out Billy* and *The More You Ignore Me* which deal with socially dysfunctional behaviour and draw on her experience in psychiatric nursing. *It's Different for Girls* looks at growing up in a one-horse seaside town. It was during a promotional tour for one of her books that the scarf met up with her in Hereford.

WALSALL FOOTBALL CLUB

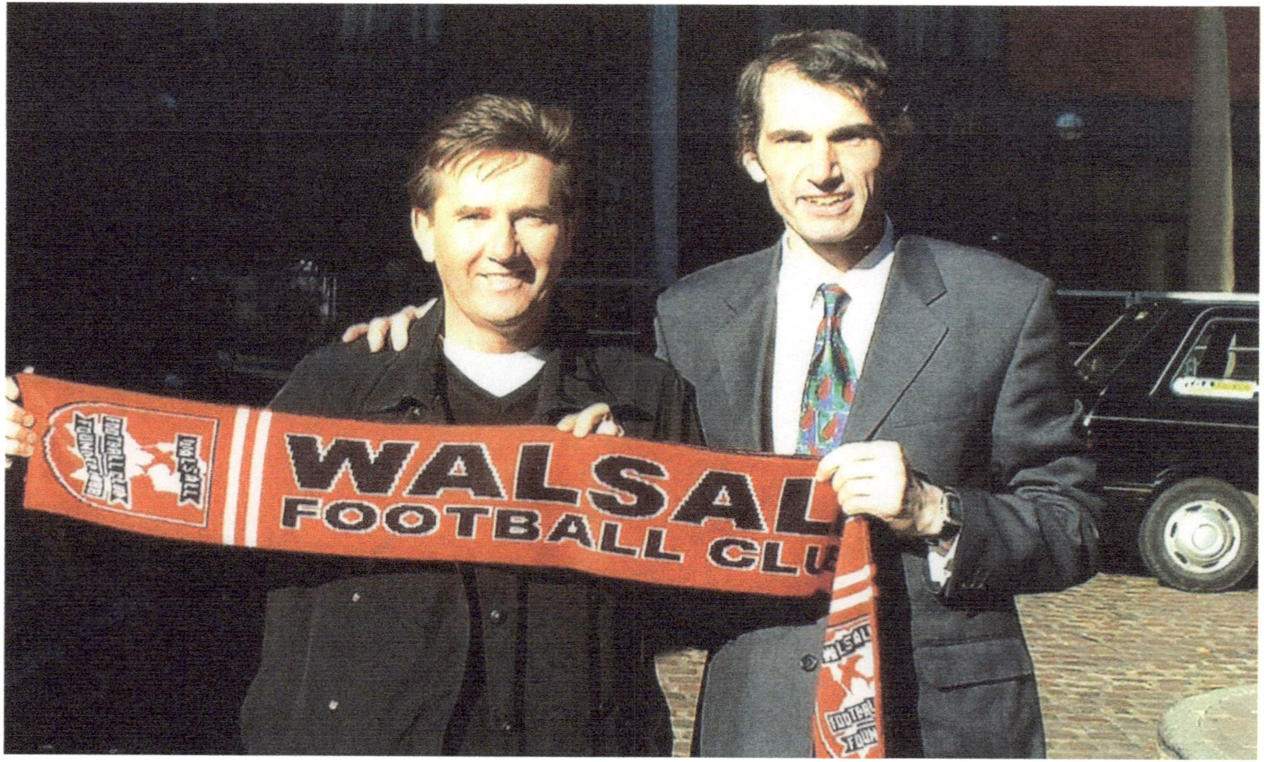
WALSAL
FOOTBALL CLU

Daniel O'Donnell.

Known for his close relationship with his fan base, coupled to his charismatic and engaging stage presence, O'Donnell's music has been described as a mix of country and Irish folk, helping him in the process to shift over ten million records to date. Recognised for his tenor voice, he is widely considered a "cultural icon" in Ireland and is often parodied in the media.

Affectionately known as "Wee Daniel", O'Donnell is a prominent ambassador for his home county of Donegal.

Not getting enough opportunities to perform solos with the band, in 1983 O'Donnell decided to record his own material. On 9 February 1983 he recorded his first single, Johnny McCauley's "My Donegal Shore", with £1,200 of his own money, selling all the copies himself. Later that year, he formed his own musical group, Country Fever. After the group disbanded, he formed The Grassroots. In 1985, the manager of the Ritz label, Mick Clerkin, saw him perform, and introduced him to Sean Reilly, who remains his manager to this day.

By the mid-1990s, O'Donnell had become a household name across Ireland and Great Britain. He appeared on popular television shows in both countries, and won various awards. Among the accolades, O'Donnell was named Donegal Person of the Year in 1989, which he still rates as the best award. He was given the Irish Entertainer of the Year award in 1989, 1992 and 1996. O'Donnell's first chart hit single in the UK was in

1992 with "I Just Want to Dance with You" (later covered by George Strait). This also led to his first ever appearance on *Top of the Pops*.

During his lengthy career, O'Donnell has made friends with his childhood idols, including Cliff Richard and Loretta Lynn. He also forged a close professional relationship with the Irish songstress Mary Duff, who regularly tours with O'Donnell.

In 2002, he was awarded an Honorary (because of his Irish citizenship) MBE for his services to the music industry. He has had twenty UK Top 40 albums as well as fifteen Top 40 singles and has sold 10 million records to date. Daniel has garnered considerable success in North America, when he starred in seven concert specials on public television stations (PBS) in the US. He has charted 18 albums in the Top 20 of the United States *Billboard*'s World Music Album Chart and also has had several entries in the Independent Albums Chart too.

It was with the help of Sean Reilly that the scarf came to be held by Daniel O'Donnell who showed his quiet and kind composure to all on a sunny day in Birmingham. He remains very much a sincere and serene human being.

WALSALL FOOTBALL CLUB

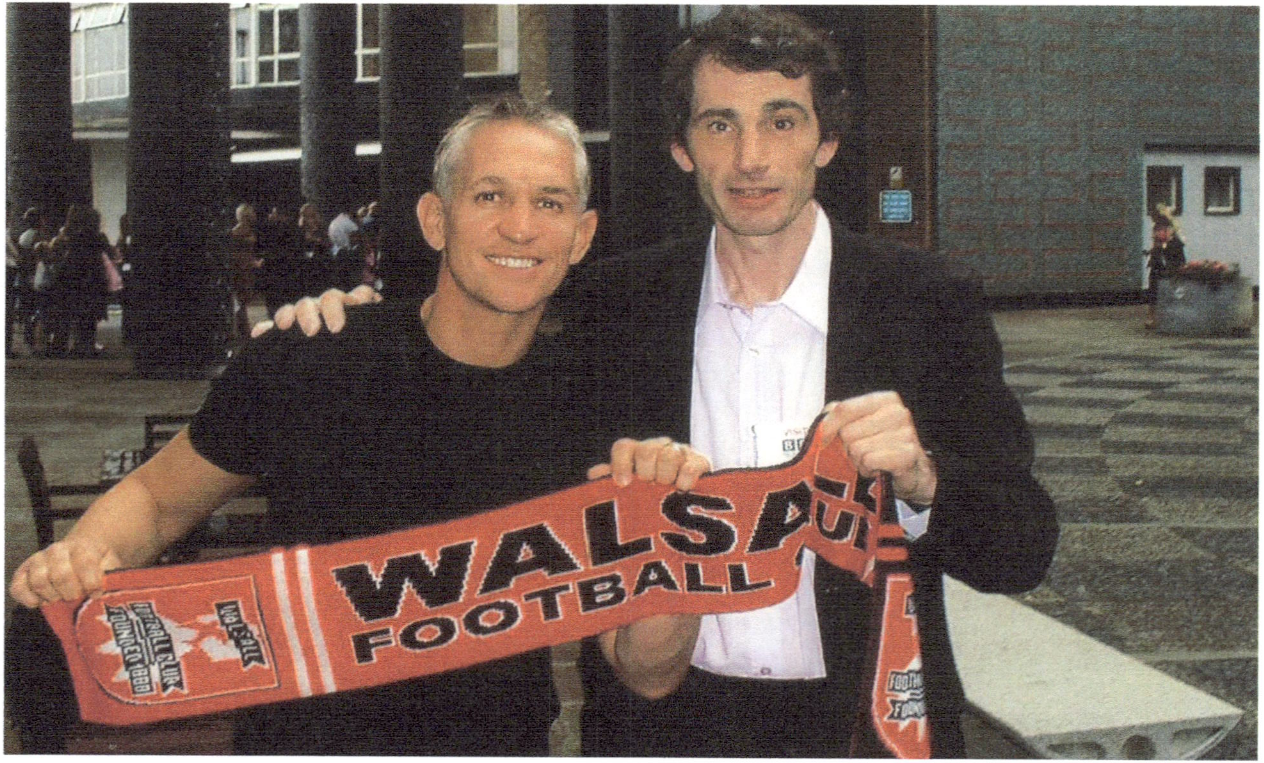
FOOTBALL
WALSALL
FOOTBALL CLUB
FOUNDED 1888

Gary Lineker

Gary Winston Lineker is an English former footballer, who played as a striker. After retiring, he became a sports broadcaster and has worked for the BBC, Al Jazeera Sports and Eredivisie Live. He remains England's top scorer in the FIFA World Cup finals, with ten goals.

Lineker began his football career at Leicester City and became known as a prolific goal scorer; despite failing to score in his first ten games, he finished as the First Division's joint top goal scorer in 1984–85 and earned his first England cap. He then moved to League Champions Everton where he remained a clinical finisher, scoring 40 goals in 57 games. His first team honours came at Barcelona, where he won the Copa del Rey in 1988 and the European Cup Winners' Cup in 1989. He returned to England that same year to join Tottenham Hotspur, and over three seasons he scored 67 goals in 105 games and won the FA Cup. Lineker's final club was Nagoya Grampus Eight and he retired in 1994 after two seasons at the Japanese side.

Lineker made his England debut in 1984 and over the following eight years earned 80 caps and scored 48 goals, finishing as England's all-time second highest scorer behind Bobby Charlton. His international goals-to-games ratio remains one of the best for the country and he is regarded as one of the all-time best English strikers. He was top scorer in the 1986 World Cup and received the Golden Boot, the only time an Englishman has achieved this feat. He is also the only player to have won the English golden boot with 3 different clubs (Leicester City, Everton and Tottenham Hotspur). After his retirement from football he was inducted into the English Football Hall of Fame. He moved in to broadcasting, working at the BBC, firstly working as a pundit on *Match of the Day* before he went on to present the flagship show. Lineker also worked on other programmes at the BBC. He led a consortium that invested in his old club Leicester, saving it from bankruptcy, and was appointed honorary vice-president. Since 1994, Lineker has featured in several television commercials for Walkers Crisps. He has four sons with his ex-wife Michelle and is now married to model Danielle Lineker.

Despite his long career, Lineker was never cautioned by a referee for foul play (never once receiving a yellow or red card) As a result of this accomplishment he was honoured in 1990 with the FIFA Fair Play Award.

In a senior career which spanned 16 years and 567 competitive games, Lineker scored a total of 282 goals at club level. Added to the 48 goals he scored in internationals, he managed a total of 330 goals.

Even though he probably owed allegiance to other teams, Gary Lineker was overwhelmingly generous with his time and allowed a meeting whilst working on *Match of the Day* to hold the scarf at the studios in London.

WALSALL FOOTBALL CLUB

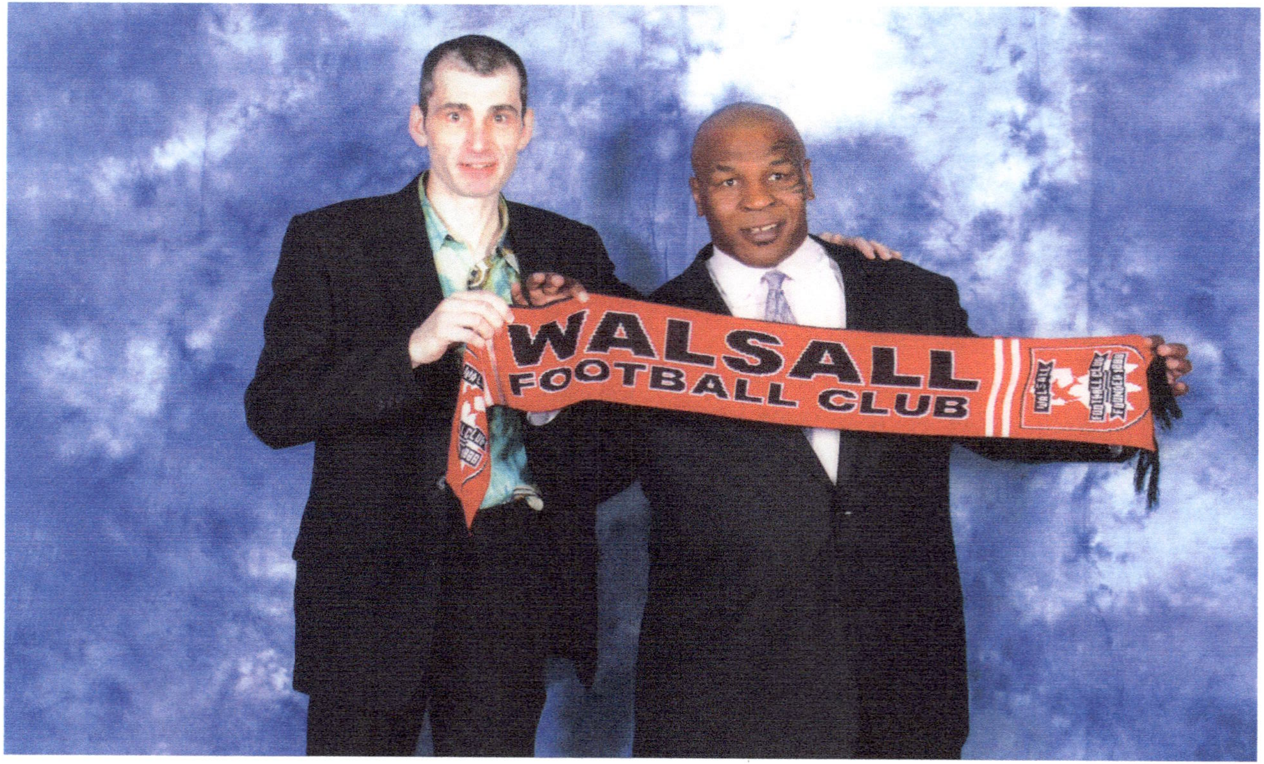
WALSALL
FOOTBALL CLUB

Mike Tyson

Michael Gerard "Mike" Tyson (also known as Malik Abdul Aziz) is a retired American professional boxer. Tyson is a former undisputed heavyweight champion of the world and holds the record as the youngest boxer to win the WBC, WBA and IBF heavyweight titles at 20 years, 4 months, and 22 days old. Tyson won his first 19 professional bouts by knockout, 12 of them in the first round. He won the WBC title in 1986 after defeating Trevor Berbick by a TKO in the second round. In 1987, Tyson added the WBA and IBF titles after defeating James Smith and Tony Tucker. He was the first heavyweight boxer to simultaneously hold the WBA, WBC and IBF titles, and the only heavyweight to successively unify them.

Tyson became the lineal champion when he knocked out Michael Spinks after 91 seconds in 1988. Tyson successfully defended the world heavyweight championship nine times, including victories over Larry Holmes and Frank Bruno. In 1990, he lost his titles to underdog James "Buster" Douglas, by a knockout in round 10. Attempting to regain the titles, he defeated Donovan Ruddock twice in 1991, but he pulled out of a fight with undisputed heavyweight champion Evander Holyfield due to injury. In 1992, Tyson was convicted of raping Desiree Washington and sentenced to six years in prison but was released after serving three years. After his release, he engaged in a series of comeback fights. In 1996, he won the WBC and WBA titles after defeating Frank Bruno and Bruce

Seldon by knockout. After being stripped of the WBC title, Tyson lost his WBA crown to Evander Holyfield in November 1996 by an 11th round TKO. Their 1997 rematch ended when Tyson was disqualified for biting Holyfield's ear.

In 2002, he fought for the world heavyweight title at the age of 35, losing by knockout to Lennox Lewis. He retired from professional boxing in 2006, after being knocked out in consecutive matches against Danny Williams and Kevin McBride. Tyson was declared bankrupt in 2003, despite having received over $30 million for several of his fights and $300 million during his career. Tyson was well known for his ferocious and intimidating boxing style as well as his controversial behavior inside and outside the ring. Tyson is considered one of the best heavyweights of all time. He was ranked No. 16 on *The Ring*'s list of 100 greatest punchers of all time, and No. 1 in the ESPN.com list of "The hardest hitters in heavyweight history".

He has been inducted into the International Boxing Hall of Fame and the World Boxing Hall of Fame.

On a visit to Wolverhampton's Civic Hall he was kind enough to hold the scarf and showed no menace whatsoever.

WALSALL FOOTBALL CLUB

Fiction

Charley Boorman

Charley Boorman is a modern-day adventurer, travel writer and entertainer. His charismatic "let's just do it" approach to challenges has won him over to a massive TV and literary audience. A little known fact is that although Charley has travelled around the world from early childhood, he spent a great deal of his youth in Wicklow in Ireland. Husband to Ollie with two young daughters, Doone and Kinvara, he's very much a family man.

His acting career started as a child. Being the son of the famous film director John Boorman, his career was already mapped out, appearing in the film *Deliverance* in 1972 and many others to follow. In 1997 he met Ewan McGregor the star of *Train Spotting*, *Star Wars* and *Moulin Rouge* amongst others, who became his co-adventurer and co-star in the *Long Way Round* and *Long Way Down* series.

In 2004 they took part in *Long Way Round*, a motorcycle trip from London to New York via Europe and Asia, which became an iconic television series, book and DVD. It was shown worldwide and became a best seller. At this time he also became involved with UNICEF as their ambassador, and has visited many of their projects during his travels, the majority of which have been integrated into his television shows.

Two years later Charley competed in the famous Dakar rally which was filmed and then became the *Race to Dakar* TV series. Injuring both his arms during the event meant that he didn't cross the finish line, however the show continued with Charley becoming team manager on the ground, and getting his team mate Simon Pavey to the end. *Race to Dakar* became a big hit, once more spurning disc and book sales.

Another journey he took with Ewan and which was televised was *Long Way Down* which took them from John O'Groats in Scotland to Cape Town, South Africa. Ewan this time brought his wife on to a section of the trip – a controversial state of affairs, but as usual Charley just took it in his stride – "...what it showed everyone is that absolutely anyone can do what we're doing – even a complete novice. It didn't sit easy with me at first – but hey, we've got families and relationships that we need to consider. It worked out well in the end and showed what could be done."

Charley Boorman has certainly carved an impressive and successful career for himself, but what most people like about him is his 'ordinary' one of the boys' attitude. Cheeky, energetic and entertaining – he's always fun to be around and he's always ready to chat to fans and have a smile, and as this occasion shows in Solihull he can hold the scarf without a motorbike!

WALSALL FOOTBALL CLUB

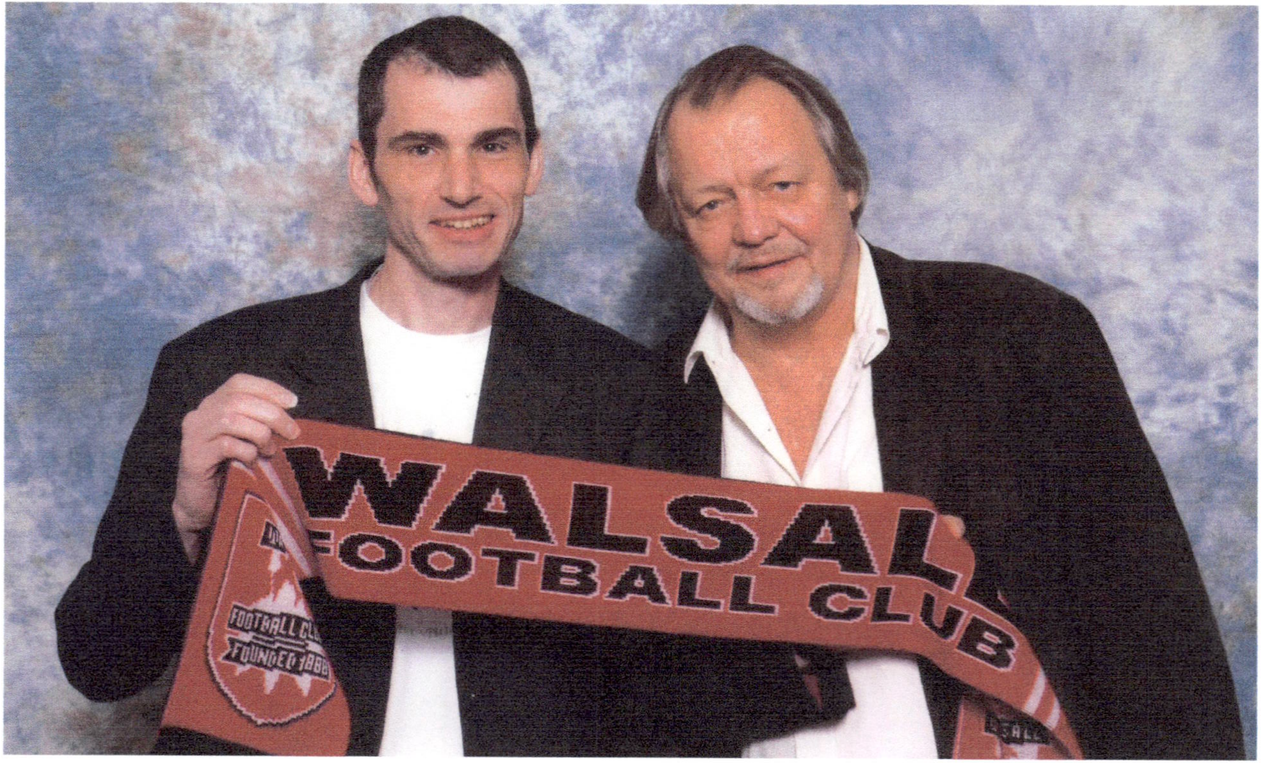
WALSAL
FOOTBALL CLUB

David Soul

Soul first gained attention as the "Covered Man" appearing on *The Merv Griffin Show* in 1966 & 1967, on which he sang while wearing a mask. He explained: "*My name is David Soul, and I want to be known for my music.*" The same year, he made his television debut in *Flipper*.

A contract with Columbia Pictures ensued and following a number of guest appearances, including the episode "The Apple" from the second season of *Star Trek*, he landed the role of Joshua Bolt on the television program *Here Come the Brides* with co-stars Robert Brown, Bobby Sherman and Bridget Hanley.

His breakthrough came when he portrayed Det. Ken "Hutch" Hutchinson on *Starsky and Hutch*, a role he played from 1975-79. Throughout his career, he has also made guest appearances on shows such as *Star Trek*, *I Dream of Jeannie*, *McMillan & Wife*, *Cannon*, *Gunsmoke*, *All in the Family*, and numerous TV movies and mini-series including *Homeward Bound*, *World War III* and *Rage*, a film that was commended on the floor of the US Senate and for which he received an Emmy Award nomination. Soul also starred with James Mason in the 1979 TV miniseries adaptation of Stephen King's *Salem's Lot*, which was also edited and released as a theatrical feature film in some countries.

During the mid- to late-1970s, Soul returned to his singing roots, ably assisted by Tony Macaulay, to record such hits as

"Don't Give Up on Us" (1976) which reached number one in the US and the UK, and "Silver Lady" (1977) which also topped the charts in the UK. During the period 1976-78, he had five UK Top 20 singles and two Top 10 albums. He toured extensively in the US, Europe, Far East and South America following the success of his albums and singing career.

In the mid-1990s, Soul moved to London, forging a new career on the West End stage including the role of Chandler Tate in *Comic Potential*. He also participated in the successful 1997 election campaign of Martin Bell who ran as an MP for Tatton, as well as Bell's unsuccessful campaign in Brentwood in Essex when he came up for re-election.

He took over playing the lead role of Jerry Springer in *Jerry Springer – The Opera* at the Cambridge Theatre in London in 2004, which was televised by the BBC the following year. He returned to the West End in 2006, playing Mack in a new production of Jerry Herman's musical *Mack and Mabel* at the Criterion Theatre. The production co-starred Janie Dee and was directed by John Doyle.

Soul became a British citizen in 2004, but retained his US citizenship. He is an avid fan of English soccer and is an Arsenal F.C. supporter; perhaps this would explain why he shied away from the scarf just a little on this occasion.

WALSALL FOOTBALL CLUB

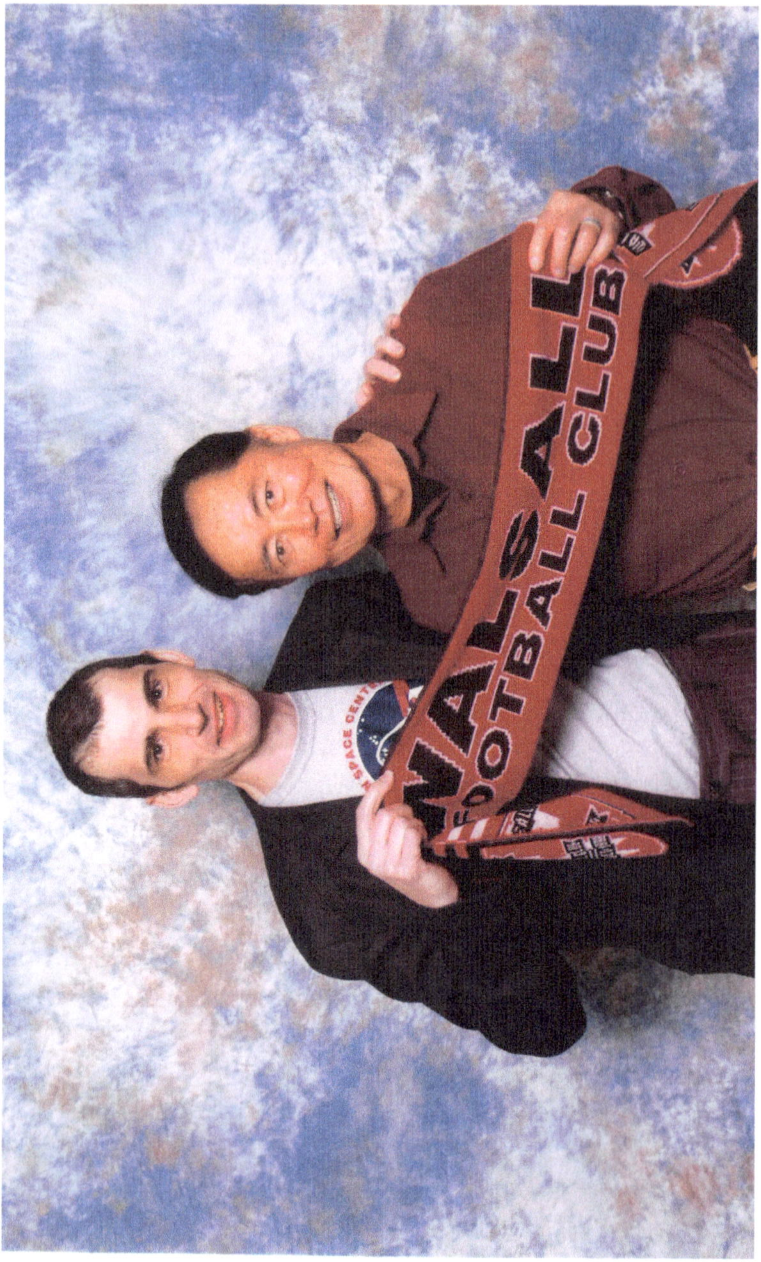
WALSALL
FOOTBALL CLUB

George Takei

George's acting career has spanned more than five decades. It began in the summer of 1957, between his freshman and sophomore years at the University of California at Berkeley, when George answered a newspaper advertisement placed by a company casting voices for a motion picture. The film was *Rodan*, a Japanese science-fiction classic about a prehistoric creature terrorizing a southern Japanese city. In a sound stage on the MGM lot in Culver City, California, he dubbed the original Japanese lines into English, creating distinct voices for eight characters.

In 1965, producer Gene Roddenberry cast him as Mr. Sulu in the second *Star Trek* pilot and eventually the *Star Trek* television series. While working on the show he appeared as Captain Nim in *The Green Berets*. It was intended that Sulu's role be expanded in the second season, but due to Takei's part in *Green Berets*, he only appeared in half the season, with his role being filled by Walter Koenig as Pavel Chekov in the other half. When Takei returned, the two had to share a dressing room and a single episode script. Takei admitted in an interview that he initially felt threatened by Walter's presence, but later grew to be friends with him, as the image of the officers sharing the ship's helm panel side-by-side became iconic.

Takei has since appeared in numerous TV and film productions, including the first six *Star Trek* motion pictures, and today he is a regular on the science fiction convention circuit throughout the world. He has also acted and provided voice acting for several science fiction computer games, including *Freelancer* and numerous *Star Trek* games. In 1996, in honor of the 30th anniversary of *Star Trek*, he reprised his role as Captain Hikaru Sulu on an episode of *Star Trek: Voyager*, appearing as a memory of Lt. Tuvok, who served on the USS *Excelsior* under Sulu, during the events of *Star Trek VI: The Undiscovered Country*.

During 1972, Takei was an alternate delegate from California to the Democratic National Convention. The following year he ran for City Council of Los Angeles, finishing second, losing by just 1,647 votes. During the campaign, Takei's bid for the city councilman's seat caused one local station to stop running the repeats of the original *Star Trek* series until after the election and KNBC-TV to substitute the premiere episode of the *Star Trek* animated series scheduled by the network with another in which his character did not appear, in attempts to avoid violating the FCC's equal-time rule. The other candidates in the race complained that Takei's distinctive and powerful voice alone, even without his image on television every week, created an unfair advantage.

He has won several awards and accolades in his work on human rights and Japanese–American relations, including his work with the Japanese American National Museum and at Coventry's Ricoh Arena stepped up to grandly hold the scarf.

WALSALL FOOTBALL CLUB

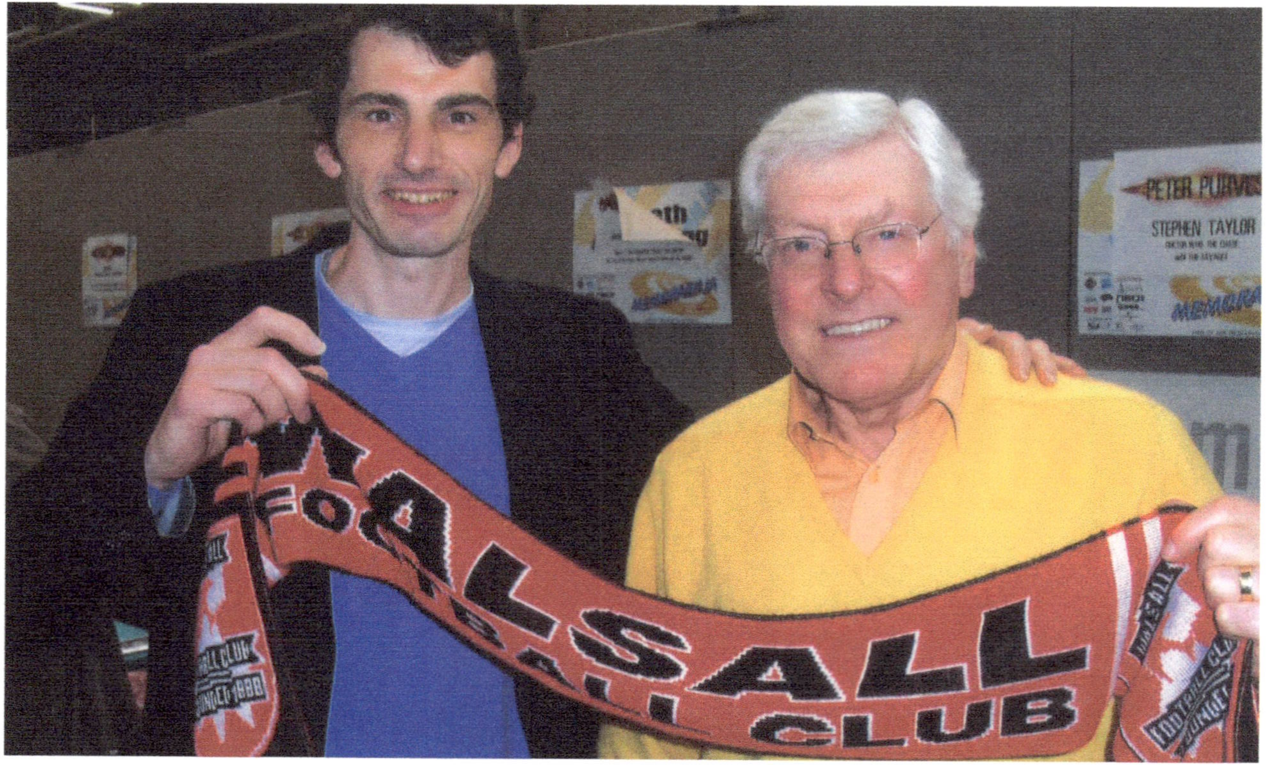
STEPHEN TAYLOR
CLUB

Peter Purves

He first became known to television audiences in the mid-1960s as Steven Taylor, one of the early time-travelling companions in the programme *Doctor Who*, when the Doctor was played by William Hartnell. After leaving *Doctor Who*, Purves became a regular presenter on the children's magazine programme *Blue Peter* for a total of 11 years. Purves maintained his connection to *Doctor Who* throughout his time on *Blue Peter*, often hosting special features on the programme and interviewing the actors. These included many clips from episodes which are otherwise now lost, most notably *The Daleks' Master Plan*, in which Purves himself had appeared. He has provided DVD commentaries for many of the surviving *Doctor Who* episodes he appeared in and documents the making of each of his *Doctor Who* stories in his autobiography, *Here's One I Wrote Earlier*. His story greatly benefited from being a good friend of the actor Jon Pertwee, who played the Third Doctor.

Peter co-presented *Blue Peter* first with John Noakes and Valerie Singleton and then with Noakes and Lesley Judd, during the programme's so called 'golden age'. After Noakes, he remains the second longest serving male Blue Peter presenter. He was so closely associated with the programme, "the sensible one", that he found his association difficult to shake off. Purves moved on to other jobs as a presenter including Blue Peter Special Assignment, "Stopwatch" and "We're Going Places" and then later a spell as the front man for darts events on the BBC, as well as being the face of the long-running BBC1 motorbike trials series *Kick Start*.

His recent TV career has included cameo appearances in episodes of the soap opera *EastEnders* and sitcoms such as *The Office* and *I'm Alan Partridge*. In *The Office* episode "Training Day" Purves played himself in a customer care training video that David Brent and his staff were being shown (incidentally, he is a qualified business trainer and a motivational speaker).

Dogs have featured in much of his career from his *Blue Peter* days. He was given charge of one of the "*Blue Peter* Pets", Petra, a German shepherd cross. This led to a thirty year association with television coverage of major dog shows such as Crufts and in 2007 his appearance as a judge on the reality TV programme *The Underdog Show*. His interested has allowed him to write for the dog press and helping out at dog award shows. It was in one of these shows that he got bitten by a West Highland terrier whilst judging a dog ceremony at a garden centre in Norwich. Purves was taken to the Norfolk and Norwich University Hospital where he received treatment to his hand.

A noted pantomime director he has enjoyed a good working relationship with the Chuckle Brothers and has now directed over 27 pantomimes at some of the UK's top theatres.

During a break in this and promoting his book in Birmingham he waived any fee for his book and signed a copy which he donated. There can be no better demonstration of his integrity, before he grasped the scarf readily enough.

WALSALL FOOTBALL CLUB

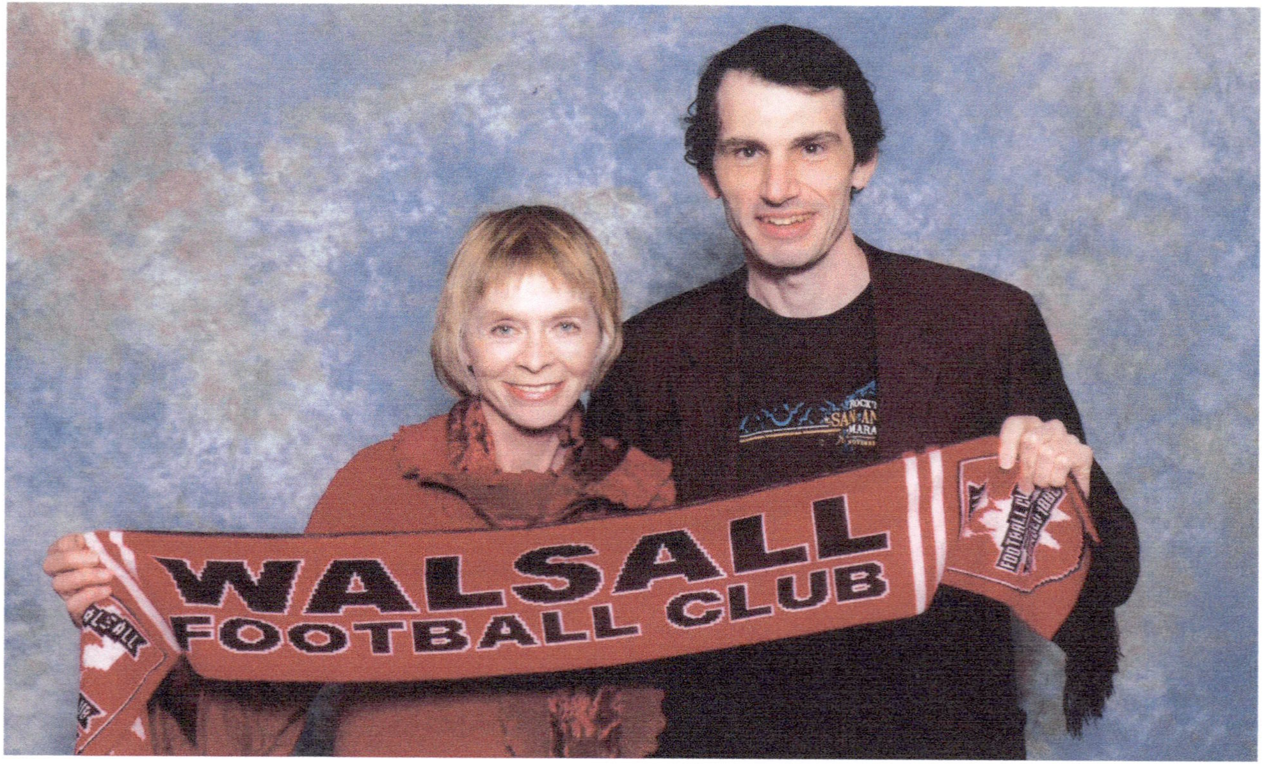
WALSALL
FOOTBALL CLUB

Susannah York

Trained at the Royal Academy of Dramatic Arts, the English-born actress became famous initially for playing dewy ingénues but went on to demonstrate an impressive range, playing everything from Shakespearean heroines to Superman's mother from Krypton.

She became an international star in 1963 as Albert Finney's true love in the lusty comedy *Tom Jones* based on the novel by Henry Fielding. Set in the 18th century, the popular film parodied the foibles of the English aristocracy and helped Ms. York, as the virginal, sharp-witted Sophie Western, establish herself as a sought-after actress.

Several years later, in 1969, she received an Academy Award nomination for her performance as a vulnerable Hollywood hopeful in Sydney Pollack's *They Shoot Horses, Don't They?*

Based on a Horace McCoy Depression-era novella about competitors in a dance marathon, the film was a bleak allegory about American life. It starred Jane Fonda and Gig Young – both of whom were also nominated for Oscars. (Young won best actor in a supporting role that year; the award for best actress in a supporting role, which York was up for, went to Goldie Hawn for her performance in *Cactus Flower*.)

Once described as being "excellent as the English girl defiantly trying to break into sordid movies," by film historian David Thomson wrote. "There is a speculative flightiness about her in that film; especially in the breakdown scene in a shower cubicle, she seemed for the first time a human animal touched to the quick," he added.

Her blond, blue-eyed allure first captured audiences' attention in 1960 when she was cast as the irresistible daughter of Alec Guinness, playing an officer in a Scottish regiment, in the drama *Tunes of Glory*. Guinness declared her "the best thing in films since Audrey Hepburn," and moviemakers began to seek her to play young beauties.

In 1961, she was "utterly lovely" as a teenager discovering her power over men in "Loss of Innocence," wrote *Washington Post* film critic Richard Coe.

Two years later, *New York Times* film critic Bosley Crowther called her "a warm little package of passions" for the role she filled in *Tom Jones*.

She also appeared in *A Man for All Seasons* in 1966 as the comely eldest daughter of Sir Thomas More, played by Paul Scofield. But she refused to be typecast.

Susannah York held the scarf shortly before she died in January 2011 of cancer at a hospital in London. She was 72.

WALSALL FOOTBALL CLUB

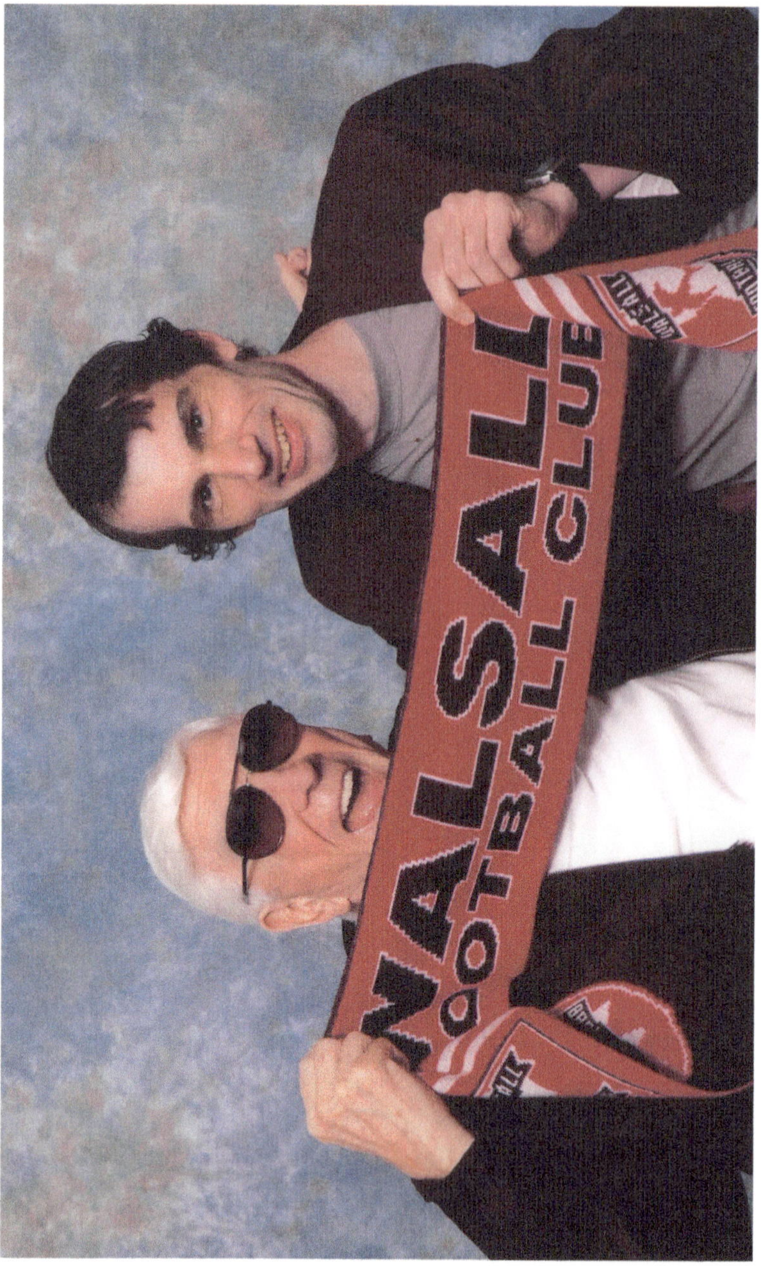

Leslie Nielsen

On the small screen, Nielsen had a recurring part on *The Virginian* before he was cast in a starring role as a deputy chief of police in the urban police drama *The Bold Ones: The Protectors*. Following the show's untimely demise, he was cast in the pilot of *Hawaii Five-O*, but when the show was picked up, he failed to make the cut. Nielsen appeared in the TV film *The Aquarians*, before joining the era's "disaster film" trend kicking off with *The Poseidon Adventure*. He played a cop in the TV film *Brink's: The Great Robbery*, a military agent on the run from involuntary chemical experimentation in the big screen thriller *Project Kill*, and remained generally prolific with guest spots on shows like *M*A*S*H* and *The Streets of San Francisco*.

In 1980, writer-director Jerry Zucker's vision of taking actors known for their unshakable seriousness and surrounding them with ludicrous site gags meant a career turning point for the 54-year-old Nielsen. He was cast alongside fellow stoics Robert Stack, Peter Graves, and Lloyd Bridges in the uproarious Zucker-Abrahams comedy *Airplane!* which parodied the "disaster film" trend and also included heavy doses of pop culture send-ups. As a doctor aboard a doomed commercial flight overcome by food poisoning, he gave a flawlessly deadpan delivery of quotable dialogue that spoofed his stolid screen persona and proved his impeccable comic timing. The film was a box office hit as well as critical success, earning a Golden

Globe nomination and a place in history as the American Film Institute's 10th "Funniest American Movie of All Time." But despite the unveiling of his previously unseen talent, he was not yet considered a comedic actor, so resumed his career with a pair of horror films, including *Prom Night* and *Creepshow*.

For *The Naked Gun – From the Files of Police Squad,* Nielsen reprised his role as Frank Drebin and a comedy film franchise was born. This time we were treated to a full 90 minutes of screen time immersed in pratfalls and bad puns – to say nothing of hilariously bad driving – and the result was wildly successful hit with both critics and audiences.

On a visit to Birmingham at the Metropole Hotel the scarf caught up with the eponymous hero to take firm hold of the scarf and did some clowning about with the prop.

In November 2010, Nielsen was admitted to a Fort Lauderdale, Florida hospital for treatment of pneumonia. On 28 November, Doug Nielsen, Nielsen's nephew, announced to the CJOB radio station that he had died in his sleep

WALSALL FOOTBALL CLUB

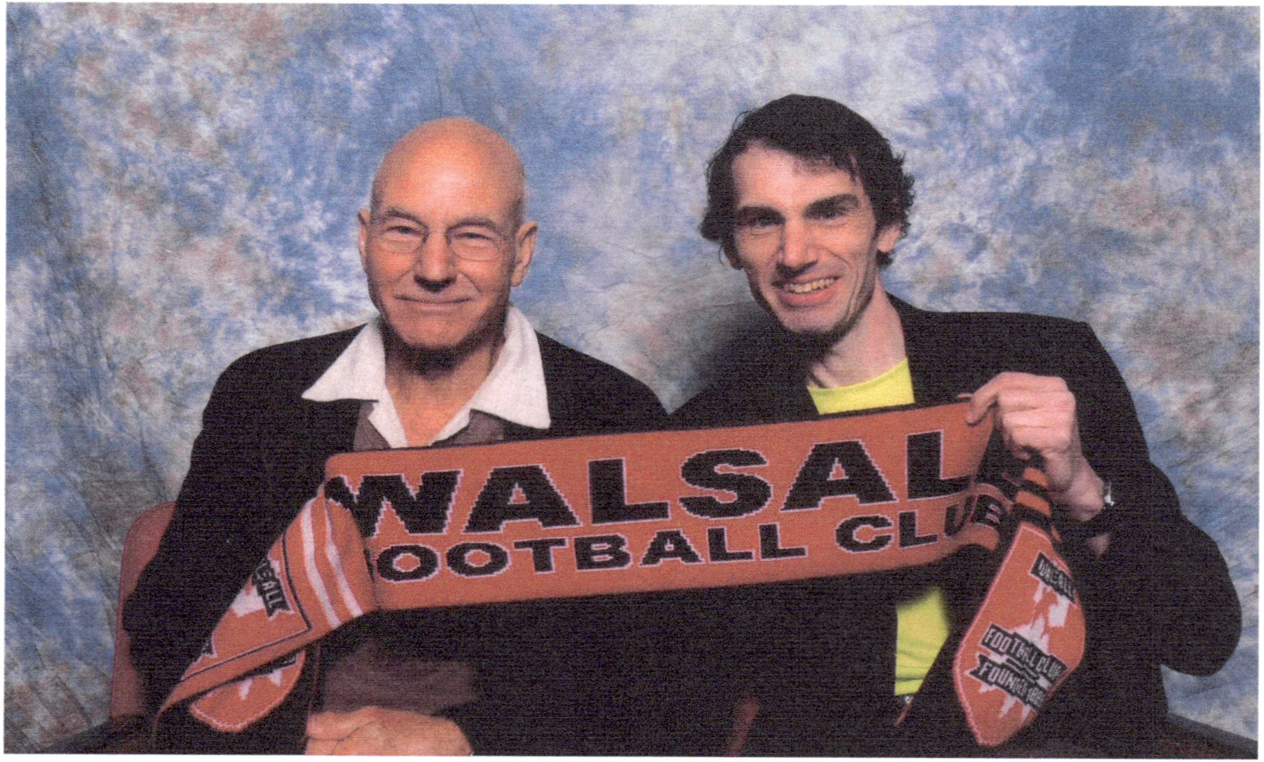
WALSAL
OOTBALL CLU

Sir Patrick Stewart

After several years working for various repertory companies, he achieved his dream of working for the Royal Shakespeare Company, and in 1967 became an associate artist. Patrick Stewart worked for the RSC for the next 20 years, which saw him develop into one of Britain's finest classical actors.

Apart from his stage work, Patrick began to be seen in TV plays during the 1970s and 80s. Productions included *Fall of Eagles* in which he played Lenin; *I Claudius*, and the adaptations of two John Le Carre novels *Tinker, Tailor, Soldier, Spy* and *Smiley's People*. He played Claudius in the BBC's *Hamlet, Prince of Denmark* and, in complete contrast, 21 episodes of the hospital series *Maybury* (1981-83) in which he took on the part as the consultant Dr Edward Roebuck.

During his time with the RSC, Stewart along with other British actors often visited American Colleges to try and improve the way Shakespeare was taught in the US. It was on such a visit in 1986, that he went on to meet Robert Justman, one of the *Star Trek* producers.

The Next Generation series was in the planning stages, with the Captain's role proving a difficult one to cast. Justman wanted Stewart for the part, but executive producer Gene Roddenbury wasn't convinced. Months passed and many actors were interviewed but, with time running out, Roddenbury finally gave in and he was given the part of Captain

Jean-Luc Picard, a role that would see him in 176 episodes of *Star Trek: The Next Generation* over seven years.

In order to avoid typecasting, Stewart developed his highly acclaimed one-man adaptation of Dickens' *A Christmas Carol*, which he performed in New York, and various other locations throughout the USA. Stewart also performed this tour-de-force of stage acting, in London in 1993.

Known for his strong and authoritative voice, he has readily lent his voice to a number of projects. In the field of narration his work has included Prokofiev's *Peter and the Wolf*, Vivaldi's *The Four Seasons*, C. S. Lewis's *The Last Battle* (conclusion of the series *The Chronicles of Narnia*), Rick Wakeman's *Return to the Centre of the Earth*; as well as numerous TV programs such as *High Spirits with Shirley Ghostman*. He also provided the narration for *Nine Worlds*, an astronomical tour of the solar system and nature documentaries such as *The Secret of Life on Earth*

More recently, he has played a recurring role as CIA Deputy Director Avery Bullock, lending his likeness as well as his voice on the animated series *American Dad!* In another animated series *Family Guy*, he chalked up eight guest appearances in total.

At *Star Trek: Destination London* he commented about the Saddlers and dutifully held the scarf in this picture.

WALSALL FOOTBALL CLUB

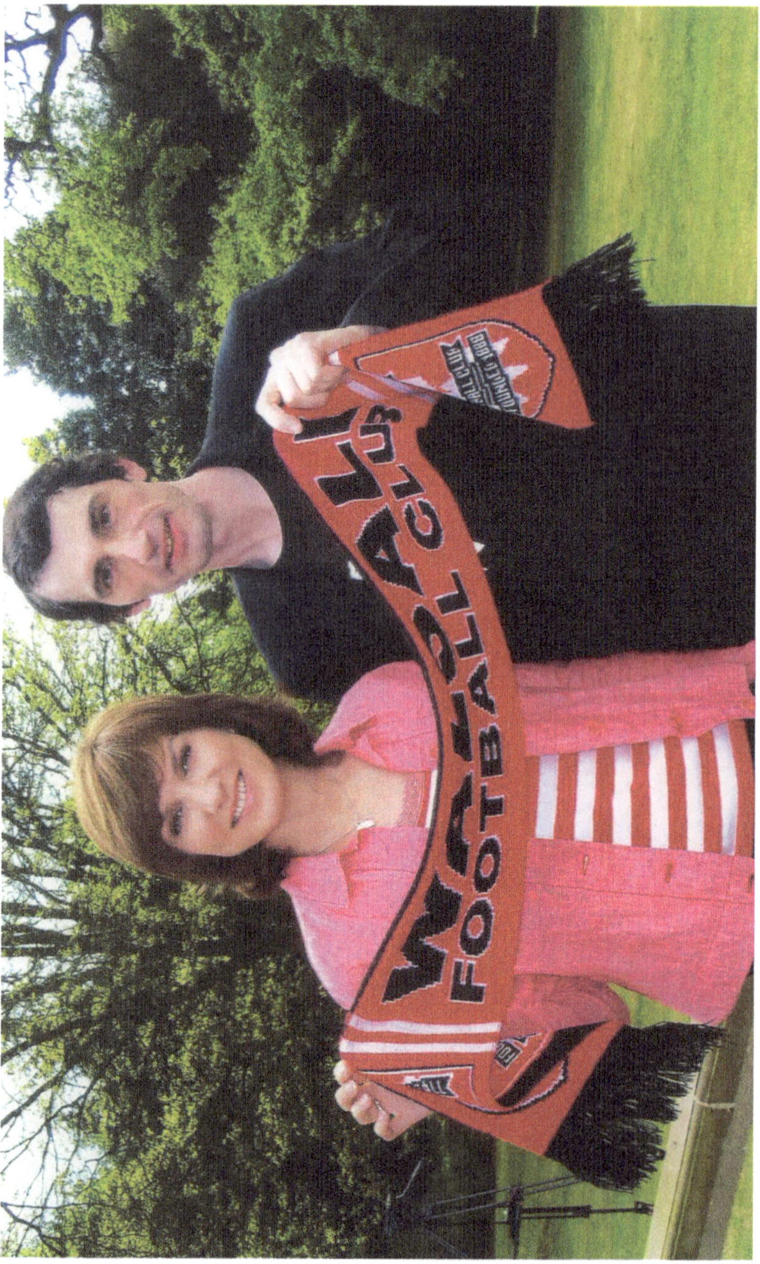

Fiona Bruce

After becoming assistant producer on *Panorama*, Fiona Bruce made the change to presenting in 1992 as a reporter for *Breakfast News*. She then moved to BBC South East, appearing as an occasional presenter and reporter on *Newsroom South East*. During this time she also appeared on some weekend main BBC News bulletins and reported for *Newsnight*. From 1994-95 she was a reporter on the BBC2 current affairs programme *Public Eye*.

A few years later, as part of a major relaunch of the BBC's news output, she was named secondary presenter of the *Six O'clock News* bulletin. She presented the programme as cover for main presenter Huw Edwards as well as regularly on Fridays until a presenter reshuffle was introduced to coincide with the retirement of Michael Buerk and the move of Peter Sissons to the BBC News channel.

Both Edwards and Bruce moved to presenting the *BBC News at Ten* and have presented the programme on their respective days since. By becoming presenter, she became the first woman to present the bulletin from launch in 2000. More recently, she has once again taken up the role of Friday presenter and main relief presenter on the BBC's Six O'clock News.

Following the murder of Jill Dando, Fiona took over the position of co-presenter on *Crimewatch* alongside Nick Ross, until both were replaced by Kirsty Young towards the end of 2007.

She also occasionally presents special editions of *The Money Programme*. In one, she profiled the entrepreneur, Sir Alan Sugar. Speaking about the experience she said "It was a bit like being in front of a hair dryer at very close quarters. He's not backwards in coming forward in his opinions." During the documentary, Bruce – who has always publicly identified herself as a feminist – challenged Sugar's view that women should openly disclose their childcare commitments to a potential employer.

In September 1998, she became the presenter for BBC2's *The Antiques Show*, which was in its fourth series. She presented it for a further two series, showing her interest in presenting antiques programmes nearly a decade before presenting the *Antiques Roadshow*.

It was during the making of an episode from *Antiques Roadshow* in Tatton Park in Cheshire that the scarf was given a rare invitation to travel there and meet with Fiona Bruce, one of the nation's favourites. In true fashion she was generous with her time that day in lending her face to the project.

WALSALL FOOTBALL CLUB

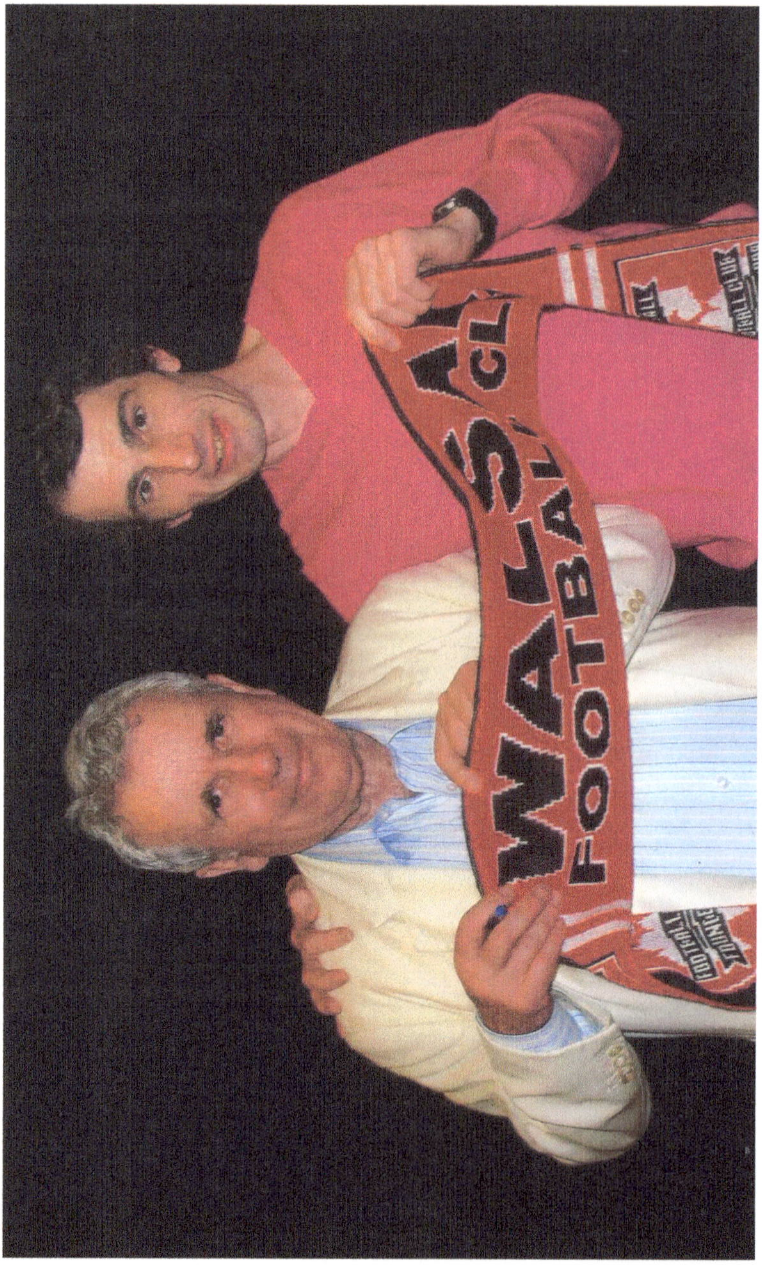

Martin Bell

Martin Bell joined the BBC as a reporter in Norwich some fifty years ago as a 24-year-old, following his graduation.

He moved to London three years later, beginning a distinguished career as a foreign affairs correspondent with his first assignment in Ghana. Over the next thirty years, he covered eleven conflicts and reported from eighty countries, making his name with reports from wars and conflicts in Vietnam, the Middle East, Nigeria, Angola and in Northern Ireland (during the "Troubles").

In 1997, twenty-four days before that year's British General Election, Bell announced that he was leaving the BBC to stand as an independent candidate in the Tatton constituency in Cheshire. Tatton was one of the safest Conservative seats in the country, where the sitting Conservative Member of Parliament, Neil Hamilton, was embroiled in "sleaze" allegations. The Labour and Liberal Democrat parties withdrew their candidates in Bell's favour in a plan masterminded by Alastair Campbell, Tony Blair's press secretary.

Hamilton was trounced, and he was duly elected an MP with a majority of 11,077 votes – overturning a Conservative majority of over 22,000 – and thus became the first successful independent parliamentary candidate since 1951.

Despite large numbers of his Tatton constituents who urged him to stand again in the 2001 general election. Bell said that the only thing which could make him change his mind would be Neil Hamilton being re-selected by the Tatton Conservative Party as candidate for the next General Election. However, future Chancellor George Osborne was selected instead as the Conservative party candidate for Tatton. Hamilton lost his libel case against Mohammed Al-Fayed at the end of 1999, ending any prospect of him making a political comeback. Though he regretted making the pledge of saying he would only serve for one term, Bell stuck to his promise.

In 2001, he was nonetheless persuaded to stand as an independent candidate against another Conservative MP Eric Pickles in the "safe" Essex constituency of Brentwood and Ongar, where there were accusations that the local Conservative Association had been infiltrated by a Pentecostal church. Having garnered nearly 32% of the vote coming second, he announced his retirement from politics, saying that "winning one and losing one is not a bad record for an amateur".

A frequent speaker around the country on many issues, Martin Bell came to Stourbridge to partly promote his latest book and found time to hold the scarf even though he is a fervent Norwich supporter.

WALSALL FOOTBALL CLUB

Waterstone's
Waterstone's
Waterstone's
Waterstone's
DAPHNE DU MAURIER
IAN McEWAN
Kazuo Ishiguro
WAR TORN
SALL
CLUB

Lynda Bellingham

Born Meredith Lee Hughes Bellingham in Montreal and brought up in Aston Abbotts in Buckinghamshire, Lynda made her debut appearance in the Pendley Open Air Shakespeare Festival. Her big break came as a nurse in an ITV afternoon soap opera of the 1970s, *General Hospital*. She went topless for her roles in *Confessions of a Driving Instructor* and *Sweeney!*

Perhaps best known as the head of the family in the Oxo television adverts during the 1980s. Her other prominent roles included the James Herriot drama *All Creatures Great and Small* (where she was the second actress to play Helen Herriot on television, replacing Carol Drinkwater) and the situation comedy *Second Thoughts* and its sequel, *Faith in the Future*.

In 1986 she appeared in the 14-part *Doctor Who* serial *The Trial of a Time Lord* as the Inquisitor. She reprised the role of the Inquisitor character for the Big Finish Productions audio series, *Gallifrey*. Other appearances have been in Gleb Panfilov's *The Romanovs: A Crowned Family* as Empress Alexandra, as well as playing Pauline Farnell, the compassionate accountant in *At Home with the Braithwaites* alongside Amanda Redman and former *All Creatures Great and Small* colleague Peter Davison. For several months in 2004, she had a recurring role in *The Bill* as villainess Irene Radford.

There was also a memorable role in the ITV comedy *Bonkers* playing Mrs. Wadlow, a man-eating suburban housewife who seduces her neighbour's teenage son and turns him into her gigolo. Later that year she filmed guest appearances in episodes of *Love Soup* and *Robin Hood*. A year later, she appeared in a play entitled *Vincent River* at the Trafalgar Studios in London. Her performance received critical acclaim, and she took the opportunity to announce on *Loose Women* in early 2008 that the show would be moving to Broadway in July of that year, although this never actually transpired.

She joined *Loose Women* during this period and continued as a regular panelist for almost four years. During that time she was one of the contestants in the seventh series of *Strictly Come Dancing*, the BBC ratings winner where she partnered Darren Bennett. However, she was voted out by the judges in the fourth week.

During 2010 she launched her book *Lost and Found*, a story of her life and career and toured the country for private readings. It was during this period that the scarf journeyed to two destinations and ended up empty handed. Finally on the third attempt it met up with her deep down in Yeovil where she proved courteous and kind personality.

Lynda Bellingham died on 19 October 2014 in her husband Michael's arms in a London hospital from colorectal cancer.

WALSALL FOOTBALL CLUB

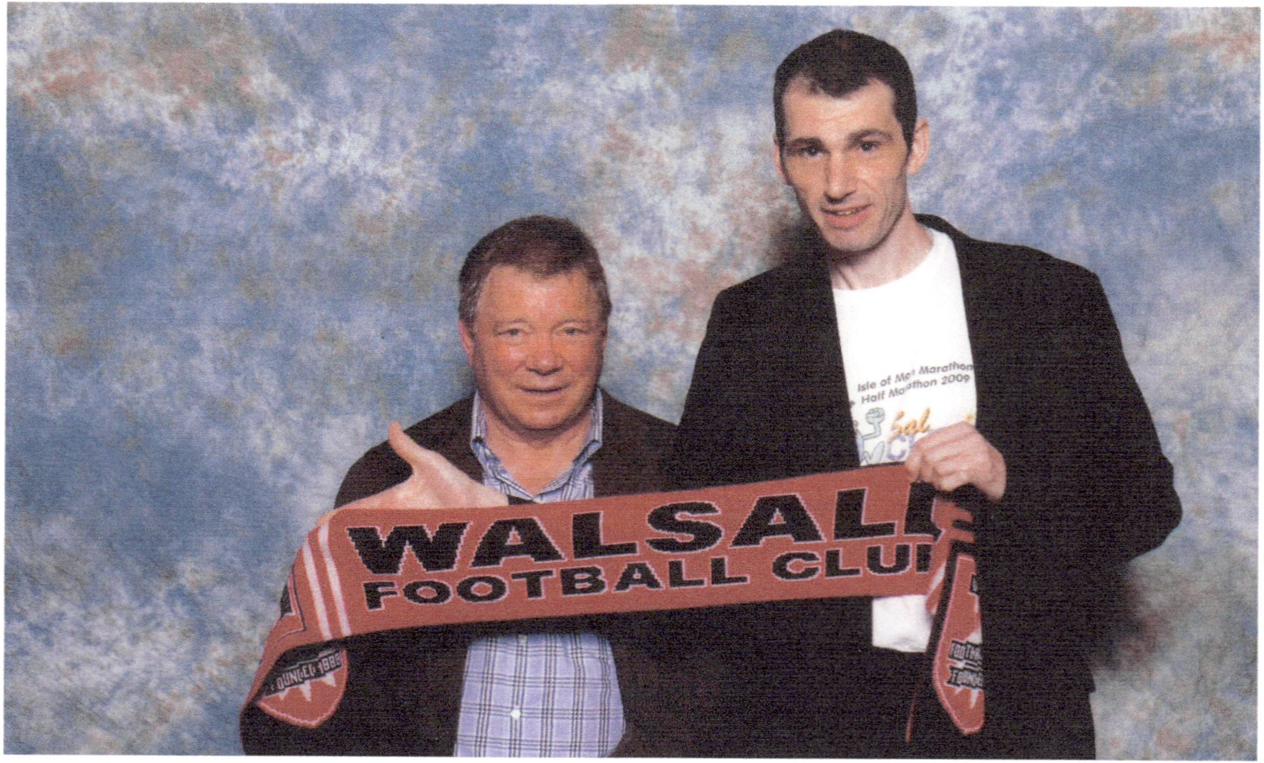
WALSALL
FOOTBALL CLUB
Half Marathon 2009

William Shatner

William Shatner made his movie debut as Alexi in *The Brothers Karamazov*, which opened in December 1957. In 1962 he appeared in the all-star cast assembled for Stanley Kramer's *Judgement at Nuremberg*, but over his long career he has worked mostly in television, including a memorable role as a bedeviled airline passenger in the *Twilight Zone* episode "Nightmare at 20,000 Feet."

His big break came when Shatner accepted the role of Captain James Tiberius Kirk that made him a pop-culture icon, in Gene Roddenberry's intergalactic science fiction series, *Star Trek*. While not exactly an emotional volcano, Kirk championed earthly empathy and compassion while his second-in-command Mr. Spock, relied upon pure logic. Shatner's long-running portrayal of this earnest, somewhat absurd figure often displayed humour and refreshing self-parody. The original television show lasted only 3 seasons, and was not a huge ratings hit. But its reputation grew in syndication, and with the special-effects breakthrough that was George Lucas's *Star Wars* (1977), a movie became possible. *Star Trek: The Motion Picture* made $175 million at the box office, and assured that there would be many sequels. In 1989, William Shatner provided the storyline and directed one of the last *Star Trek* films with the original cast: *Star Trek, The Final Frontier*. After 7 films made over 15 years, Shatner finally put the Captain Kirk role to rest in *Star Trek: Generations* (1994).

Other memorable television roles include the lead in the police drama *TJ Hooker*; (he also directed some episodes of the show), and the recurring character The Big Giant Head in *Third Rock from the Sun*, which earned him an Emmy Award nomination. In the early 1990s, he wrote a series of sci-fi novels under the title *TekWar*. Four cable films based on the books were made, and Shatner served as executive producer and the occasional star of the series of the same name

He hosted the series *Rescue 911* from 1989 to 1996, and after playing the role of attorney Denny Crane in the final season of the series *The Practice* in 2004, he successfully transported the character to the popular series *Boston Legal*. He hosted the weekly programs *William Shatner's Raw Nerve*, a celebrity interview show, and *Weird or What?*, which examines the unusual and unexplained; he stars in the sitcom *$#*! My Dad Says* as a shoot-from-the-hip retiree.

During May 2011, he was honoured with the Governor General of Canada's Performing Arts Award for Lifetime Artistic Achievement, recording a humorous short film *William Shatner Sings O Canada* for the occasion.

During this period he toured extensively including England and made appearances in London where he gladly posed with the scarf albeit whilst he was sitting down.

WALSALL FOOTBALL CLUB

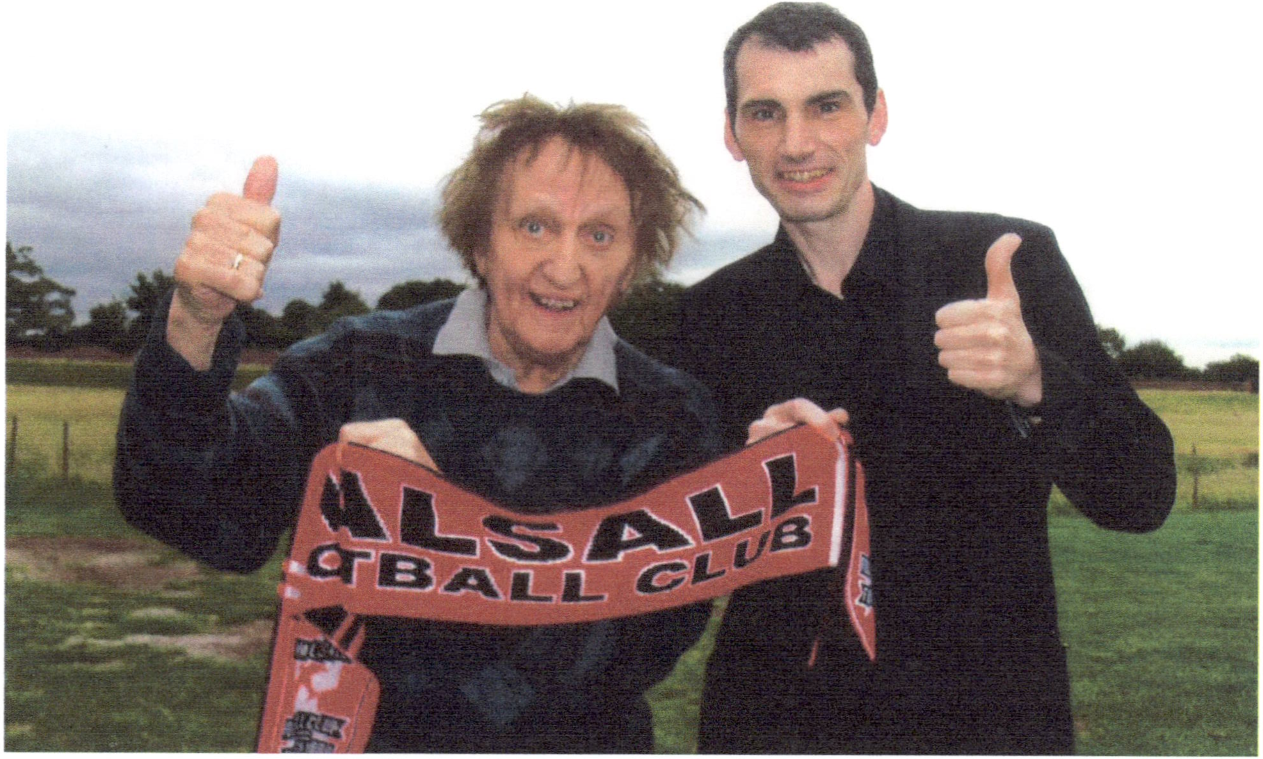
ALSALL
TBALL CLUB

Ken Dodd

Ken Dodd is known to millions through his trademark frizzy hair or "fluff dom" and buck teeth or "denchers", his favourite cleaner, the feather duster (or "tickling stick") and his greeting of "How tickled I am!", as well as his send-off "Lots and lots of happiness!".

Dodd's stand-up comedy style is fast and relies on the rapid delivery of one-liner jokes. He has claimed that his comic influences include other Liverpool comedians like Arthur Askey, Robb Wilton, Tommy Handley and the "cheeky chappy" from Brighton, Max Miller. He intersperses the comedy with occasional songs, both serious and humorous, in an incongruously fine light baritone voice.

In addition he has had many recording hits, charting on nineteen occasions in the UK Top 40, including his first single "Love Is Like a Violin", produced on Decca Records by Alex Wharton, which charted at number 8, and his song "Tears", which topped the charts for five weeks in 1965, selling over a million copies. At the time it was the country's biggest selling single by a solo artist, and remains one of the UK's biggest selling singles of all time. Dodd was selected to perform the song on *A Jubilee Of Music* on BBC One as part of a celebration of the key pop successes of Queen Elizabeth II's first twenty-five years as Britain's monarch.

He is renowned for the length of his performances, and during the 1960s he earned a place in the *Guinness Book of*

Records for the world's longest ever joke-telling session: 1,500 jokes in three and a half hours (7.14 jokes per minute), undertaken at a Liverpool theatre, where audiences were observed to enter the show in shifts. In 2006, he appeared at the Royal Variety Performance in front of Prince Charles and his wife Camilla, where he reprised some of his famous jokes, including those about tax accountants as well as singing his famous song "Happiness".

An example of his schedule can be seen from his prolific touring and, despite his age, his shows still frequently do not finish until after midnight. In 2012 at the age of 84, he played the Princes Theatre in Clacton-on-Sea, Essex on 7 July. Starting at 7.15pm he continued until just before 9.00pm when Sybie Jones took to the stage. Returning at 9.30pm he continued until 10.00pm. The second support act performed until Dodd's return just before 11.00pm when he continued well past midnight.

A statue depicting Dodd with his feather duster was unveiled in Lime Street Station, Liverpool 2009. During the later part of the year in Congleton Cheshire he invited the scarf backstage at a performance where after some obvious clowning about held the scarf and kept the one-liners coming.

WALSALL FOOTBALL CLUB

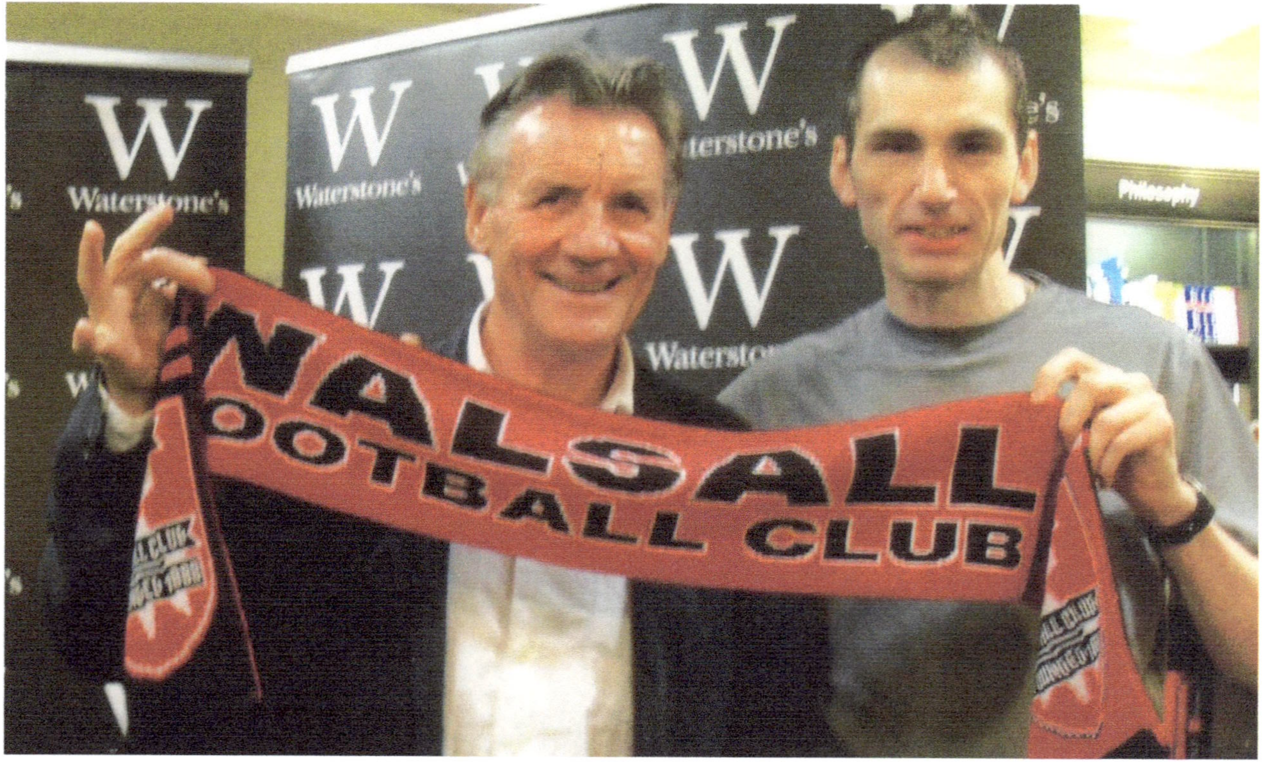
WALSALL
OOTBALL CLUB
Waterstone's
Philosophy

Michael Palin

Having graduated from Oxford University in 1965 with ambitions to be a writer and performer of comedy, Michael Palin made his first television appearance as the rather unlikely sounding host of a regionally-produced pop show for children, *Now*.

Meanwhile, Palin began writing sketch material with Terry Jones (whom he had befriended at university) for various television shows, in addition to working in cabaret with him as a double-act. Their major breakthrough arrived when they were recruited to the writing team of *The Frost Report*. Not only was the series itself a huge success, it brought the pair into contact with fellow writers John Cleese, Graham Chapman and Eric Idle.

Monty Python's Flying Circus (BBC, 1969-74) finally saw Palin and Jones united with Cleese, Chapman, Idle and Gilliam to create what was to become one of British television's most influential series, comedy or otherwise. Launched without any fanfare, the show quickly drew a cult audience for the sheer originality of its humour, turning the writers/performers into arguably the most important and internationally influential comedy team ever to work in television.

Palin followed *Monty Python's Flying Circus* with his own superbly realised series, *Ripping Yarns* in the late seventies. Palin starred in each episode of this anthology series parodying early twentieth century Boys' Own adventure stories, and co-wrote all the stories with Terry Jones. However, despite the success he enjoyed with *Ripping Yarns* (it won a BAFTA award in 1980 for best light entertainment series) it was the only post-*Python* comedy television series in which Palin appeared.

Although he co-starred in the Alan Bleasdale-scripted drama series *G.B.H.*, playing a teacher in this story of political corruption, acting, whether in comedy or straight drama, increasingly took a back seat from the late 1980s, as he began to steer his career into new territory.

Since the phenomenal success of the documentary series *Around the World in Eighty Days*, in which he followed the route taken by the fictional Phileas Fogg in Jules Verne's novel, Palin has enjoyed renewed success with a spate of travel documentaries. All self-penned as well as presented, they include *Pole to Pole with Michael Palin*, *Full Circle with Michael Palin*, *Michael Palin's Hemingway Adventure*, *Sahara with Michael Palin*, *Himalaya with Michael Palin*, *Michael Palin's New Europe*.

He has also enjoyed a degree of success with the publication of his diaries, covering the years 1969 to 1987, in two volumes published in 2006 and 2009. During which time he stopped off at Bristol and managed to sign a book and hold a scarf for the Saddlers.

WALSALL FOOTBALL CLUB

P.P.S
Positive Protection Solutions
DRAGON
PROMOTIONS
www.dragonpromotionswales.co.uk
Safe Style UK
WWW.P4PPHOTOS.IFP3.COM
P4P
EVENT PHOTOGRAPHY
WALSALL
FOOTBALL CLUB

Roberto Duran and Thomas Hearns

Thomas Hearns was born October 18, 1958 and is a retired American boxer. Nicknamed the "Motor City Cobra" and more famously "Hitman", Hearns became the first boxer in history to win world titles in four divisions. He would also become the first fighter in history to win five world titles in five different divisions. Named *Ring Magazine* fighter of the year in 1980 and 1984 he is best known for his fights with Sugar Ray Leonard, Marvin Hagler and Roberto Duran.

In 1981, Hearns the WBA champion, with a 32-0 record (30 KOs), fought WBC champion Sugar Ray Leonard (30-1) to unify the World welterweight championship in a bout dubbed "The Showdown". In this legendary fight, he suffered his first professional defeat when Leonard stopped him in the 14th round. In the 13th round, Leonard, behind on points on all 3 judges' scorecards needed a knockout to win. He came on strong and put Hearns through the ropes at the end of the round. Although he was visibly dazed, totally out of gas and received a count but he was saved by the bell. Leonard, with his left eye shut and time running out, resumed his attack in the 14th. Hearns started the round boxing and moving, but after staggering Hearns with an overhand right, Leonard pinned him against the ropes. After another combination to the body and head, referee Davey Pearl stopped the fight.

He went on to win six world titles in five weight classes during his pro career, defeating future boxing hall of famers such as Pipino Cuevas, Wilfred Benítez, Virgil Hill and Roberto Durán.

Roberto Duran is a retired Panamanian professional boxer, widely regarded as one of the greatest boxers of all time. A versatile brawler in the ring, he was nicknamed "Manos de Piedra" ("*Hands of Stone*") during his career.

He controversially defeated Ken Buchanan in Madison Square Garden, New York for the WBA Lightweight Championship. Durán, as a 2-to-1 underdog, scored a knock down against the defending champion just fifteen seconds into the opening round and battered him throughout the bout.

On June 20, 1980, Durán captured the WBC Welterweight title by defeating Leonard via a 15-round unanimous decision. The fight became known as "The Brawl in Montreal". Following this he earned a crack at the light middleweight title, this time against WBA Champion Davey Moore, the fight was stopped in the eighth round with Duran the victor.

In 2001, he traveled to Argentina to promote a salsa music CD that he had just released. While there, he was involved in a car crash and required life-saving surgery. After that incident, he announced his retirement from boxing at the age of 50.

Both fighters stood toe to toe with the scarf in Wolverhampton during a boxing dinner.

WALSALL FOOTBALL CLUB

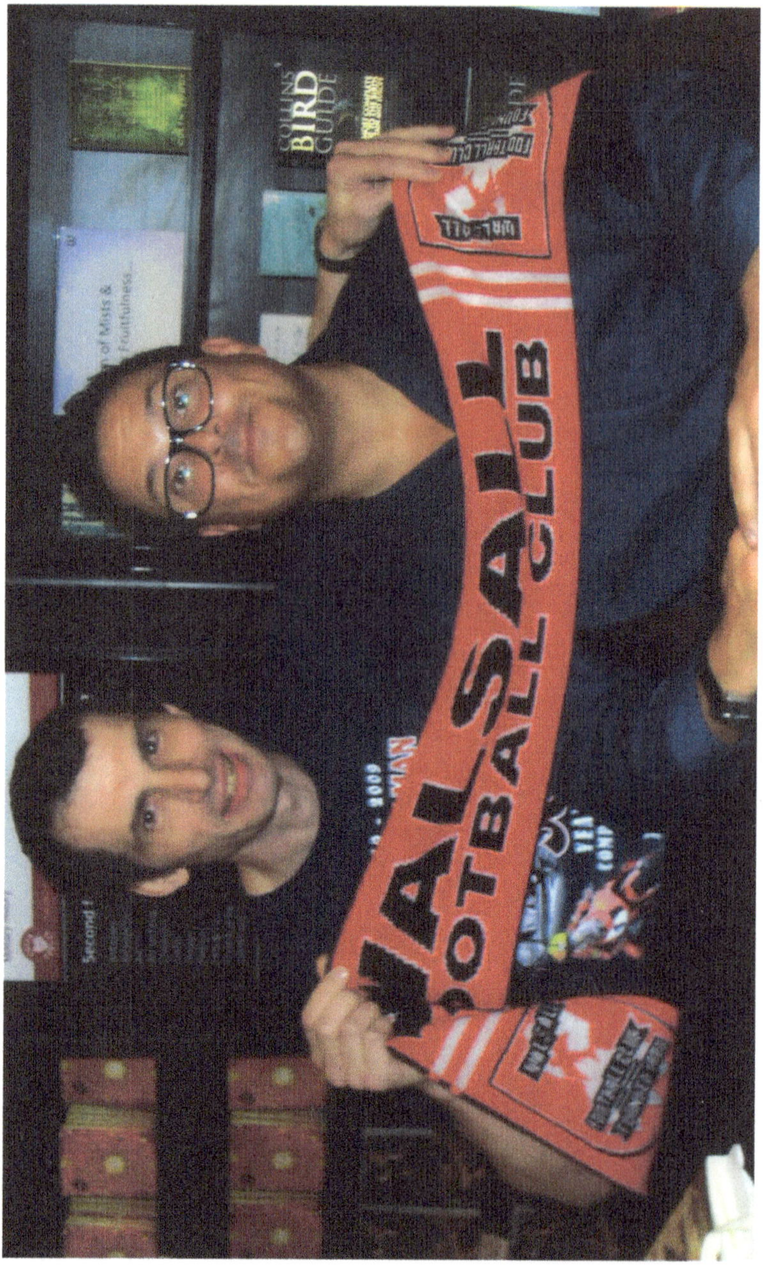
COLLINS BIRD GUIDE
OTBALL CLUB

Dom Joly

Beiruit-born Dom Joly moved to Britain as a teenager, and started his professional career as a political producer for ITN. After being recruited to work as a producer on the show *House to House*, a political discussion programme on Channel 4, Joly went on to work for *The Mark Thomas Comedy Product* because of his political knowledge.

From there he went on to create his own show for the Paramount Comedy Channel called *War of the Flea*. Discovering that working in comedy was both easier and more fun than his previous employment, Joly began to develop *Trigger Happy TV* which had a similar structure to *War of the Flea*.

He started doing hidden camera stunts as 'bumpers' between adverts and programmes on the Paramount Comedy Channel, and in 1998, made a pilot of *Trigger Happy TV* for Channel 4's Comedy Lab strand, which was commissioned for two full series, which scooped a silver Rose at the Montreux TV festival.

Following the success of *Trigger Happy TV* on Channel 4, Joly was secured by the BBC for a rumoured £1 million. However, his first show for the BBC, *This is Dom Joly*, a spoof chat show in which he played an appallingly egotistical media character who had the same name as him, thereby confusing a lot of the audience as to what was real and what wasn't, did not achieve the same success as *Trigger Happy TV*, leading to the hidden camera format being revamped on BBC1 as *World Shut*

Your Mouth. It featured all new material and an increased budget relative to *Trigger Happy*, allowing for pranks to be performed in different countries.

Early on his career he was the singer in an Indie band called "Hang David" in the early 1990s. He was a Goth and said that he looked more like Robert Smith than Robert Smith. Joly personally selects all the soundtracks for his TV shows.

He has also turned his attention to authoring several books in his time, as well as becoming an award-winning travel writer for both the *Sunday Times* and the *Mail On Sunday*. He writes several regular columns for various UK nationals and periodicals including a weekly sports column for *The Independent* and an eclectic weekly column for the *Independent on Sunday*.

Amongst many books he published the *The Dark Tourist* in 2010, about dark tourism.Dom travels beyond the radius of Ryan Air's reach and gives us a literary photo album of his exploits travelling through the atmospheric North Korea (to the extent possible for a foreigner), Cambodia, Lebanon, Iran and USA.

On a promotion tour for the book, the scarf crossed paths with him not once but twice, firstly in Nottingham, then in Birmingham where the scarf was "warned off" in typical Joly style!

WALSALL FOOTBALL CLUB

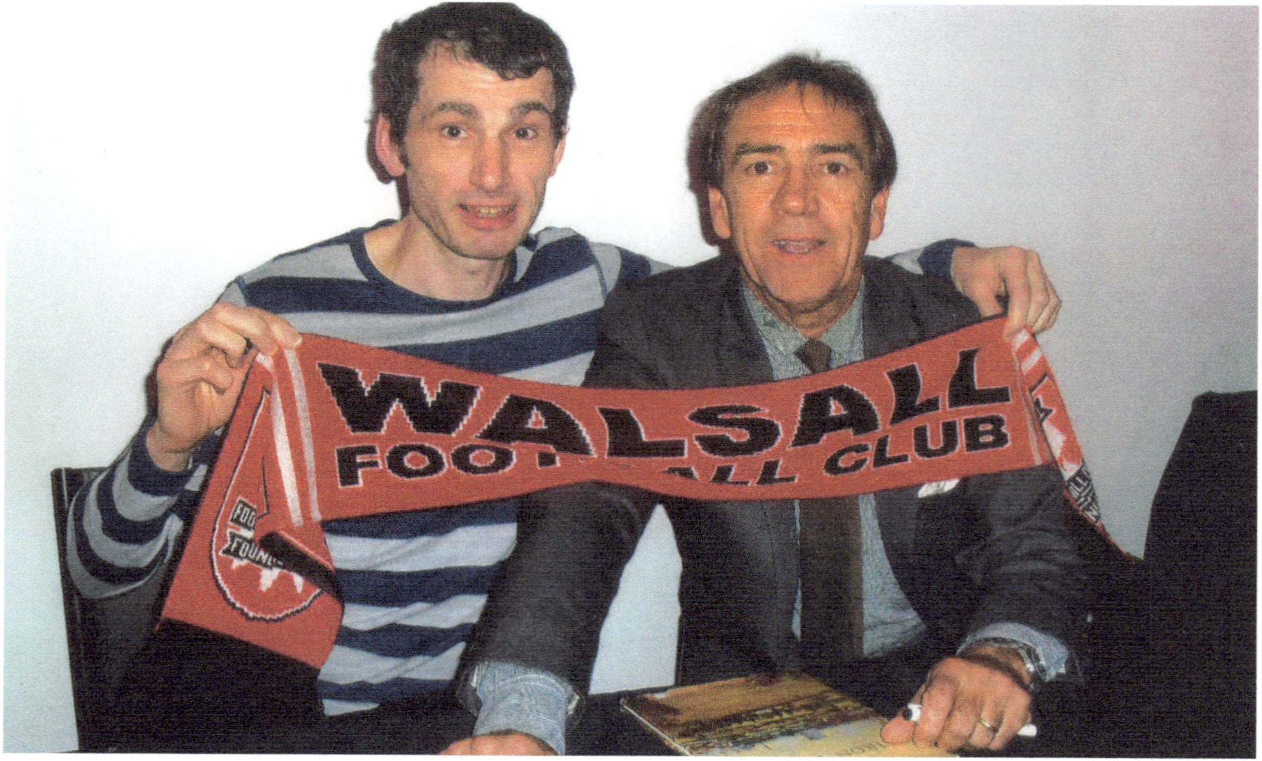

Robert Lindsay

It was whilst attending school that Robert was introduced to the world of performing arts by an enthusiastic arts teacher who recognised his potential and steered him towards a career in acting.

Lindsay was a huge fan of the poet DH Lawrence who was born in Eastwood – only five miles away from Ilkeston – and he says he was inspired by Lawrence's achievements.

Upon graduating from RADA, Lindsay's first job was as a dialect coach for a repertory company in Essex, before joining a regional theatre group and then graduating to roles in the West End.

But in was in 1977 that the breakthrough came when Lindsay was cast as Wolfie Smith in the BBC sit-com *Citizen Smith*. The comedy, about a would-be revolutionary, made Lindsay a household name and even lead to a national catch-phrase:Power to the People!

Lindsay then appeared in another comedy series *Seconds Out* in 1981. He played a boxer who fought his way from local bouts to the British Middleweight Championship.

During the eighties, Lindsay appeared in five BBC Shakespeare adaptations: Fabian in *Twelfth Night*, Lysander in *A Midsummer's Night's Dream*, Iachimo in *Cymbeline*, Edmund in *King Lear* and Benedick in *Much Ado About Nothing*.

He also joined with Paul McGann in the TV series *Give Us a Break* and played the title role in the movie *Bert Rigby, You're a Fool*. In 1991 came another career highlight for Lindsay when he won a BAFTA for his leading role in Alan Bleasdale's dark comedy *G.B.H.*

Robert's most recent screen appearances include Fagin in Alan Bleasdale's ITV adaptation of *Oliver Twist* and as Ben, the main character in the BBC sit-com *My Family*.

Lindsay is also noted for his stage appearances and he won both a Tony and Olivier award for his performances in the musical *Me and My Girl* which travelled from the West End to Broadway in the mid-nineties.

It can be argued that he is probably Ilkeston Town's most famous supporter – having grown up in the town, the football club is understandably close to his heart. Another link with a local football club is that of Derby County F.C. for whom he sings the recorded version of the anthemic song "Steve Bloomer's Watchin'", played and sung by the fans at the beginning of every home game, and usually at the start of the second half and after a good win.

In spite of these ties and obvious loyalties he faithfully allowed Walsall FC into the frame at a talk he gave in Derby.

WALSALL FOOTBALL CLUB

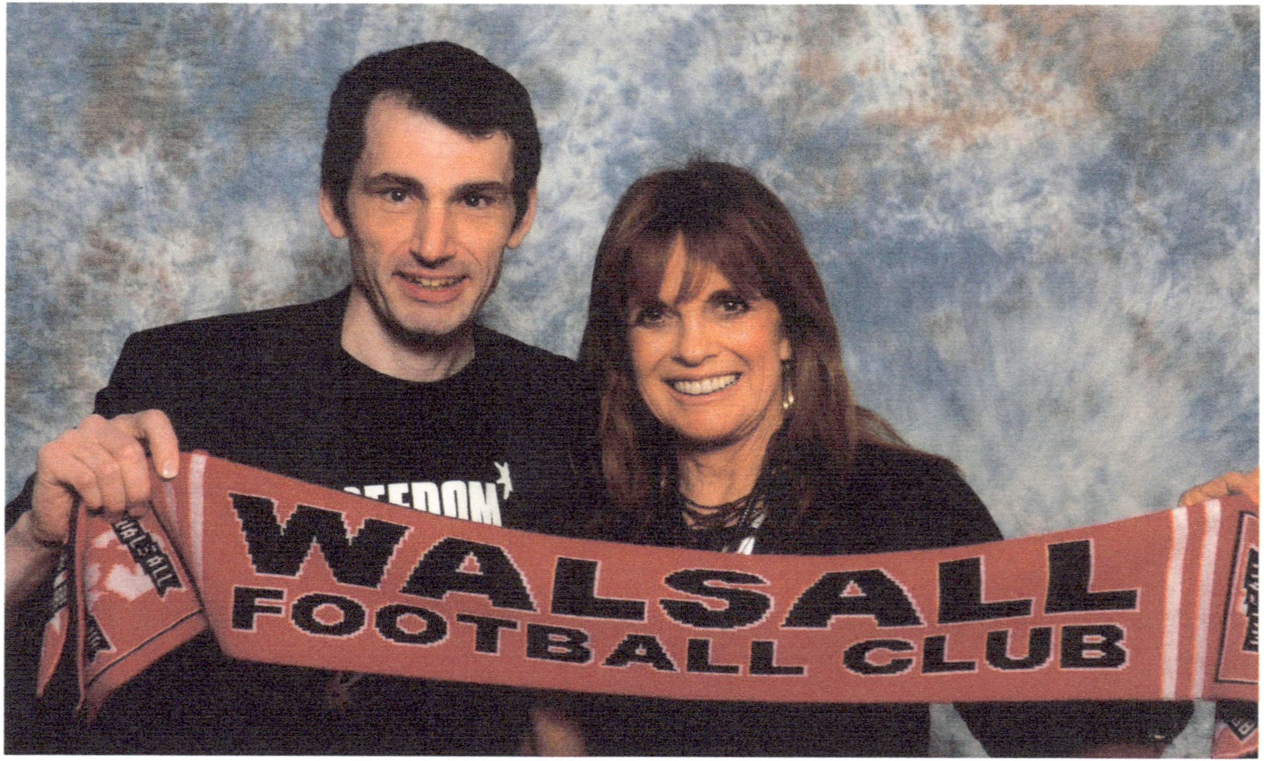
WALSALL
FOOTBALL CLUB

Linda Gray

As an introverted child, Linda grew up a mere block away from the movie studios where she would hang around the studio gates and daydream about being a child star. Her Catholic parents, leery of the influence of the seamy spheres of show business, sent her to nearby all-girls Notre Dame Academy, but she nevertheless gravitated to the school's performing arts offerings. Tall and graceful upon graduating high school, she landed work as a model. One of her earliest jobs took her to Capitol Records, then looking for hot new talent to grace album covers. It was there she met Ed Thrasher, an art director with the label, and the two began dating and married in 1962.

Restless with modeling, Gray had begun taking acting lessons and, in the 1970s, she urged her agent to start looking for dramatic work. She began with bit parts, eventually securing her first featured role on the shamus series *McCloud*, and her first regular TV series work in *All That Glitters*, a short-lived attempt at a soap opera satire produced by Norman Lear.

Gray was relieved to win the role of Sue Ellen Ewing, even though the character, the onetime beauty queen wife of central oil magnate J.R. Ewing played by the late Larry Hagman, was initially written as little more than pretty window dressing for the show, sniping at J.R. from the couch. By her later account, her character initially did not even have a name, and she and

Hagman merely vamped their scenes as she played it as a dissatisfied one-time trophy wife. Producers liked their chemistry enough that they began beefing up her part. The show became a major hit, even as Sue Ellen's gross discontentment and her own schemes became one front on which the caddish J.R. did battle, even as he scrapped with business nemeses and his own goody-two-shoes brother Bobby.

For her work, Gray earned an Emmy nomination for Best Actress in a Drama in 1981, but she very nearly did not make it through the show's long run. Gray reportedly ran foul of producers in 1986 when she told them she wanted to direct episodes as had co-stars Hagman and Duffy, and, when they fired her, Hagman threatened to leave the show until they hired her back and acceded to her request.

In the meantime, she would make a stab at comedy, playing opposite Sylvester Stallone in his attempt at screwball comedy, *Oscar*, star in a flurry of soapy made-for-TV movies, then return to nighttime soaps in 1994 with a recurring role as the mother of Heather Locklear's character on Fox's hit *Melrose Place*. That set the table for a new Fox show for the fall which was the premiere of *Models, Inc.*, revolving around a modeling agency run by Gray's character and the backstabbing, sexual conquests and power-plays behinds the scenes.

Gray returned full time to the role that made her a star – a "reboot" of *Dallas* and during a promotion run she greeted the scarf in London at the Thistle Hotel in Hounslow.

WALSALL FOOTBALL CLUB

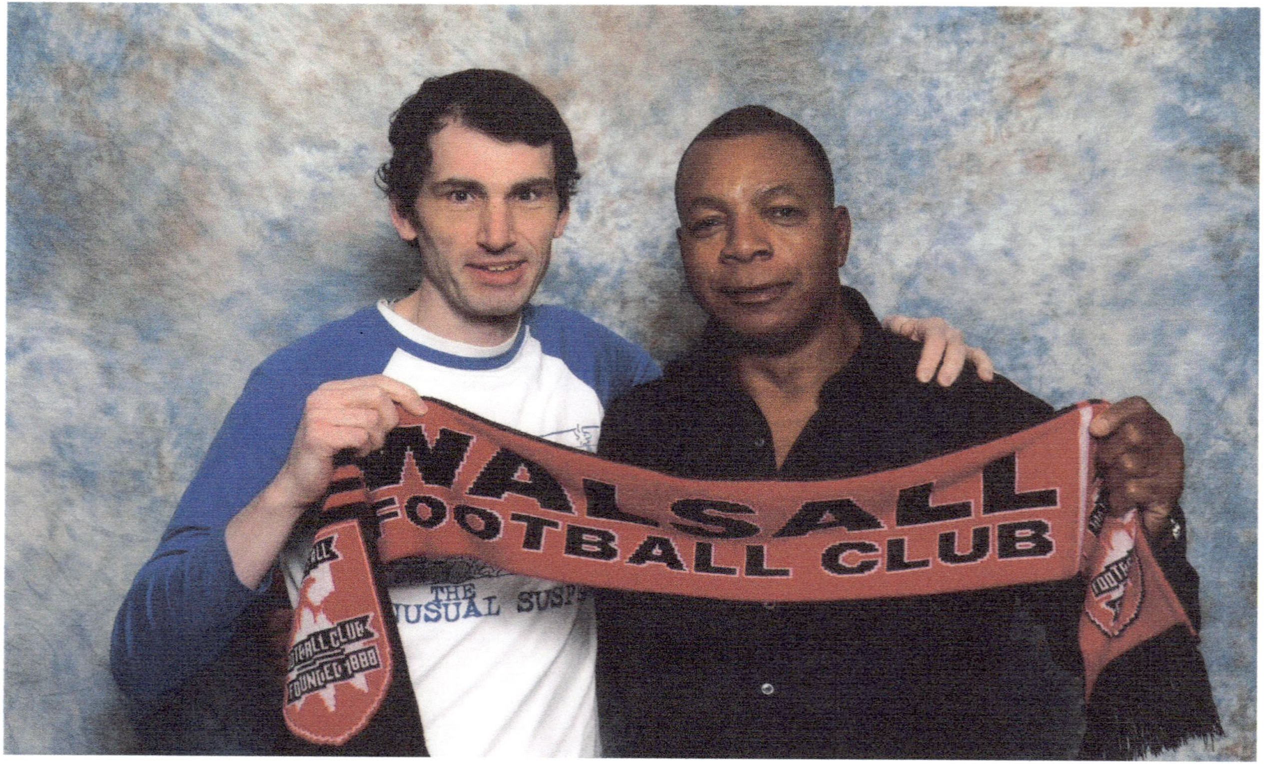
WALSALL
FOOTBALL CLUB

Carl Weathers

Weathers started out playing football both collegiately and professionally as a linebacker. He began his college career at Long Beach City College, where he did not play in 1966 due to an ankle injury suffered when he tripped over a curb surrounding the running track while warming up for practice with another linebacker, Paul Snow. He then transferred and played for San Diego State University, becoming a letterman in 1968 and 1969. This led to a brief professional career with the Oakland Raiders, where he played 7 games in 1970 and one game in 1971. He joined the BC Lions of the Canadian Football League in 1971 and played until 1973, 18 games in total. In his football career, he played for Hall-of-Fame coaches Don Coryell (at San Diego State) and John Madden with the Oakland Raiders. It was perhaps this reputation with the team that led him to be chosen as the narrator of the NFL Films' season recap of the 2001 Raiders season.

He retired in 1974 and became an actor.

In 1976, he starred alongside Sylvester Stallone in *Rocky* as the iconic Apollo Creed, a role he would reprise for the next three *Rocky* movies. For the final film in the *Rocky* series, *Rocky Balboa*, Sylvester Stallone asked Weathers, Mr. T, and Dolph Lundgren for permission to use footage from their appearances in the earlier Rocky movies. Mr. T and Dolph Lundgren acquiesced, but Weathers wanted an actual part in the movie, even though his character died in *Rocky IV*. Stallone refused and Weathers decided not to allow Stallone to use his image for Rocky flashbacks from the previous movies. They instead used footage of a fighter who looks similar to Weathers.

As a member of the cast of *Predator*, Weathers worked with future California governor Arnold Schwarzenegger and future Minnesota governor Jesse Ventura. Many years later he appeared in a spoof segment on *Saturday Night Live*, announcing that he was running for political office and urging viewers to vote for him on the basis that "he was the black guy in Predator".

He also appeared in Michael Jackson's "Liberian Girl" music video, and co-starred in the Adam Sandler comedy *Happy Gilmore*, as Chubbs, a golf legend teaching Happy how to play golf. He reprised the role nearly four years later in the Sandler comedy *Little Nicky*.

The start of the millennium proved a fruitful year for Weathers as he received a career revival as a comedic actor beginning with appearances in 3 episodes of the comedy series *Arrested Development* as a cheapskate caricature of himself, who serves as Tobias Fünke's acting coach. He was then cast in the comedies *The Sasquatch Gang* and *The Comebacks*.

He has since turned his hand to making commercials for Bud Light in which he introduces plays from the "Bud Light Playbook". During a trip to Milton Keynes he aligned himself with Walsall F C in this shot.

WALSALL FOOTBALL CLUB

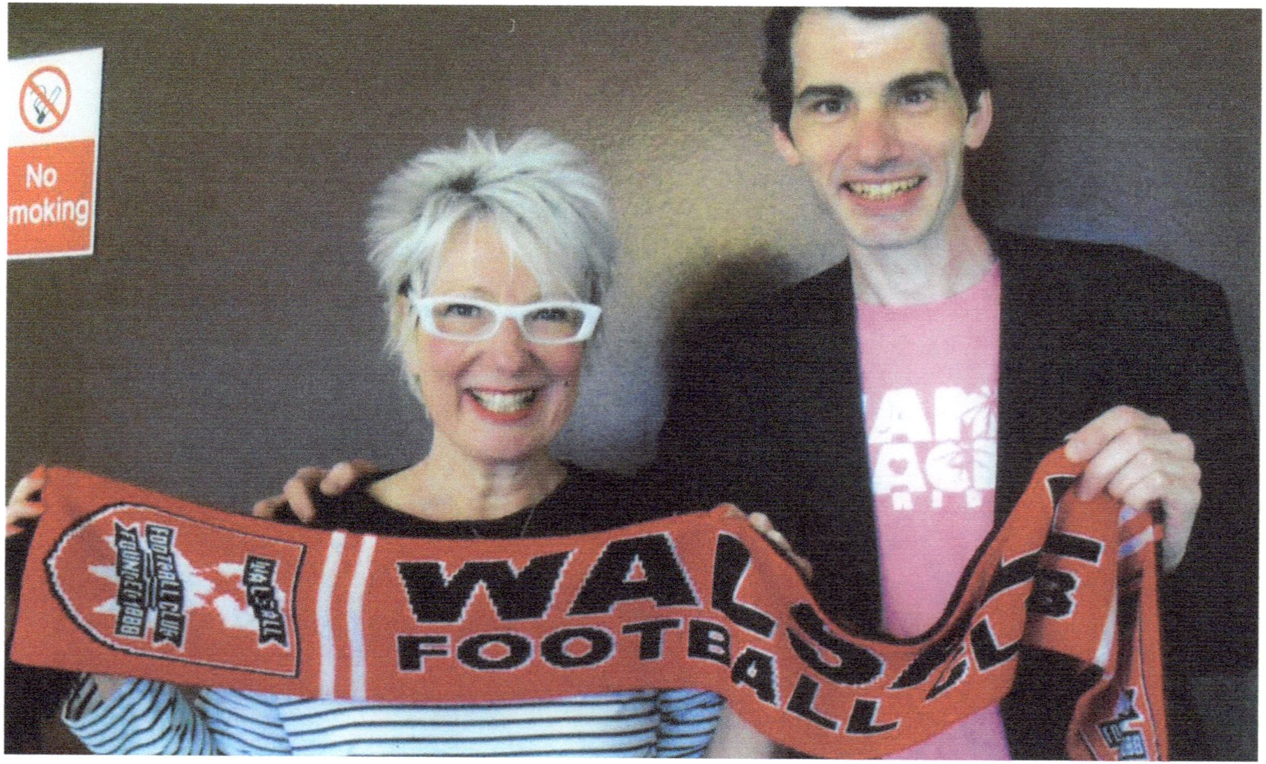
No
moking
FOOTBALL CLUB

Jenny Éclair

Jenny Hargreaves became a punk performance poet in the 1980s. According to legend, she acquired the name 'Eclair' while pretending to be French at a Blackpool nightclub.

After moving to London her first job was at Camberwell Arts College as a life model which she did for about 2 terms. Then she saw an advert in 'The Stage' looking for novelty acts, and she found work doing punk poems. In 1989, when she was named the *Time Out Cabaret Award* winner, she said it "was nice because it's the first time I've ever won without having to run 100 metres balancing an egg on a spoon."

Jenny Eclair, has been a standup comic for many years, she was the first woman to win the coveted Perrier Award and hasn't stopped banging on about it ever since. She still gigs regularly and is on tour around the UK in the autumn with her new show *Eclairious*.

She is most recognizable to the public for her regular television work and some of her small screen highlights include, *I'm A Celebrity... Get Me out Of Here*, the *Grumpy Old Women* series, plus the *Grumpy Guides'*, '*Grumpy Holidays* and *It's Grim up North*. She also occasionally crops up on day time telly and gets very excited about doing things like *This Morning* and *Loose Women*.

Stage wise, Eclair's biggest hit to date has been co-writing (with Judith Holder) and starring in *Grumpy Old Women Live* and *Grumpy Old Women Live: 2 Chin Up Britain*, a two hour extravaganza that toured the UK, Australia and recently opened in Helsinki, the show enjoyed success when it transferred to DVD. *Grumpy Old Women Live 2: Chin Up Britain* enjoyed an 8 week West End run at the Novello Theatre.

Eclair is a writer as much as a performer. She has co-written a number of one-woman plays including the critically acclaimed *Andy Warhol Syndrome*, which was also adapted for Radio 4. She is the author of two novels *Camberwell Beauty* and *Having a Lovely Time*, whilst her nonfiction books include, *Chin Up Britain*, *The Book of Bad Behaviour*, plus *Grumpy Old Couples* and *Wendy The Bumper Book of fun for Women of a certain age* (both of which were co-written with Judith Holder) Radio writing credits include the two series of *Twilight Baby* for Women's Hour on BBC Radio 4.

She lives in South London with St Geof of Camberwell and has a daughter at university.

During her sell out *Eclairious* tour the scarf was invited backstage at Stafford Gatehouse theatre before the show, where she joked and exhibited some colourful language before taking a firm grip of the scarf, and signing a copy of her book.

WALSALL FOOTBALL CLUB

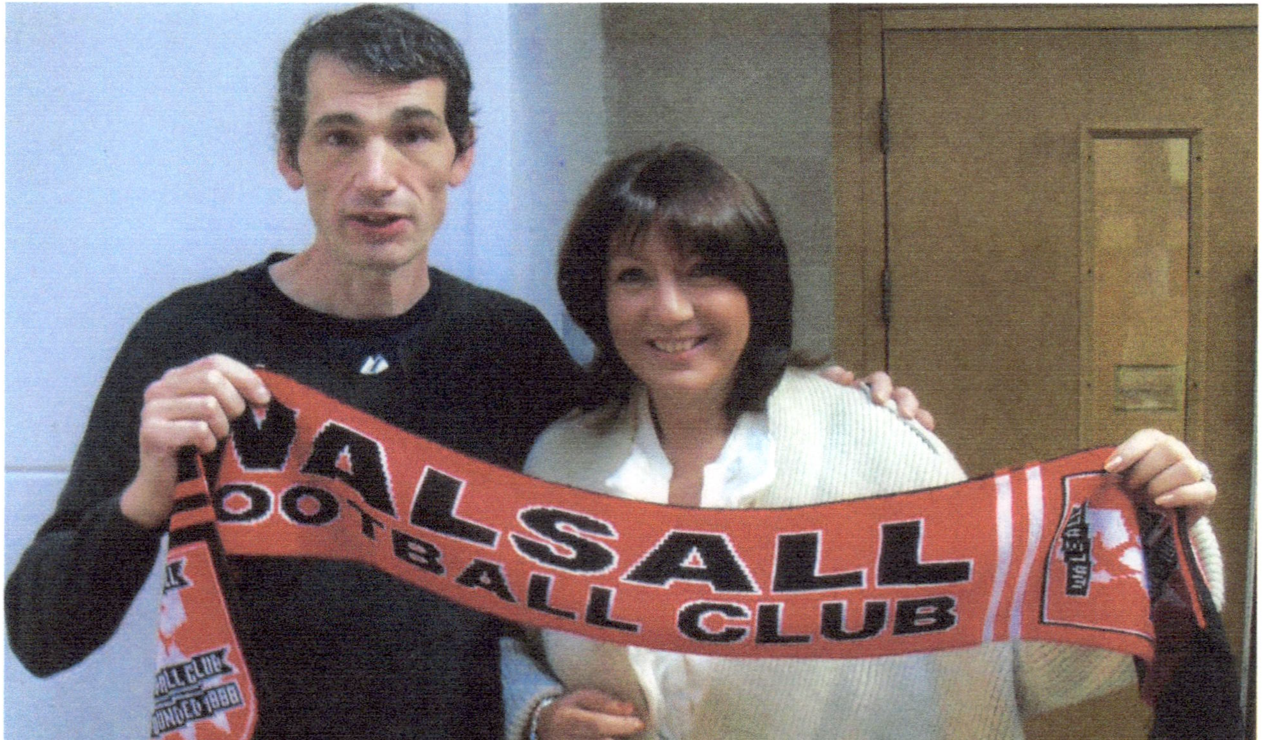
CLUB

Jayne MacDonald

In her early days McDonald toured many clubs in the north of England, with her father acting as her roadie. She provided all of her own equipment, which she had to replace after it was destroyed in a large bar-fight. Her first position on a cruise ship was on the *Black Prince*, and following that, the *Horizon*. After her father's death, she returned to sea and began working on the *Zenith*. Later she cruised on the *Century*, where she met Henrik Brixen who was the Ships Plumber. She confesses that this period of her life was not a happy one, due to pay delays, technical difficulties, and stressful working conditions. After this she took some time off with Henrik, but was eventually tempted back to sea as a headliner on the *Century's* sister-ship, the *Galaxy*.

Shortly after accepting the position, Jayne was contacted by Chris Terrill of the BBC, who asked her to be the star of his docusoap. The *Cruise* was watched regularly by 14 million viewers, and after years of hard work, she became a celebrity overnight. Her wedding to Henrik Brixen was televised by the BBC and watched by a large audience, although the couple have since divorced.

After signing a major-label recording contract, she began to carve out a mainstream showbiz career, first as a guest presenter on BBC's National Lottery and subsequently with her debut album *Jane McDonald*, which spent three weeks at Number 1 in the UK Albums Chart.

As well as appearing on *The Cruise*, Jayne presented the television programme, *Star for a Night*, which helped launch the singer Joss Stone and also showed us the first glimpse of 2008's *X Factor* winner Alexandra Burke. She has also appeared on the reality shows, *Have I Been Here Before*, *All Star Family Fortunes* and *Celebrity*. Unbeknown to many; Jane's first TV performance, was as a 'Guest' Dancer on the 1983 'Black Lace' video for their hit single 'Superman' which was shot at the 'Casanova's' night club in Wakefield, where she worked as VIP lounge manager.

She has since become known for her commentary as a panelist and a regular presenter on the ITV daytime television programme *Loose Women*, appearing on the show three times a week. It was confirmed in July 2010 that McDonald would depart *Loose Women* in the summer, taking at least a year's break to concentrate on her music career and to tour Australia and New Zealand. She left at the end of the 2010 series, only to return after a two year hiatus. During this period off she maintained her profile as a regular on *The Wright Stuff* for a few seasons.

Her 2011 UK tour began with a preview night at Potters Leisure Resort in Great Yarmouth and took in Cornwall, Bristol, Bournemouth and Essex in the south, before heading to Birmingham where she met up with the scarf before her performance at the Symphony Hall.

WALSALL FOOTBALL CLUB

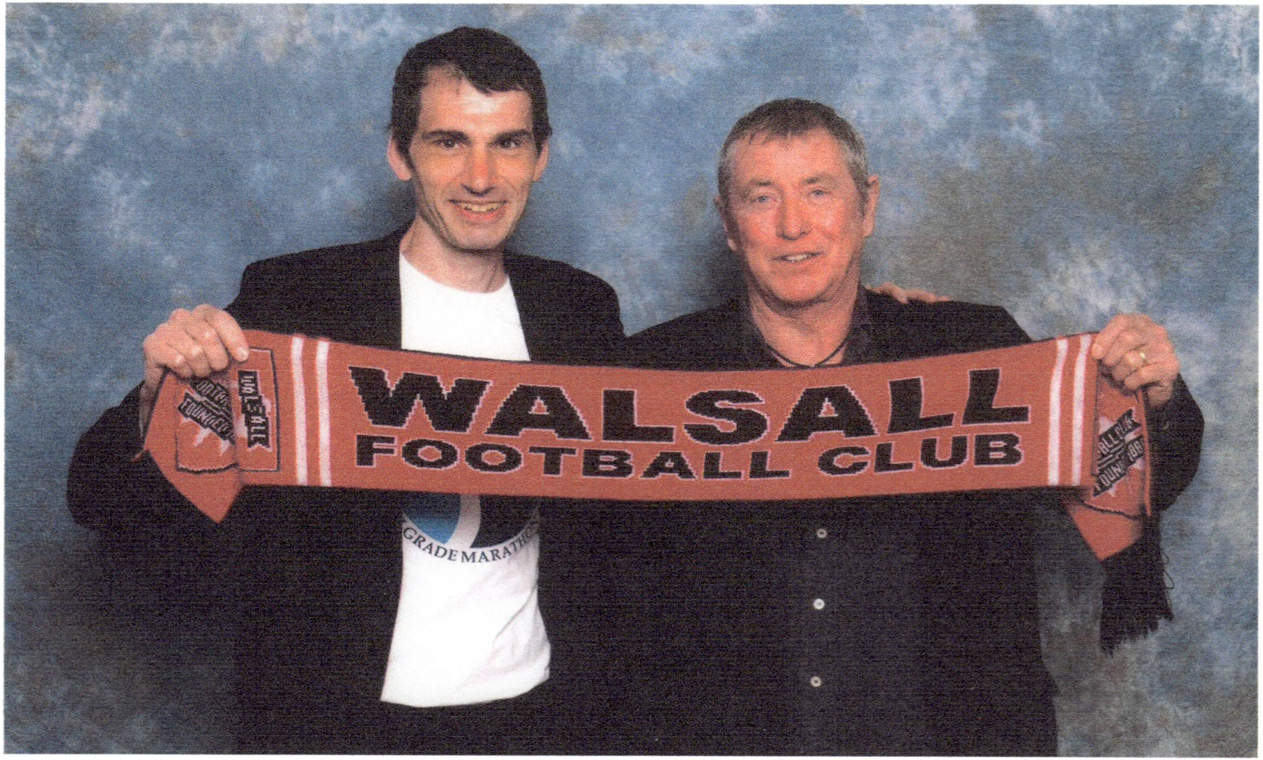

John Nettles

Nettles grew up in Cornwall and went on to study history and philosophy at the University of Southampton as he had hoped to become a teacher. While at the university, he discovered acting and played mostly small parts in Royal Court Theatre productions. He left school to pursue a career in the theatre and became a member of the Royal Shakespeare Company in Stratford-upon-Avon.

He made his first television appearance on the BBC comedy series *The Liver Birds* in the early 1970s. In 1981, he took the role that would make him a star in Great Britain and several other countries. As Detective Sergeant Jim Bergerac on *Bergerac*, he solved crimes and caught crooks on the British island of Jersey in the English Channel. The series lasted for ten years and even boosted tourism to the island. After the show ended, Nettles immediately returned to the Royal Shakespearean Company and his first love of performing on the stage.

In the late 1990s, Nettles was offered another crime-fighting, mystery-solving role. This time he became Detective Chief Inspector Barnaby who watches over a quiet, beautiful English county filled with dangerous inhabitants in *The Midsomer Murders*. The first episode aired in England in 1997, and the show shot its fiftieth episode in 2006. The series has remained popular for nearly ten years and has featured murder by almost any means imaginable, including a slide projector and bottles of relish. It was announced that John Nettles would be leaving

Midsomer Murders after two further series were made and viewers saw him in his final appearance on-screen was in February 2011, by which time he had appeared in 81 episodes.

Besides his television and theatre performances, Nettles has lent his distinctive voice to several documentaries. He has also written several books, including *Bergerac's Jersey*, *John Nettles' Jersey* and the comedic *Nudity in a Public Place*. In which Nettles takes a humorous look at his experiences as a "semi-celebrity" and how he became a reluctant heart-throb to women viewers.

Married twice, Nettles has a daughter, Emma, from his first wife Joyce. He and his current wife Cathy live near Stratford-upon-Avon, where he likes to attend the theatre whenever he can.

In 2012 John wrote *Jewels and Jackboot* about the German Occupation of the British Channel Islands 1940-1945. He said "I wanted to re-visit the hot topics brought up in the documentary *(The Channel Islands at War)* and look at them in more detail in book form". He also produced a YouTube video talking about his views on this publication.

A visit to Chenies in Buckinghamshire brought a meeting with Nettles, who was only too pleased to talk about Walsall and its football team.

WALSALL FOOTBALL CLUB

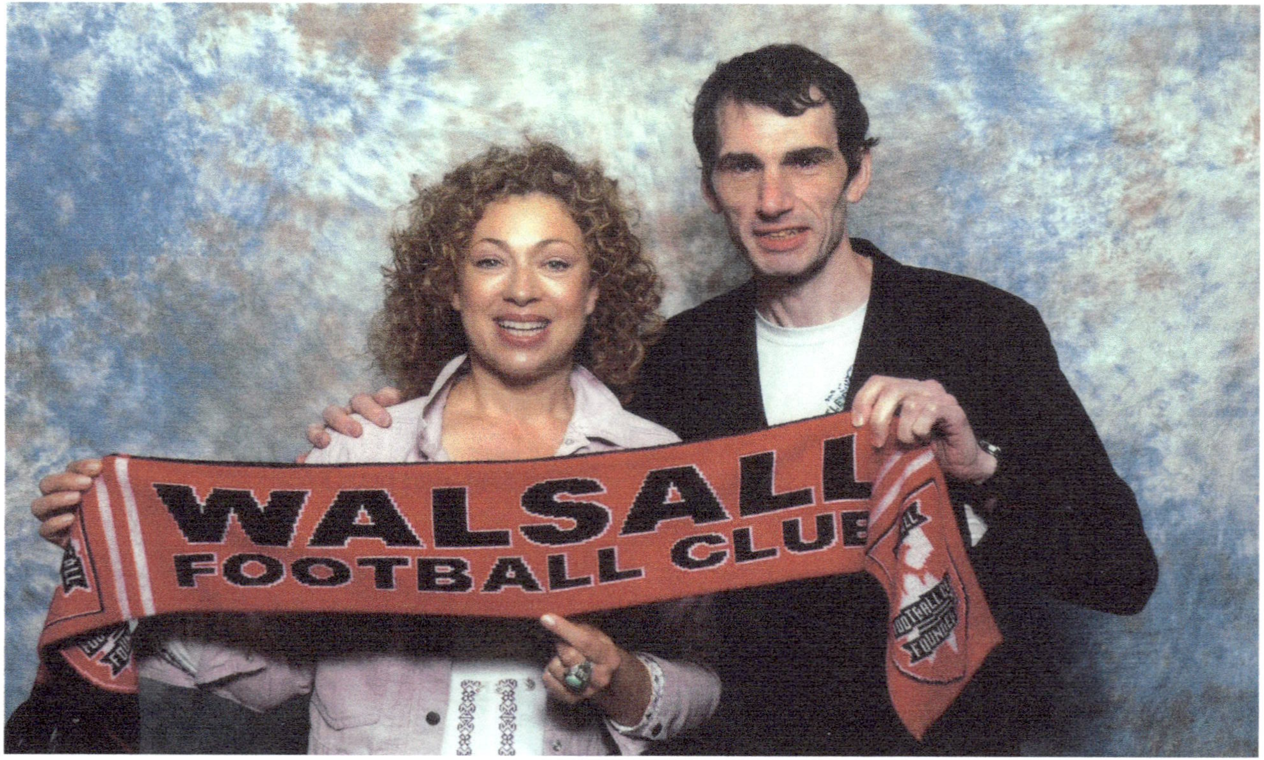
WALSALL
FOOTBALL CLUB

Alex Kingston

Kingston was inspired to pursue acting by one of her teachers at Rosebery School for Girls. She auditioned and performed in the Surrey County Youth Theatre production of *Tom Jones*, as Mrs Fitzpatrick alongside Sean Pertwee, as Captain Fitzpatrick and Thwackum played by Tom Davison. She later completed a three-year programme at the Royal Academy of Dramatic Art and went on to join the Royal Shakespeare Company.

It was not until the late nineties that she gained fame on the North American television circuit after being cast on the long-running medical drama *ER*. Her first appearance was in the premiere of the fourth season which was the award-winning live episode "Ambush". She portrayed Elizabeth Corday, a surgeon arriving from Britain. Kingston played this role for just over seven seasons until leaving in 2004, in an episode entitled "Fear". Five years later she made a dramatic return to *ER* during its 15th and final season for two episodes the first being: in the episode "Dream Runner" and a two hour series finale called "And in the End...".

After such extraordinary highs, Kingston starred as Nurse Ratched, opposite Christian Slater as Randle Patrick McMurphy, in the Garrick Theatre's West End production of *One Flew Over the Cuckoo's Nest*. She revealed that had been turned down for a role on ABC's *Desperate Housewives*, as Lynette Scavo, for being too curvy. In the same article, she admitted to considering and nearly attempting suicide after her separation from her ex-husband Ralph Fiennes.

Another challenge for her came when she secured the part of Miranda Pond, a defence attorney in two episodes of the legal drama *Law & Order: Special Victims Unit*. This guest spot reunited Kingston with her former cast mate from *ER*, Mariska Hargitay. Hargitay had a recurring role during the fourth season of *ER*. In June, Kingston starred as the lead character Ellie Lagden, one of four former convicts in the BBC One drama series *Hope Springs* until it was cancelled less than a month later. That same year she had a recurring role in *Flash Forward*, playing Inspector Fiona Banks.

Other roles came her way when she was a cast member on the British supernatural series *Marchlands*. She played the character Helen Maynard. The series ended in 2011. She followed this up by guest-starring in the *Grey's Anatomy* spin-off, *Private Practice* as Marla Tompkins, about a psychiatrist who writes book reviews for newspapers. She went on to appear in Friedrich Schiller's *Luise Miller* at the Donmar Warehouse in London.

A rare appearance at a *Doctor Who* fixture led to her holding the scarf in Birmingham before a second meeting in Earls' Court, both of which proved to be hugely popular with the scarf and fans alike.

WALSALL FOOTBALL CLUB

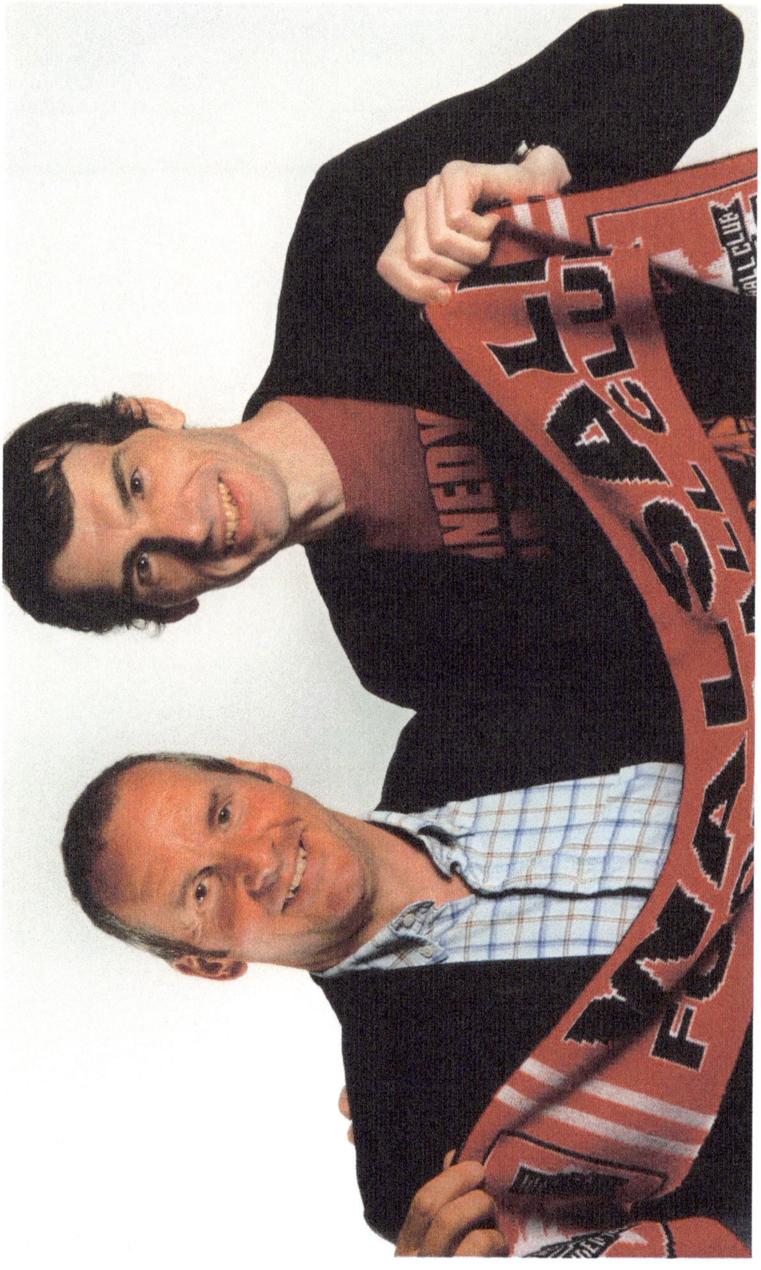

Chris Barrie

To his legions of fans across the world, Chris is best known as Rimmer – the *Red Dwarf* character who made love only once in his life. To others he is Hilary, Angelina Jolie's butler in *Tomb Raider*; but to many he will forever be remembered as Gordon Brittas, the most irritating manager in the history of the British leisure centre industry.

After moving to London from his native Northern Ireland, Chris started out in the comedy clubs as an impressionist. It wasn't long before he was picked up by the producers of *Spitting Image*, and he went on to provide the voices for a stream of characters from HRH Prince Charles to Paul Daniels.

For live audiences, Chris performs after dinner, as a speaker or in cabaret. He also hosts awards and lightens up conferences. It's not unknown for him to toss the audience a curved ball, particularly in relation to those all-important health and safety issues: "What would you do if faced by a tiger rampaging through your office?"

Barrie played the character Arnold Rimmer in ten series of *Red Dwarf*. A central character, Barrie appeared as Rimmer in almost every episode of the series, absent only for a brief period during series 7. For most of the series the character of Arnold Rimmer was a hologram, requiring Barrie to wear an "H" on his forehead during filming. The character is described as self-centred, neurotic, cowardly and hopeless with women.

When a pilot for an American version of the show was produced, Barrie was invited to reprise his role as Rimmer. He passed up the offer because of the constraint of the five-series contract which is standard for American television. Robert Llewellyn was the only cast member of the British show to participate in the pilot, which was not picked up.

He is also well known for his role as Gordon Brittas, the title role in *The Brittas Empire*, a BBC sitcom running from January 1991 to February 1997 for seven series, with 52 episodes, including two Christmas specials. It centred on the life of a well-meaning but incompetent manager of Whitbury New Town Leisure Centre. Quite different from his character in *Red Dwarf*, Barrie was accompanied by a supporting cast who played the other staff members of the leisure centre. Each episode revealed a disastrous occurrence, which Brittas was sure he could sort out, the truth being that he was normally one of the causes of all the trouble that went on.

Chris most recent TV work includes *Britain's Greatest Machines with Chris Barrie*, screened on the *National Geographic Channel* in 2009. Each of the four episodes features some of the most notable air, sea and land vehicles along with equipment of the 1930s, 1950s, 1960s and 1980s respectively. The series explores almost every invention in mechanised transport from trains to airships. As the proud owner of several classic cars, motorcycles and trucks, it played perfectly to one of his biggest obsessions.

This meeting with the scarf took place in the Welsh town of Wrexham.

WALSALL FOOTBALL CLUB

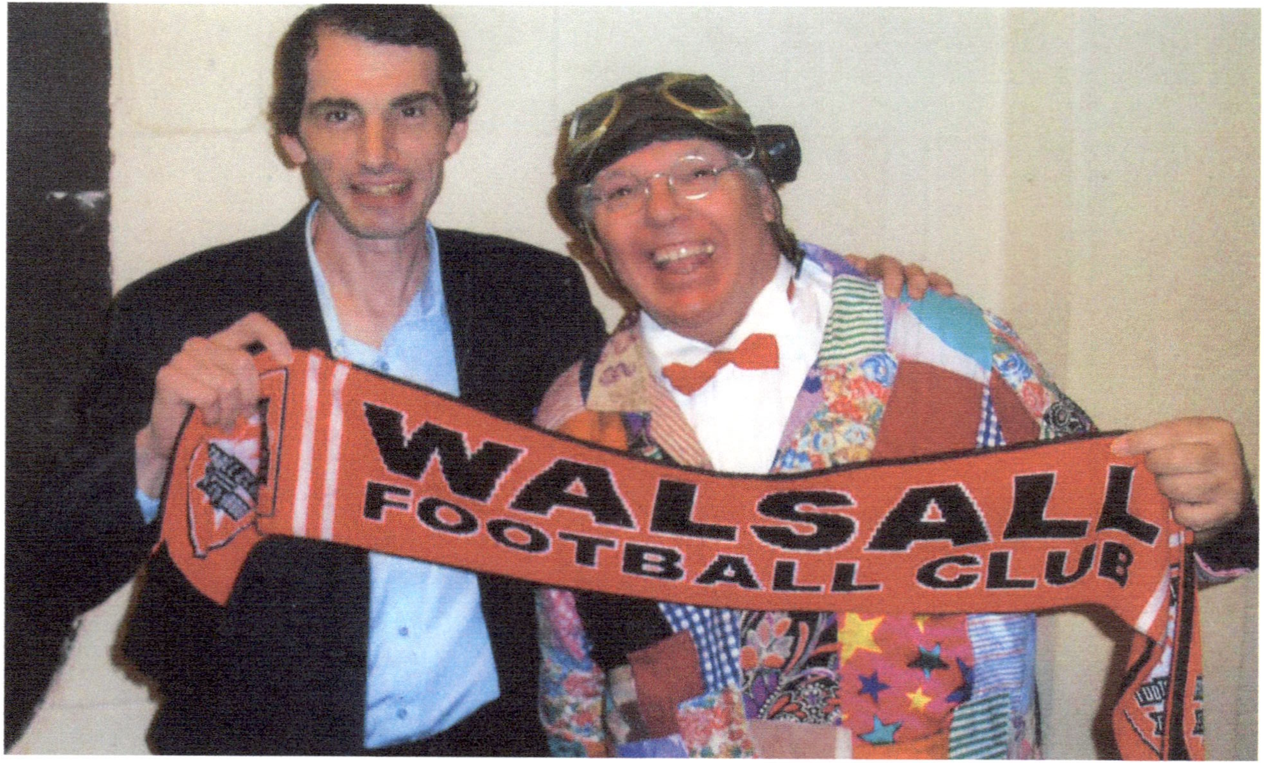
WALSALL
FOOTBALL CLUB

Roy "Chubby" Brown

An English stand-up comedian, Chubby Brown has built up a reputation for his sarcastic blue humour. The controversial nature of his act means he rarely appears on major television channels, and Brown has attracted accusations that his comedy style is outdated, whilst also being described as "the most important comedian of the past 25 years".

Hailing from the small town of Grangetown in the North Riding of Yorkshire, he has a sister named Barbara. Leaving home at the age of fourteen, he spent time living rough and moved from job to job and at one point joined the Merchant Navy. He served time in a young offenders' institution colloquially named borstal and also prison. He later found work as an entertainer in working men's clubs during the 1960s, first as a drummer and later as a comedy act under the name "Alcock & Brown".

Brown's image is characterised by a clown-like stage costume consisting of a flying helmet and goggles, a multicoloured patchwork jacket and trousers, a white shirt, a red bow tie and moccasin slippers.

During his long career, he has caused offence by mocking various groups and individuals, including ethnic minorities, women, the Queen Mother (whose death occurred hours before the recording of his show *Standing Room Only*) and himself, yet he maintains a loyal fan base. Brown's live shows are rarely seen on television, as many of his jokes are either sexist or racist, and he relies on strong language.

His real name, Royston Vasey, was used as the name for the fictional town in the comedy television show *The League of Gentlemen*. He also made several cameo appearances as the foulmouthed mayor of the town.

In 1993 Brown released a film called *U.F.O.* starring himself and Roger Lloyd Pack; in it he is abducted by aliens while staying in a hotel in Blackpool during his live shows. In another acting role viewers saw him appear as a talking lamppost in Robin Sheppard's film adaptation of Richard Milward's book, *Apples*.

One of his best known songs is "Living Next Door to Alice (Who the Fuck is Alice?)" — A cover version of "Living Next Door to Alice" recorded with Smokie. The record spent 19 weeks in the UK Singles Chart, peaking at number 3. He released a solo single in the winter of 1996 called "A Rocking Good Christmas", written by Ray Hedges; this reached number 51. Brown has also released two albums, *Take Fat and Party* and *Fat Out of Hell*; which went on to achieve positions 29 and 67 in the UK Albums Chart respectively.

His tours are legendary and each year he covers thousands of miles around the country. The scarf was accorded a rare honour in meeting him in full stage costume, which his manager informed us that he usually likes to put on immediately before going on stage, so this proved quite a meeting at Cannock's Prince of Wales theatre.

WALSALL FOOTBALL CLUB

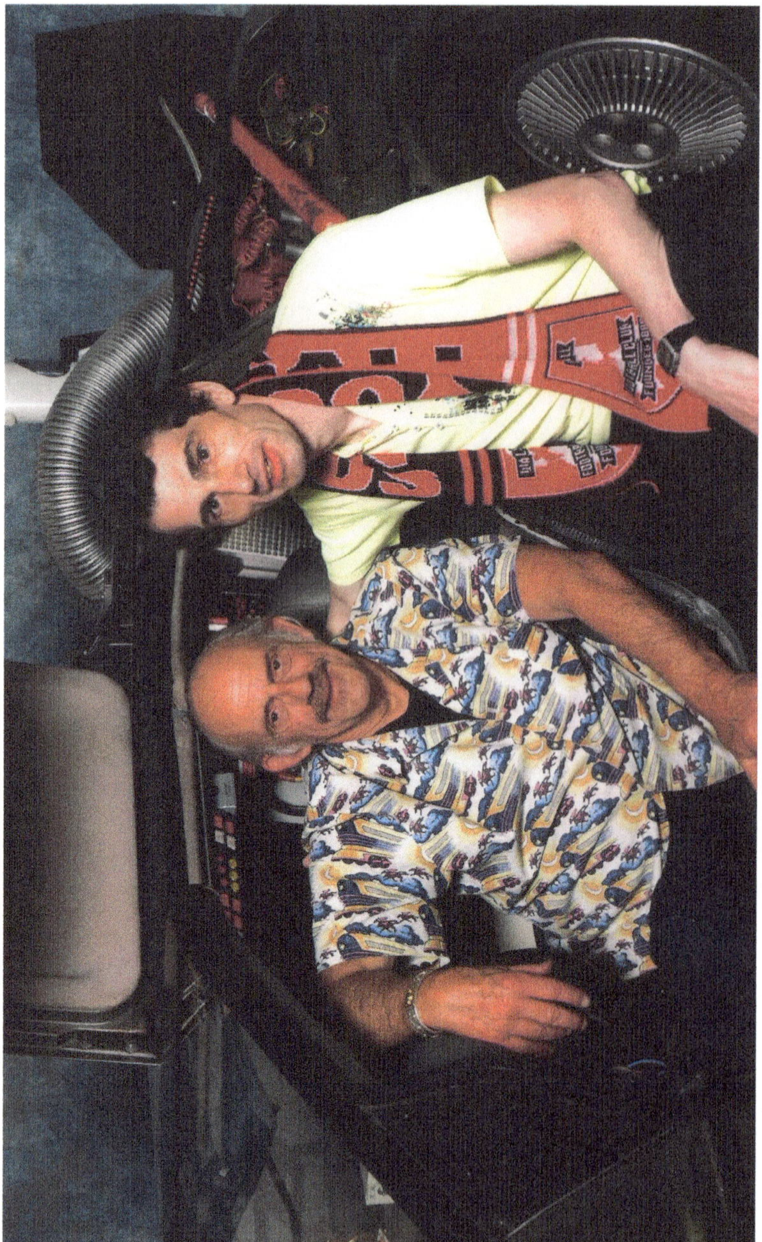

Christopher Lloyd

Christopher Lloyd is among Hollywood's busiest and best character actors and has created a number of unforgettable roles on television and in film. Lanky, dark-haired, gravel-voiced, hollow-eyed, and possessing almost skeletal facial features that belie their flexibility, he takes after Lon Chaney in his ability to transform himself into a variety of odd personages ranging from malevolent villains to lovable cooks, most of which are comical. Lloyd is also a versatile theatrical actor known for his ability to improvise in inventive, often outrageous ways. This is despite the fact that in his personal life he is known to be famously reclusive and shy.

Raised in New Canaan and Westport, CT, Lloyd became interested in acting at age 14 and started out in summer stock at age 16. Following high school, he moved to New York to study acting with such noted drama coaches as the Neighborhood Playhouse's Sanford Meisner. Beginning in 1969 with a Broadway appearance in *Red, White and Maddox*, he went on to appear on and off-Broadway and with several New York Shakespeare Festivals; in one production of *A Midsummer Night's Dream*, Lloyd starred opposite Meryl Streep. In 1973, he won an Obie and a Drama Desk Award for his work in *Kaspar*.

He became interested in being a film actor after making a memorable debut as the cynical, sadistic mental patient Taber in *One Flew over the Cuckoo's Nest*. He moved to Los Angeles a year later, but did not get his big break until he walked into an audition for the innovative comedy *Taxi*. They were looking for someone to play Reverend Jim Ignatowsky, a burned-out nut case who took one drug too many during the '60s and never recovered. Lloyd shuffled into the audition wearing a faded, funky jean jacket, with his hair all askew, and his eyes bleared: he was instantly cast. His character was only meant for one episode, but proved so popular that he was written in as a regular character. Between 1979 and 1983, Lloyd won two Emmy's for Reverend Jim and the actor remains closely identified with him.

His success on *Taxi* led Lloyd to larger film roles, but he did not become a big name in pictures until he portrayed the crazy but lovable inventor Doc Emmett L. Brown opposite Michael J. Fox in *Back to the Future* and its sequels.

Some of his other memorable roles from the '80s include that of a Klingon in *Star Trek II: The Search for Spock*, the sneaky Professor Plum in *Clue*, and the nefarious Judge Doom in *Who Framed Roger Rabbit?* He played his third most recognizable role, that of Uncle Fester opposite Angelica Huston's Morticia and Raul Julia's Gomez in both *Addams Family* films. Occasionally Lloyd plays "normal" people in such films as *Eight Men Out*. In regard to his hermit-like tendencies, Lloyd insists on signing a contract for every project that frees him from all promotion duties so he won't have to do interviews and have people pry into his private life.

Lloyd seldom appears in public or gives interviews, which made it all the more special for this appearance he gave in London with a Delorean as the backdrop.

WALSALL FOOTBALL CLUB

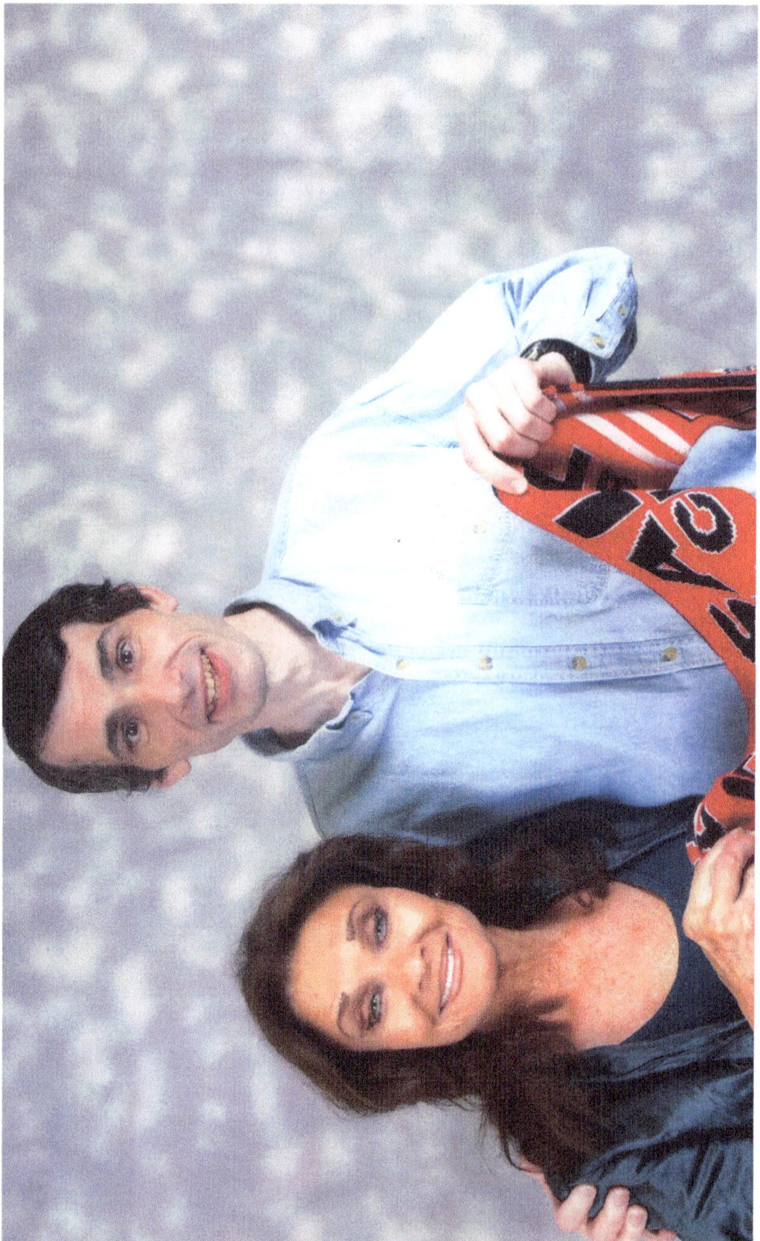

Kate O'Mara

Kate made her stage debut in a production of *The Merchant of Venice* in 1963. Her earliest television appearances included guest roles on *Danger Man*, *Adam Adamant Lives!*, *The Saint*, *Z-Cars* and *The Avengers* in the 1960s. She continued to appear in classical works throughout the next two seasons until TV series spots started coming her way. Kate attracted gothic notice in Hammer Studio horror flicks as tawdry, darkly alluring femmes in both *The Horror of Frankenstein* and *The Vampire Lovers*, but her film load over the years would remain sporadic. In 1975, she had a regular role in the BBC drama series *The Brothers* as Jane Maxwell.

In the early 1980s, O'Mara starred in the BBC soap opera *Triangle*. Whilst making the first episode she had to endure a scene in which she sunbathes topless on a clearly freezing deck.

During this rather fruitful period, she played the Rani in the *Doctor Who* adventure "The Mark of the Rani" before going on to be cast as Caress Morrell in the American primetime soap opera *Dynasty*. Playing the sister of Alexis Colby (Joan Collins), O'Mara appeared in 17 episodes of the sixth season and 4 episodes of the seventh. After returning to the UK, she appeared in her second *Doctor Who* story, "Time and the Rani" in 1987. She was then later cast as another scheming villain, Laura Wilde, in the BBC soap *Howards' Way* which proved a great success in the later stages of the 1980's.

She continued to make television appearances throughout the 1990s, including *Cluedo* and *Absolutely Fabulous*. In 2001, she had a recurring role in the ITV prison drama series *Bad Girls* before appearing in the short-lived revival of the soap opera *Crossroads*. She continued to perform on stage and in March 2008 she played Marlene Dietrich in a stage play entitled *Lunch with Marlene*. From August to November of that same year, she played Mrs Cheveley in Oscar Wilde's stage play 'An Ideal Husband' directed by Peter Hall and produced by Bill Kenwright.

O'Mara has also performed in radio and audio plays. In 2000 she reprised her role as the Rani in the BBV audio play *The Rani Reaps the Whirlwind*, and in 2006 she made a guest appearance in the radio comedy series *Nebulous*.

Speaking about her bouts of depression, later in her life, O'Mara said: "... I've since learnt a cure for depression: listening to J.S. Bach and reading P.G. Wodehouse. This got me through the break-up of my second marriage 17 years ago. The great thing about Wodehouse is that his books are full of romantic problems and yet so hilarious that it puts things in perspective ..."

It was in nearby Birmingham that she starred with the scarf and they met up one final time a few months before she died on 30 March 2014, in a Sussex nursing home, at the age of 74.

WALSALL FOOTBALL CLUB

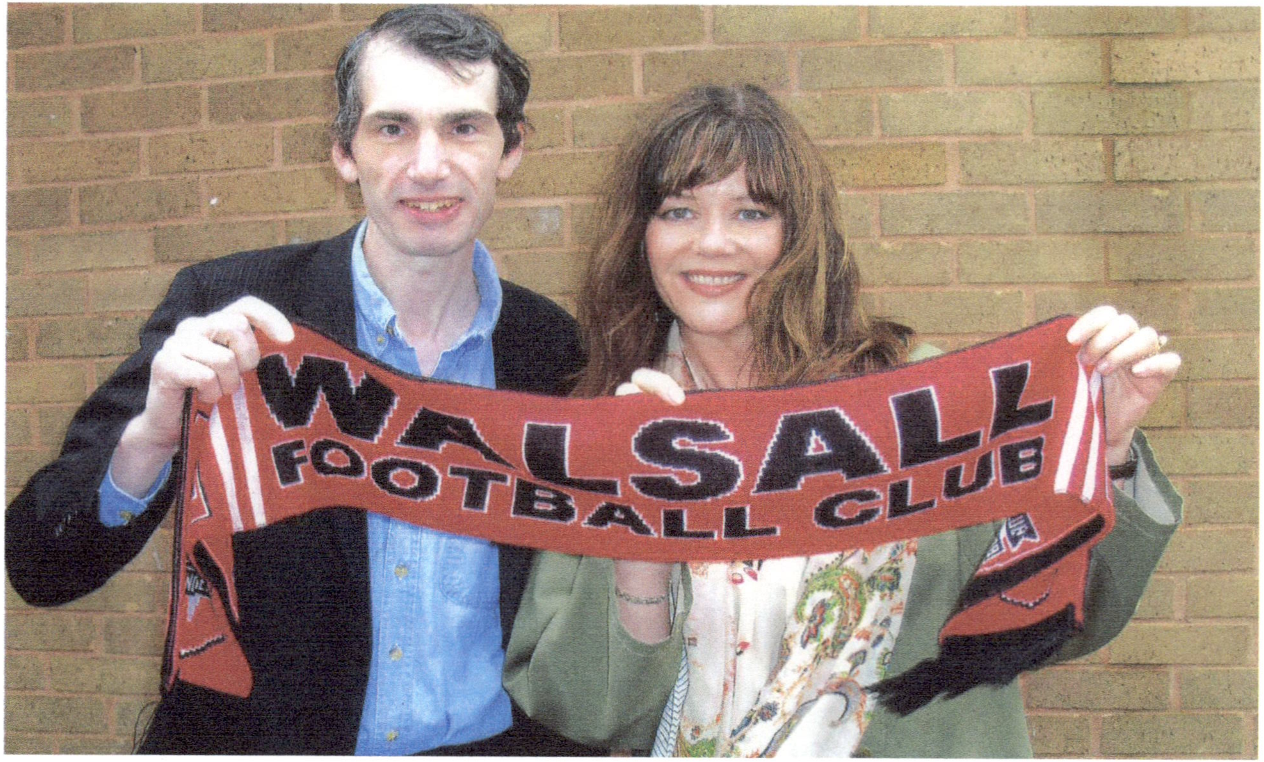
WALSALL
FOOTBALL CLUB

Josie Lawrence

Josie Lawrence was born Wendy Lawrence in Old Hill. She has a brother, John, and sister, Janet, 10 years older who are twins. They were brought up in nearby Cradley Heath, where her father worked for British Leyland and her mother as a dinner lady. She says everyone in her family has a wicked, dry sense of humour. She knew she wanted to be an actress at the early age of 5 and by the time she was 16 she joined the Barlow Players in Oldbury.

Her first acting role was as a young boy in a production of *The Ragged Trousered Philanthropists* at the Half Moon Theatre. During the 1980s, she was also involved in a play called *Passionaria* at the Newcastle Playhouse, starring Denise Black and Kate McKenzie, and they later formed the jazz group Denise Black and the Kray Sisters.

From there she began to work in comedy as a result of starring in a Donmar Warehouse play called *Songs For Stray Cats* and hearing the audience invited to supply lines and ideas for improvisers appearing in after-show cabaret.

She first came to public attention as a regular guest on the Channel 4 improvisational comedy series *Whose Line Is It Anyway?* When it was launched in 1988, she was known as a talented singer; Lawrence's specialty on the show was her ability to improvise songs on the spot. She was the first female performer to regularly perform and featured on the show for almost a decade. When the final show UK series to be made in

London was aired in 1999 she could also be seen in two episodes of the American edition..

During 1991, she had her own short-lived comedy series *Josie*, also on Channel 4. The next year she starred in *Enchanted April* a British remake of the 1935 film based on Elizabeth von Arnim's novel. Her other television work includes the comedy series *Not with a Bang* and *Downwardly Mobile*, and she is remembered for her performances as Maggie Costello in the cricketing comedy drama *Outside Edge* alongside Timothy Spall and Brenda Blethyn, for which she was awarded the Spectacle Wearer of the Year award in 1993. She went on to perform in *Sealed with a Loving Kiss* and *Lunch in the Park* as part of the *Paul Merton in Galton and Simpson's...* series in February 1996 and October 1997. She appeared in the 1999 made-for-TV movie *The Flint Street Nativity* as both Debbie Bennett and Debbie's mother. In 2001 she played Camilla in *A Many Splintered Thing*.

Lawrence starred in three series of the improvised comedy series *The Masterson Inheritance* on BBC Radio 4 alongside Paul Merton, Phelim McDermott, Caroline Quentin, Lee Simpson and Jim Sweeney. Each episode comprised a different time period, and the plots were improvised based on suggestions from the studio audience.

A frequent visitor to Tile Hile this meeting took place there whilst she took time out from opening the carnival to snatch a picture with the scarf, although she was somewhat befuddled as to what the fuss was all about.

WALSALL FOOTBALL CLUB

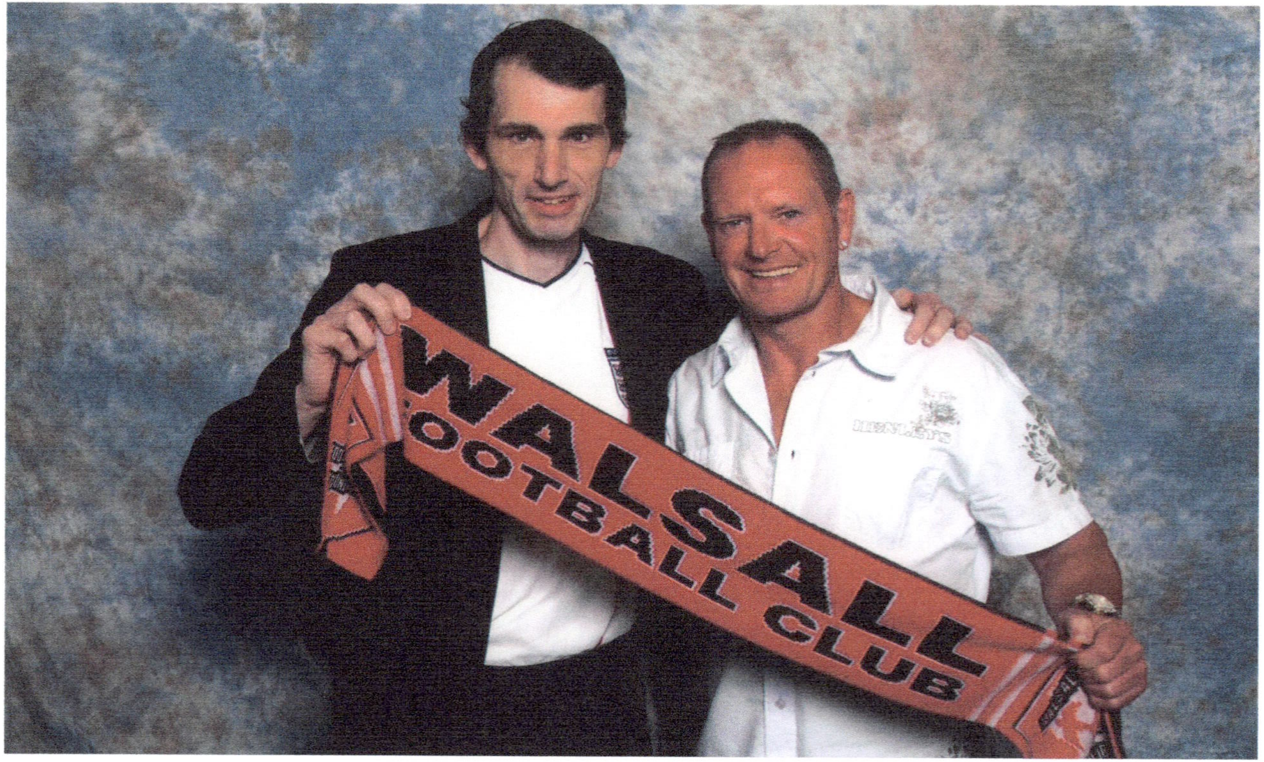
WALSALL
OOTBALL CLUB
HENLEYS

Paul Gascoigne

Paul John Gascoigne is known to the nation by his sporting moniker – Gazza, is a former England international footballer.

Playing as a midfielder, he began his professional career with local club Newcastle United in 1985. Three years later he was sold on to Tottenham Hotspur for a £2 million fee. He won the FA Cup with Spurs in 1991, before he was sold to Italian club Lazio for £5.5 million the following year. In July 1995, he was transferred to Rangers for £4.3 million, and helped the club to two league titles and two trophies. He returned to England in a £3.4 million move to Middlesbrough in March 1998. He made his debut in the Premier League in the 1998–99 season, having already featured in the 1998 Football League Cup Final. He switched to Everton in July 2000, and later had spells with Burnley, Gansu Tianma (China), and Boston United.

Though well-known throughout Europe for his club career, his football career is particularly remembered for his 57 England caps. He also won 13 caps for the England under-21s and four caps for the England B team. He was part of the England squad that reached fourth place in the 1990 FIFA World Cup, and was famously reduced to tears after receiving a yellow card in the semi-final with West Germany, which meant he would be suspended for the final itself had England won the game. He also helped the team to the semi-finals of UEFA Euro 1996, and again embedded himself in the national consciousness with a spectacular goal against Scotland that was coupled with a memorable goal celebration.

After retiring from professional football, his life became dominated by his mental and emotional problems, particularly his alcoholism. His problems have received regular coverage in the British press, especially during his various run-ins with the law. He has attempted to live without alcohol on numerous occasions, though numerous rehabilitation programmes have provided only temporary relief. His problems have curtailed his coaching career, particularly his 39-day spell as Kettering Town manager in late-2005.

One thing we should certainly do is celebrate him. He was both a footballing genius, and an extraordinary character. Gazza is what happens when you bless a man with both wonderful sporting talent and the playful naivety of a child. His displays on the pitch dazzled, but his career was blighted by injuries that allowed his demons to overcome him.

His self-destructive nature harmed those around him and damaged Gazza beyond repair, but it is still impossible to forget those glimpses of magic he exhibited throughout his career. We can only hope that he manages to regain his strength and banish the personal demons that have haunted him all his life, while we honour one of England's all time footballing greats.

For all too short a brief moment he stepped out with the scarf in Milton Keynes, but we are thankful to him for this.

WALSALL FOOTBALL CLUB

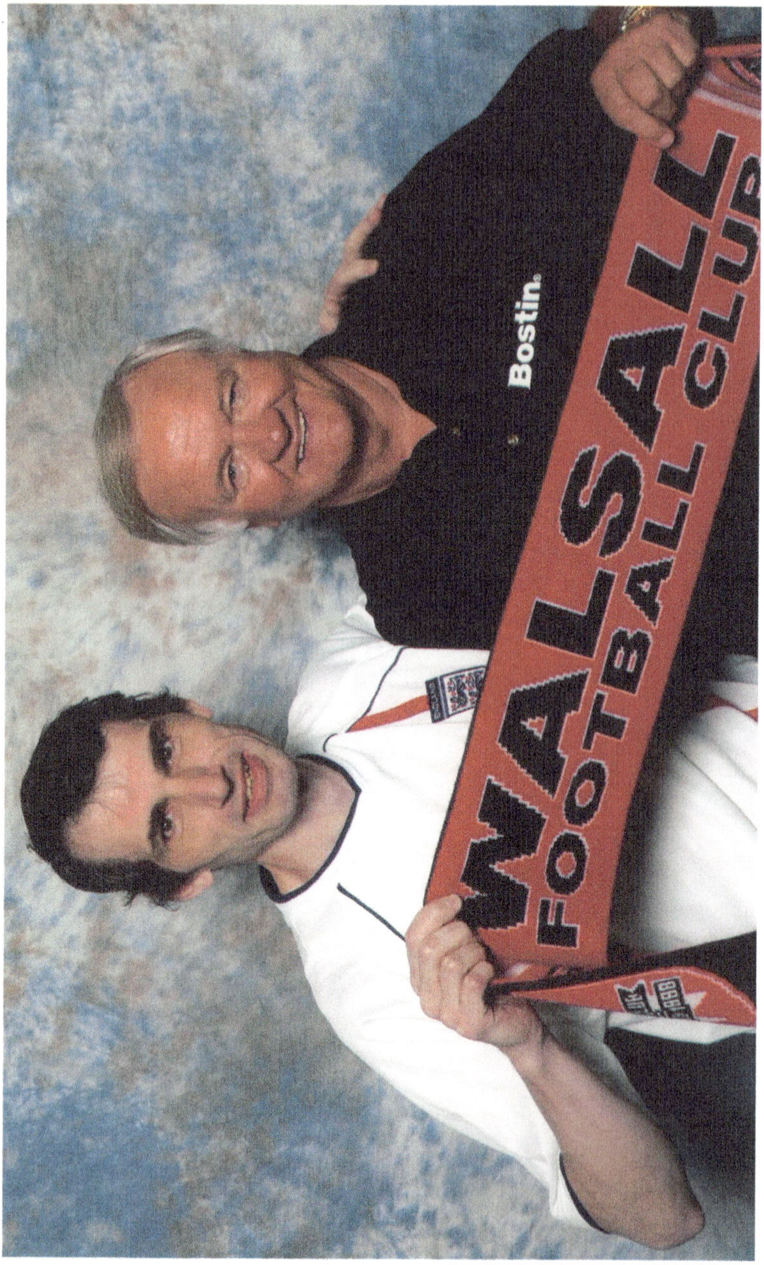
Bostin
WALSALL
FOOTBALL CLUB

Ron Atkinson

Ronald Atkinson was born in 1939 and is a former English professional football player and manager. Well known for his time in football management, he was born in Liverpool and possesses great charisma and sparkle. He is also well known for his time as one of the country's most loved football pundits. His idiosyncratic use of the English language has led to the term Ronglish to be used for his unusual terminology and phrases. He has two nicknames – 'Big Ron' and 'Bojangles'!

Although a Merseysider by birth Ron grew up in Birmingham and he signed for Aston Villa at the age of seventeen. However, he never played a first team match for them and in 1959 he transferred to Oxford United. His younger brother Graham also played for Headington, as the team was known in those days. Ron made hundreds of appearances for the club and earned himself the nickname of 'The Tank'. He became captain of the club and saw their rise from Southern League to the Second Division in only six years. This was a somewhat impressive achievement!

Although Ron's time as a player at Oxford United does not often get the recognition that it deserves, it is his role in management that he is best remembered for. Ron managed a number of clubs during the late twentieth century and had considerable success in the process. His first managerial role was at Kettering Town in 1971. At the young age of thirty two he demonstrated that he was very capable in this role, and in

1974 he moved to Cambridge United. Here he was also successful and in 1978 he took on the role as manager of First Division West Bromwich Albion. He guided the team to third place in the league in 1979 and also to the UEFA Cup quarter-finals.

In 1981 Ron became the manager of Manchester United. A complete opposite to his predecessor David Sexton, he was easy going and possessed an extrovert character. He did well in his five seasons for the team – in fact they never finished worse than fourth in the league! In the 1982-1983 seasons they won the FA Cup, and in 1983-1984 they reached the semi-finals of the European Cup Winners Cup. Ron is also credited with signing one of Manchester United best ever players – Bryan Robson. He was eventually replaced by Sir Alex Ferguson and he returned to West Bromwich Albion where he spent one year.

Following this brief return to West Bromwich, Ron had a high profile move to Atletico Madrid. He subsequently went on to manage Sheffield Wednesday, Aston Villa, Coventry City and Nottingham Forest.

Atkinson was already working as a pundit for ITV Sport and after leaving management he continued in this role. For a number of years he covered most of the channel's live matches, sometimes as a studio guest, but more often as the "ex-football insider" member of a two-man commentary team.

Here he holds the scarf in Milton Keynes.

WALSALL FOOTBALL CLUB

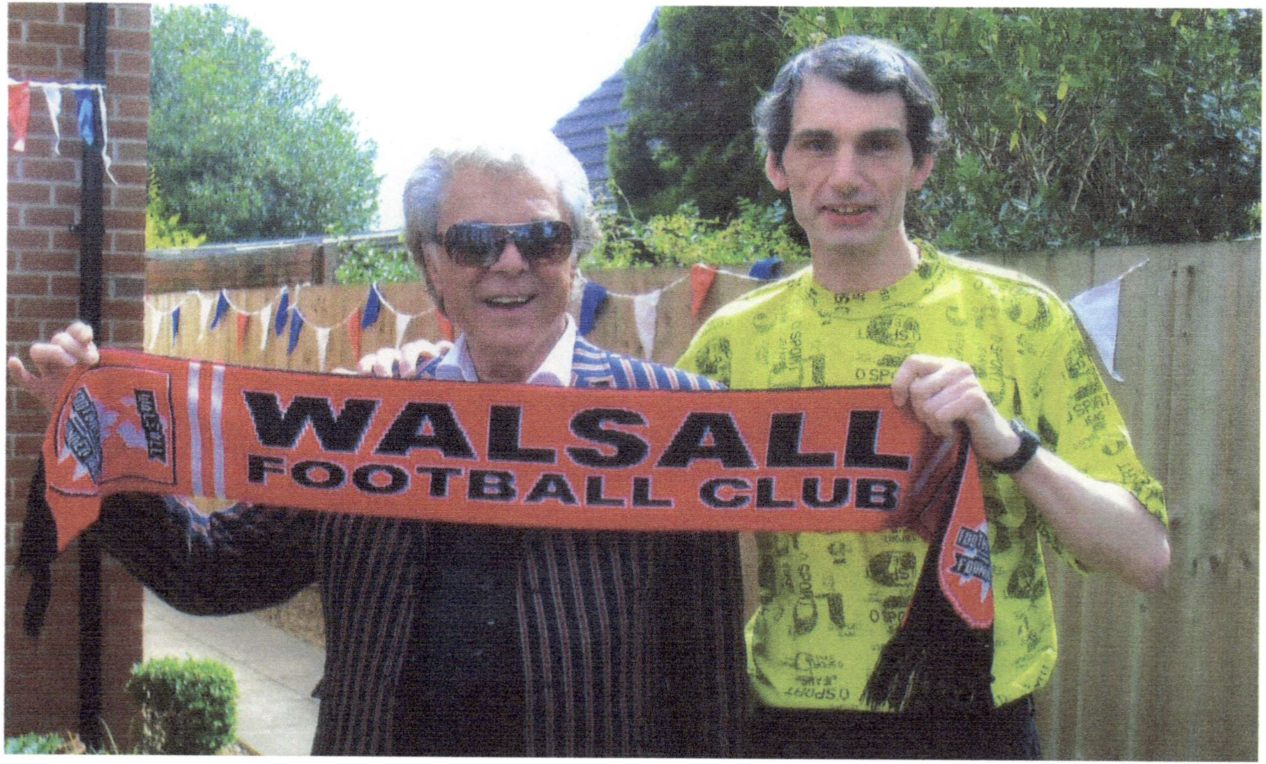
WALSALL
FOOTBALL CLUB

Lionel Blair

Blair came to Britain when he was just one year old. His first public performances were with his sister Joyce in London Underground Station air raid shelters during World War II. He attended the Royal Shakespeare Theatre in Stratford in 1944, followed by London's University of East London, where he majored in Ethnography. Blair eventually rekindled his passion for musical theatre and joined the West End. He gave up acting for dancing in 1947 although he subsequently appeared in the fringe production, *Out of the Blue* and *Who Killed Agatha Christie* (national tour) amongst other acting credits.

He came to the fore in the 1960s, when, with his dance troupe, he appeared on television variety programmes. He also appeared in the films *A Hard Day's Night* and *Absolute Beginners*, cameoed in an episode of *The Persuaders!* and in television comedy, including the short film, *The Plank*. In addition, he choreographed films such as *Jazz Boat* and *The Magic Christian*.

Perhaps he is best known for being one of the team captains on the game show *Give Us a Clue* from 1979 until the early 1990s and for being the second presenter of the British version of *Name That Tune* in the 1980s.

Blair's camp public persona is regularly mocked in the introduction to the game Sound Charades on BBC Radio 4's comedy show *I'm Sorry I Haven't a Clue*, normally by double entendre during over-the-top accounts of Blair's skills on *Give*

Us A Clue. In one episode the host, Humphrey Lyttelton, introduced the game: "The expert's expert was, of course, Lionel Blair. Who could ever forget opposing team captain, Una Stubbs, sitting open-mouthed as he tried to pull off *Twelve Angry Men* in less than two minutes?"

He was one of the celebrities taking part in the 2005 Channel Five reality series, *The Farm*. Until then he had appeared extensively in pantomime, for which he was earning up to £15,000 a week. Blair appeared in a Christmas special of the Ricky Gervais show *Extras*, as himself, portraying the end-stages of his showbiz career by trying to keep up his profile by appearing on *Celebrity Big Brother* alongside Lisa Scott-Lee and *X Factor* contestant Chico. Another reality slot came about when he appeared in the "Great British Dog Walks" feature on ITV1's *This Morning* with his dog Lola.

Further projects he took part in was the BBC's *The Young Ones* series, in which six celebrities in their 70s and 80s attempt to overcome some of the problems of ageing by harking back to the 1970s. He continued in comedy scenes when he appeared briefly in a sketch with Ronnie Corbett and Rob Brydon for BBC1's *The One Ronnie*. Blair also appeared as the celebrity darter for charity on *Bullseye*.

At an event celebrating Age Concern Sutton which he launched to change its name to Age UK Sutton, he cheerily supported the scarf during the garden party.

WALSALL FOOTBALL CLUB

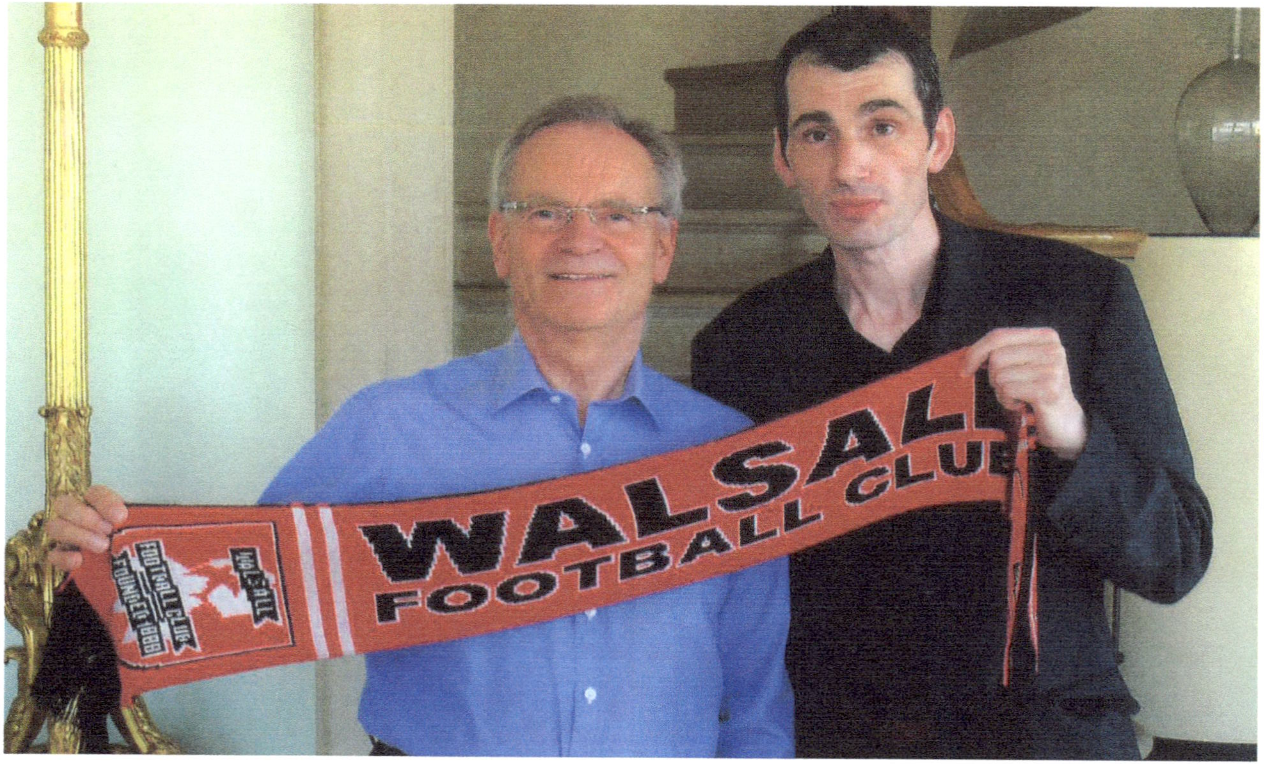
WALSALL
FOOTBALL CLUB
WALSALL
FOOTBALL CLUB
FOUNDED 1888

Jeffrey Archer

Jeffrey Howard Archer was born in the City of London Maternity Hospital. He was two weeks old when his family moved to the seaside town of Weston-super-Mare. In 1951, he won a scholarship to Wellington School, in Somerset (it has been noted that the blurbs in Archer's earlier books are ambiguous enough to lead to confusion with the public school Wellington College).

Just shy of his 30th birthday, he was elected Member of Parliament for the Lincolnshire constituency of Louth, holding the seat for the Conservative Party in the 1969 by-election. He succeeded in beating off Ian Gow to the selection after winning over a substantial proportion of younger members at the selection meeting. The national party had concerns about Archer's selection, but these were dismissed by the local Conservative association after representatives made a journey to party headquarters to discuss the matter. Archer's campaign colour was a day-glow orange/pink with a blue arrow; the political parties in Lincolnshire had not yet abandoned local colours, which were different from the party national colours.

In 1974, he was a casualty of a fraudulent investment scheme involving Aquablast, a Canadian company, a debacle which lost Archer his first fortune. Fearing imminent bankruptcy, he stood down as an MP at the October 1974 general election. By this time the Archers were living in a large five-bedroom house in The Boltons, an exclusive street in South Kensington.

His first book, *Not a Penny More, Not a Penny Less*, was picked up by the literary agent Deborah Owen and published first in the US, then eventually in Britain in the fall of 1976. The book was an instant success and Archer avoided bankruptcy, never being legally declared bankrupt. A BBC Television adaptation of the book was broadcast in 1990, and a radio adaptation was aired on BBC Radio 4 in the early 1980s.

Kane and Abel proved to be his best-selling work, reaching number one on the *New York Times* bestsellers list. It was made into a television mini-series by CBS in 1985, starring Peter Strauss and Sam Neill. The following year, Granada TV screened a ten-part adaptation of another Archer bestseller, *First Among Equals*, which told the story of four men and their quest to become Prime Minister.

Archer's political career revived once he became known for his novels and as a popular speaker among the Conservative grassroots. He was made deputy chairman of the Conservative Party by Margaret Thatcher in 1985.

Eventually he was made a life peer in 1992 as Baron Archer of Weston-super-Mare, of Mark in the County of Somerset. Prime Minister John Major recommended him largely because of Archer's role in aid to the Kurds. The scarf was kindly invited to his plush Thamseside apartment, overlooking Parliament, for a private showing.

WALSALL FOOTBALL CLUB

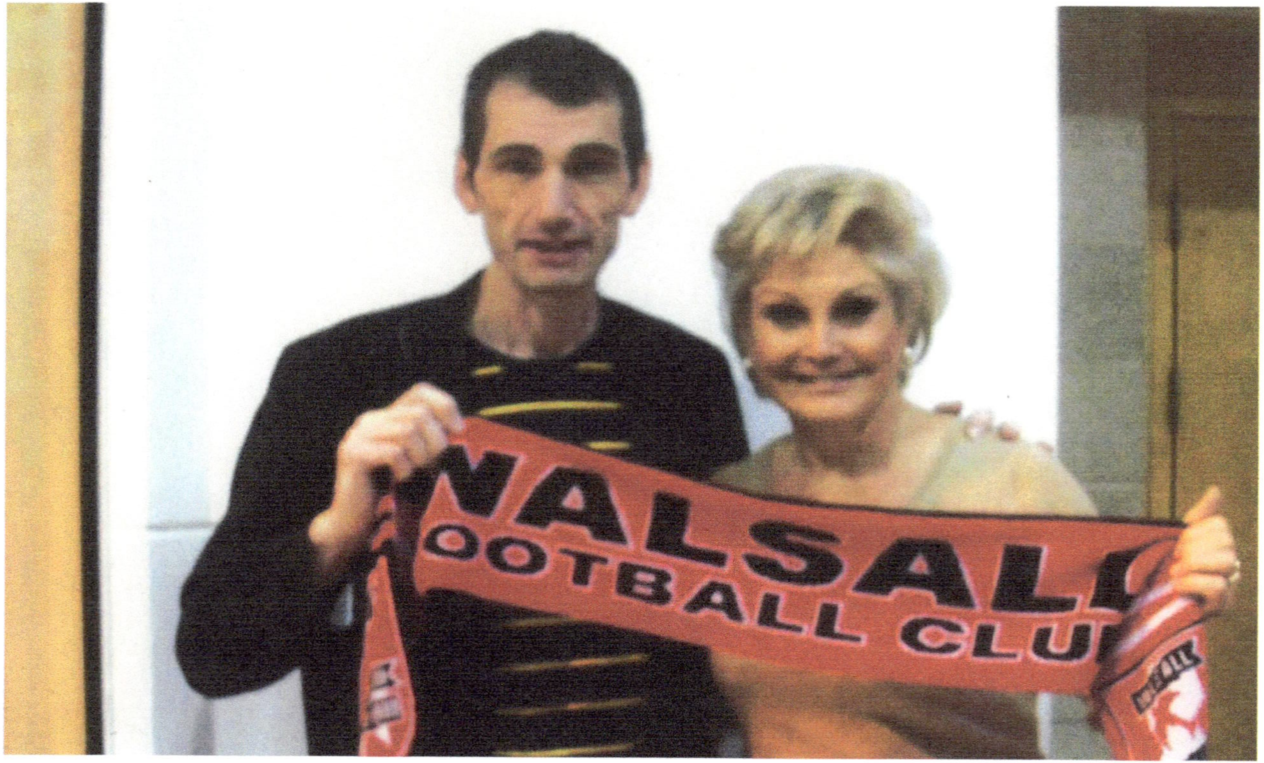
NALSALI
OOTBALL CLU

Angela Rippon

In the same week that Mrs Margaret Thatcher became leader of the Tory Party in 1975, Angela Rippon began reading the *Nine O'Clock News* on BBC1. Often referred to as the first woman television newsreader – though not quite correctly; Barbara Mandell appeared on ITV in 1955 and Nan Winton on BBC in 1960 – Rippon was the face of BBC evening news for five years, winning the Newsreader of the Year award for three of them.

Leaving the grammar school system with an appetite for journalism, she served an apprenticeship as a junior reporter with Plymouth's Sunday paper, the *Independent*, eventually managing a young people's page and a women's page, and as a Services Correspondent in Aden in 1964.

She stayed with Westward for four years before she was lured away from an increasingly desk-bound producer's life by the prospect of work as a national news reporter for BBC Television. After two years on the reporter's job came the offer to read the *Nine O'Clock News* and later to present the current affairs programme *Newsday*.

She also did a spell as presenter of the *Antiques Roadshow* by joining expert Arthur Negus in 1980.

Along with fellow newsreader Anna Ford, Rippon became one of the 'Famous Five' presenters (with Michael Parkinson, Robert Kee and David Frost) who launched Britain's second breakfast television series, *Good Morning Britain* (1983-92), for TV-am.

Despite the glittery line-up of celebrities who had helped win TV-am a breakfast slot franchise, in just two months the company was running at a loss (*Good Morning Britain* achieving a peak viewing figure of only 400,000, compared to the 1,700,000 gained by the BBC rival *Breakfast Time*).

Chief executive and chairman Peter Jay was ousted and Timothy Aitken took over as chief executive. He fired both Anna Ford and Rippon (for 'breach of contract'). While Ford was snapped up to read the news on the BBC, Rippon was out of work for a year. The experience came close to wrecking her career.

Following her return to British broadcasting, Rippon hosted the popular quiz shows *Masterteam* and *What's My Line?* as well as the perennial *Come Dancing*.

In more recent years Rippon has alternated presenting jobs on the health issues magazine *Watchdog: Healthcheck*, as guest host on *Open House with Gloria Hunniford* and *The Wright Stuff*.

At Birmingham Symphony Hall Angela Rippon proved what a wonderful and kind lady she is by patiently waiting for a somewhat late scarf to arrive. The scarf was thankful she did.

WALSALL FOOTBALL CLUB

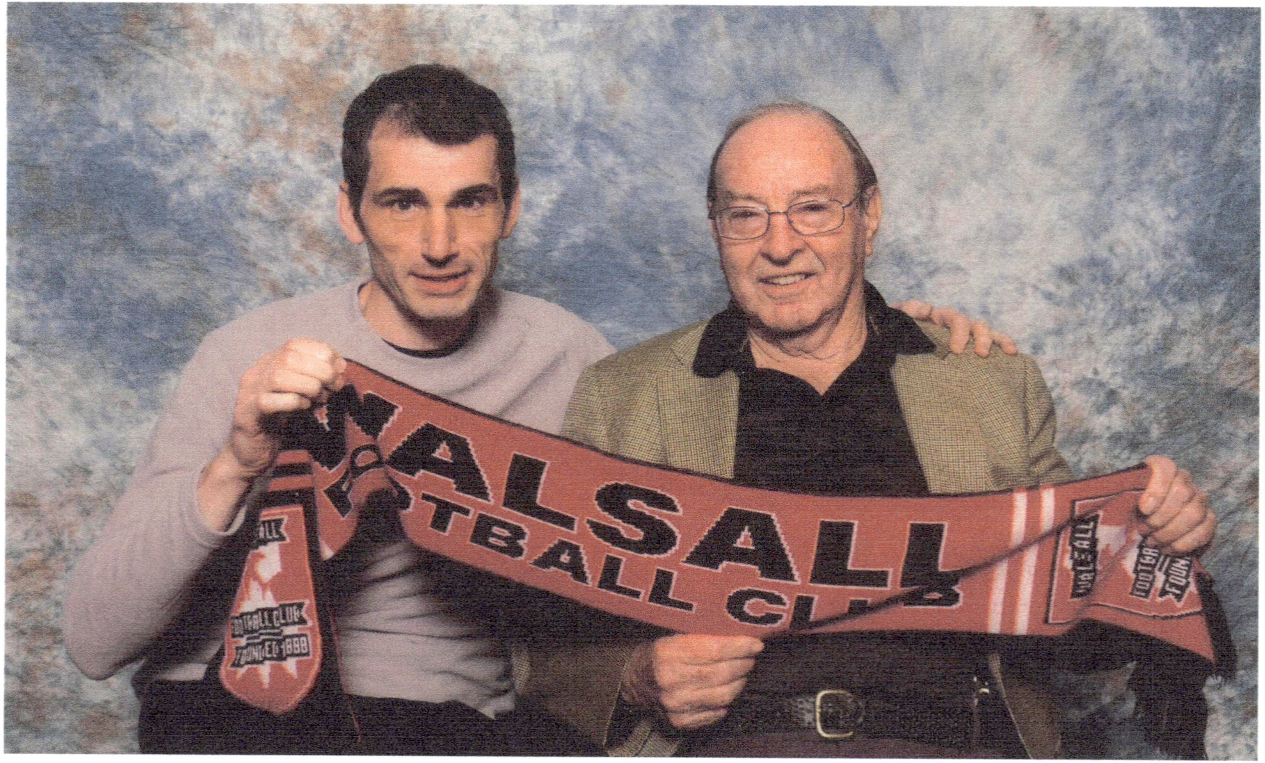
ALSALL
TBALL CLUB

Ed Mitchell

Edgar Mitchell was born in Hereford, Texas He was active in the Boy Scouts of America where he achieved its second highest rank, Life Scout. He was also a member of DeMolay International and has been inducted into its Hall of Fame.

He earned a Bachelor of Science degree in industrial management from Carnegie Institute of Technology in 1952 The following year he joined the U.S. Navy, where he trained as a pilot and flew off the aircraft carriers USS *Bon Homme Richard* and USS *Ticonderoga*. He later qualified as a research pilot and taught at the Navy's research pilot school. While on active duty in the Navy, he earned a Master of Science degree in aeronautical engineering from the U.S. Naval Postgraduate School and a Doctor of Science degree in aeronautics and astronautics from the Massachusetts Institute of Technology.

Mitchell was selected to be an astronaut in 1966 and was seconded from the Navy to NASA. He was designated as backup lunar module pilot for Apollo 10, and flew as lunar module pilot on Apollo 14, where he spent nine hours working on the lunar surface in the Fra Mauro Highlands region, making him the sixth person to walk on the Moon.

Apollo 14 was Mitchell's only spaceflight. He remained with NASA until 1972, when he retired from the Navy.

Deeply interested in consciousness and paranormal phenomena he has claimed that on his way back to earth during the Apollo 14 flight he had a powerful Savikalpa samadhi experience, and also claimed to have conducted private ESP experiments with his friends on Earth. The results of said experiments were published in the Journal of Parapsychology in 1971. In early 1973, he founded the nonprofit Institute of Noetic Sciences (IONS) to conduct and sponsor research into areas that mainstream science has found unproductive, including consciousness research and psychic events.

During 2011, the United States Government filed a lawsuit against Mitchell in the United States District Court in Miami, Florida after discovering that he possessed a camera used by the Apollo 14 crew on the moon, and had put the camera up for auction at the British auction house Bonhams. The litigation asked that the camera be returned to NASA. Mitchell's position was that NASA had given him the camera as a gift upon the completion of the Apollo 14 mission. Bonhams withdrew the camera from auction. In October, 2011, prosecutors and Mitchell reached a settlement agreement, under which Mitchell gave up any claims to the camera and agreed to return it to NASA, which in turn would donate it for display at the National Air and Space Museum.

On a visit to Birmingham Ed Mitchell became another one of a select group of moon walkers who have also held the Walsall scarf.

WALSALL FOOTBALL CLUB

John Hurt

Despite being advised by his headmaster not to pursue an acting career, John Hurt gave up a course in painting to attend the London Royal Academy of Dramatic Art (RADA).

In 1962, he made both his professional stage debut in 'Infanticide in the House of Fred Ginger' and his feature film debut in 'The Young and the Willing'.

And it was while appearing in a London production of *Little Malcolm* in 1965 that he came to the attention of director Fred Zinnemann.

The young actor was given a small role in the film version of *A Man for All Seasons* and when the film clinched six Oscars, he found himself thrust into the spotlight.

Over the next ten years came a mixture of TV and film roles, including *The Pied Piper* and *10 Rillington Place*. Then in 1975 came the role that would take Hurt's acting career up a level – playing Quintin Crisp in the series, *The Naked Civil Servant*.

His acclaimed performance in the lead role brought about a period of fine performances over the next few years.

These included Caligula in the BBC's *I, Claudius*, Max the Englishman in *Midnight Express*, Kane in *Alien* (including the famous scene where an alien burst from his stomach), and the lead role in *The Elephant Man*.

His role as the disfigured John Merrick required him to spend seven hours in make-up and critics were amazed at how he managed to produce such an expressive performance despite being beneath layers of prosthetic skin.

The nineties saw Hurt mix lead roles in independent and low-profile films and plays, whilst taking handpicked roles in more well-known movies such as *Rob Roy*, *Contact* and *Even Cowgirls Get the Blues*.

Recently, in the last few years we have seen an ageing Hurt make acclaimed appearances in *Captain Correlli's Mandolin* and as Mr Ollivander in *Harry Potter and the Philosopher's Stone*, a role John described as 'a lot of fun'.

His rich tones have also been tapped into frequently with a number of animated features and documentaries, often serving as narrator.

A journey down to London at Earl's Court saw him resplendent in a beard for his latest role, where he gave the scarf the big thumbs up.

WALSALL FOOTBALL CLUB

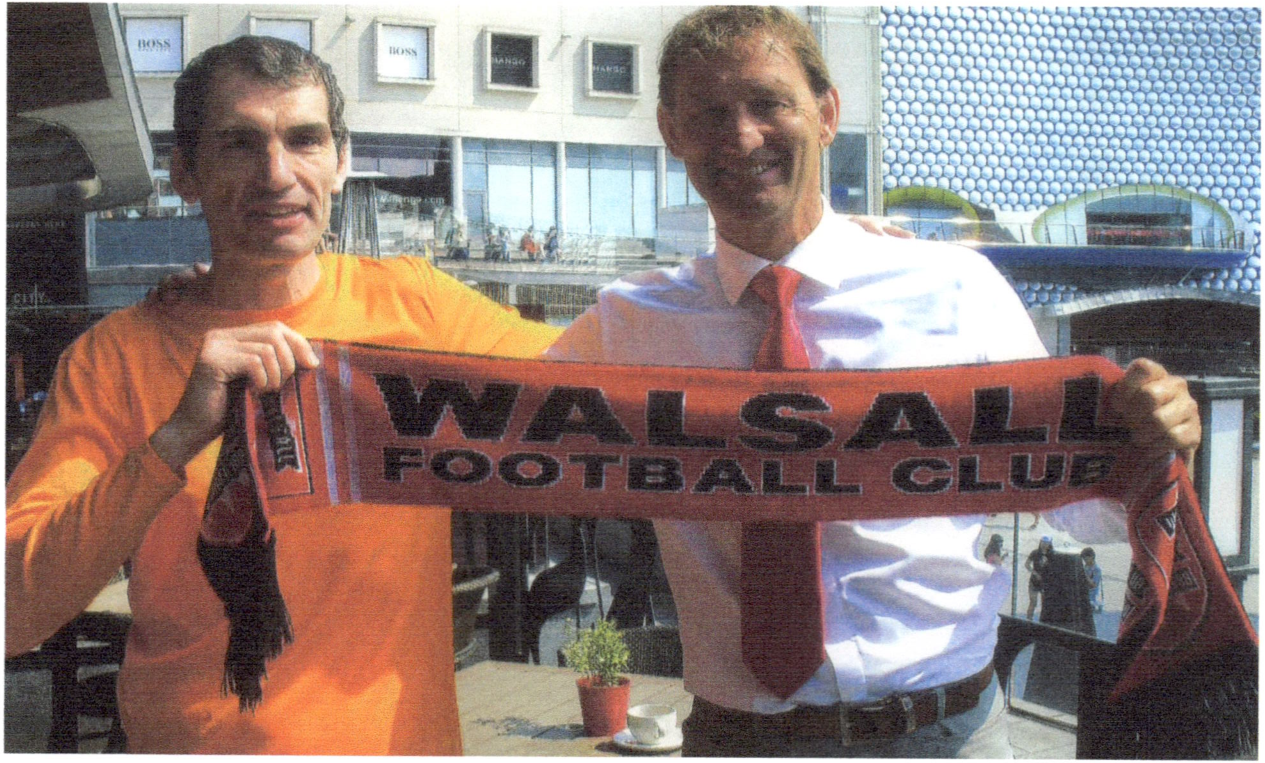
WALSALL
FOOTBALL CLUB
BOSS
BOSS

Tony Adams

It was clear that Adams was a bit special from the moment he signed for Arsenal as a schoolboy in 1980. Three years later he made his debut against Sunderland, four weeks after his 17th birthday. It was hardly an auspicious start – Adams was partly to blame for a 2-1 home defeat – but he soon found his feet at the top level.

Eight months after winning his first medal at the 1987 Littlewoods Cup Final, Adams became Arsenal's youngest ever skipper at the age of 21. It was a position he would hold until his retirement but, in those early days of captaincy, Adams had to endure plenty of stick. The *Daily Mirror* famously depicted Adams with donkey ears the morning after he scored at both ends in Arsenal's 1-1 draw at Manchester United. Opposition fans soon latched on.

Eight weeks after his Old Trafford experience, the Arsenal captain led his team to the title on that famous night at Anfield. Two years later he had his hands on the same trophy and a domestic Cup Double would follow in 1993. The taunts continued – a spell in prison from December 1990 fuelled the fire – but Adams always seemed to have the last laugh.

He scored 48 goals during his Arsenal career including the header which beat Tottenham at Wembley in 1993 as well as in the Cup Winners' Cup Quarter-Final a year later against Torino. Adams was arguably at his peak during that European campaign.

By 1996 Adams was the England captain too but that year was dominated by revelations of his alcoholism. It proved a turning point on and off the pitch. Away from the action Adams matured and showed great dignity. On the field, the arrival of Wenger was perfect timing. The Frenchman's focus on diet and preparation helped Adams fend off his old habits while Wenger's footballing ethos allowed the Arsenal skipper to express himself more on the pitch.

Whereas Graham had favoured a more direct style, Wenger encouraged Adams to be more expansive. He flourished, showing more poise in possession, initiating attacks from the back and even getting forward when he could. That approach manifested itself most emphatically on the final day of the 1997/98 season when Adams, put through by Bould (of all people), rifled a shot into the corner to put the top hat and tails on another title. Adams' celebration in front of an adoring North Bank remains one of the iconic moments in Arsenal's rich history. The FA Cup – and the Double – duly followed.

When in his 30s, Adams was increasingly hampered by injuries but, like so many Arsenal greats, he managed to go out on a high note. In Adams' case it was another Double, this time in 2002, clinched in style with a win at Old Trafford. Since retiring he has moved into management, most notably the Azerbaijani club Gabala FC of the Azerbaijan Premier League. This meeting between Adams and the scarf came about from a competiton win which saw them link up at Browns Bar and Brasserie Two to attend an exclusive Talking Tactics session with him in Birmingham city centre

WALSALL FOOTBALL CLUB

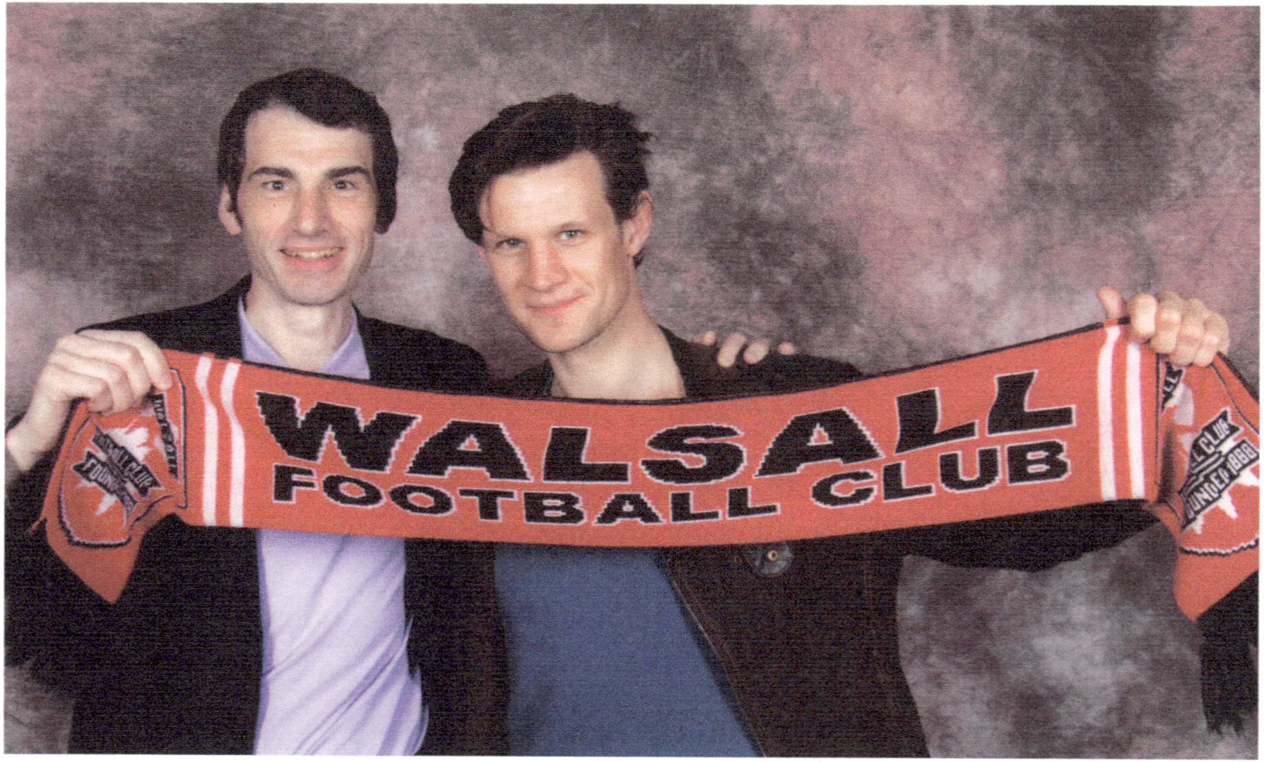
WALSALL
FOOTBALL CLUB

Matt Smith

Matt Smith grew up with his family including one sister in Northampton. He was head boy at Northampton School for Boys where he excelled at sports, music and drama.

Initially, Matt wanted to be a professional footballer and played for Northampton Town under 11 and 12s, Nottingham Forest under 12,14s and Leicester City under 15 and 16s before a back injury forced him out of the game.

Following his injury, and with the encouragement of one of his teachers, Jerry Hardingham, he decided to join the National Youth Theatre. It was during this time that Matt first gained attention at the Royal Court Theatre when he was cast in the play *Fresh Kills*, directed by Wilson Milam, whilst still at the University Of East Anglia where he was studying Drama and Creative Writing.

Already a stalwart of the National Youth Theatre, his performance at the Court led to a variety of theatrical experiences at the National Theatre: in the award winning *History Boys* (directed by Nick Hytner), *On The Shore Of The Wide World* (directed by Sarah Frankcom) and also in the acclaimed trio of plays *Burn / Citizenship / Chatroom* (directed by Anna Mackmin).

These roles led to his first outings on the small screen, alongside Billie Piper in Phillip Pullman's period detective stories, *The Ruby in the Smoke* and *The Shadow in the North*, where he played Jim, right hand man to Billie's detective heroine Sally

Lockhart. These pieces were followed by the lead role of Danny in the BBC Two series *Party Animals*, the brilliantly observed drama set in the world of young politicians.

In a dazzling return to the Royal Court in 2007, he played Henry in Polly Stenham's award winning first play *That Face*, opposite Lindsay Duncan. His performance gained Matt an *Evening Standard* Best Newcomer nomination and a year later the play had a second life in the West End at the Duke of York's Theatre. In between the two runs, he played Guy opposite Christian Slater's Buddy in *Swimming With Sharks*, Mike Leslie's searing West End adaptation of the Hollywood film. In this time he also played a lead role in the BAFTA winning BBC 1 series, *The Street*, opposite Gina McKee and Lorraine Ashbourne.

Matt has recently completed work on *Moses Jones* for BBC 2, directed by Michael Offer, in which he plays the lead role of Dan Twentyman, alongside Shaun Parkes in the title role.

He is an atheist and an avid Blackburn Rovers supporter and in spite of this cheered the Saddlers by holding the scarf.

WALSALL FOOTBALL CLUB

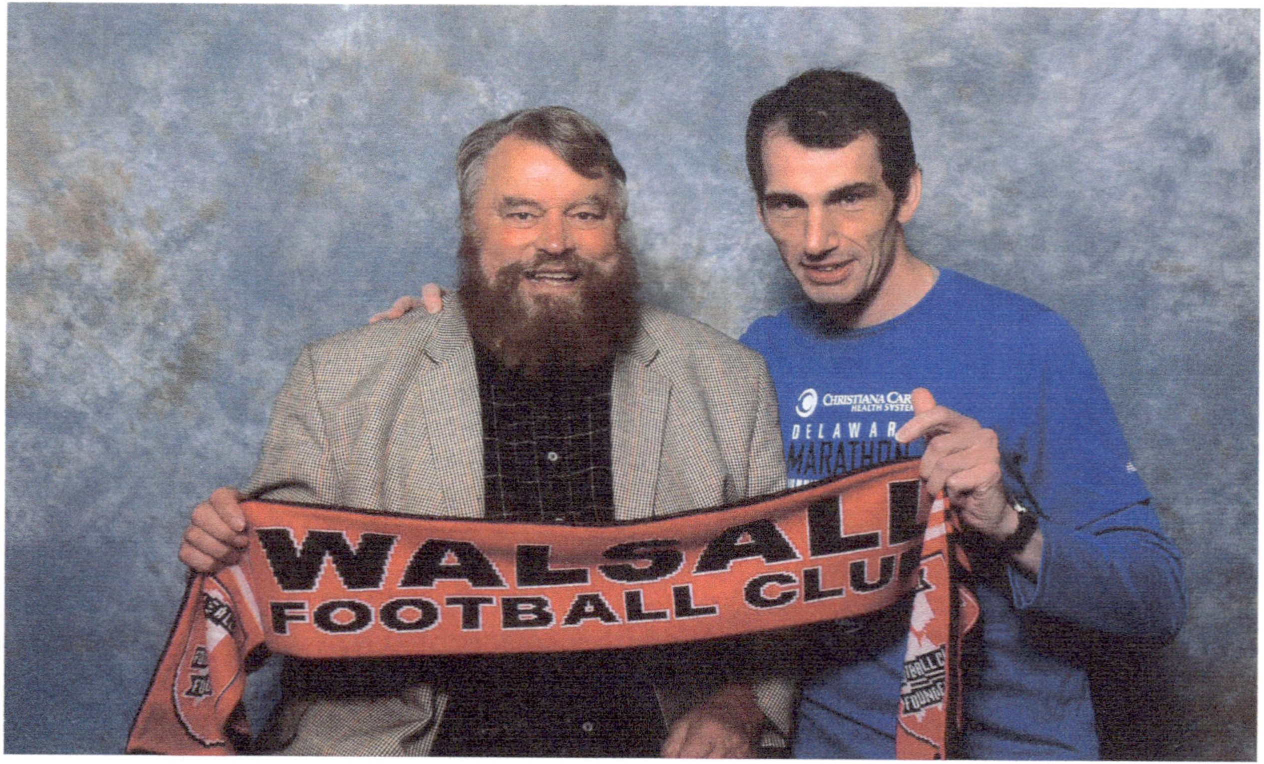
WALSALL
FOOTBALL

Brian Blessed

Blessed trained as an actor at the Bristol Old Vic Theatre School. Although his later acting work, particularly on screen, tends to be of a rather ebullient type, his talents have scored him a wide variety of roles such as the surprisingly subtle portrayal of Caesar Augustus in the BBC series *I Claudius* (for which he won the New York Critics Award). He has also enjoyed numerous roles on stage as a member of the RSC including a stint as Claudius in *Hamlet*.

His earliest TV work consisted of bit-parts in such cult shows as *The Avengers* and the original *Randall and Hopkirk (Deceased)*. But the part for which he is best remembered – by older viewers at least – is the firm-but-fair PC 'Fancy' Smith in the BBC's acclaimed police drama *Z Cars* – a part he played for a total of three years.

Despite the many roles Brian has played over the years, he is often called upon to play a variation of one particular part – that of Vultan, leader of the Hawkmen in *Flash Gordon*. This enthusiastic, bombastic performance has since been mirrored or revised in parts such as the raucous Richard IV in *Blackadder* and King Yrcanos in the *Doctor Who* story 'The Trial of a Time Lord'. However, he has continued to play a variety of subtler parts on stage and screens big and small. Witness his portrayals of Lord Locksley in the Kevin Costner-starring film version of *Robin Hood – Prince of Thieves*, Sir Tunbelly Clumsey in *The Relapse*, Baron Bomburst in the stage version of *Chitty Chitty Bang Bang*, Clayton the hunter in Disney's *Tarzan* and Old Deuteronomy in Andrew Lloyd Webber's stage musical, *Cats*.

Brian has also performed with, among others, the London Symphony Orchestra and Bolshoi Symphony Orchestra in works such as *Peter and the Wolf* and Prokofiev's *Ivan the Terrible*. Blessed's fame and cult status has been boosted enormously by his work on *Star Wars: Episode 1 – The Phantom Menace* – where he provided the voice of the character Boss Nass, a connection which has now caused the rate of his fan mail to become unmanageable.

Among his personal heroes are George Mallory and Ernest Shackleton. As an adventurer and explorer himself, he has climbed many mountains including Mount Kilimanjaro and Aconcagua in the Andes. He has made three attempts to reach the summit of Mount Everest, becoming – at the age of 65 – the oldest man to reach the dizzy altitude of 28,000ft without oxygen.

He also holds the record for being the oldest man to trek (on foot) to the magnetic North Pole and has made an expedition deep into the jungle interior of Venezuela to the plateau of Mount Roraima – a boyhood dream instilled in him by a BBC Radio production of Sir Arthur Conan Dolye's *The Lost World*, which is set on that plateau.

A new honour he achieved was in Milton Keynes when he held on tightly to the scarf, his voice booming away as ever!

WALSALL FOOTBALL CLUB

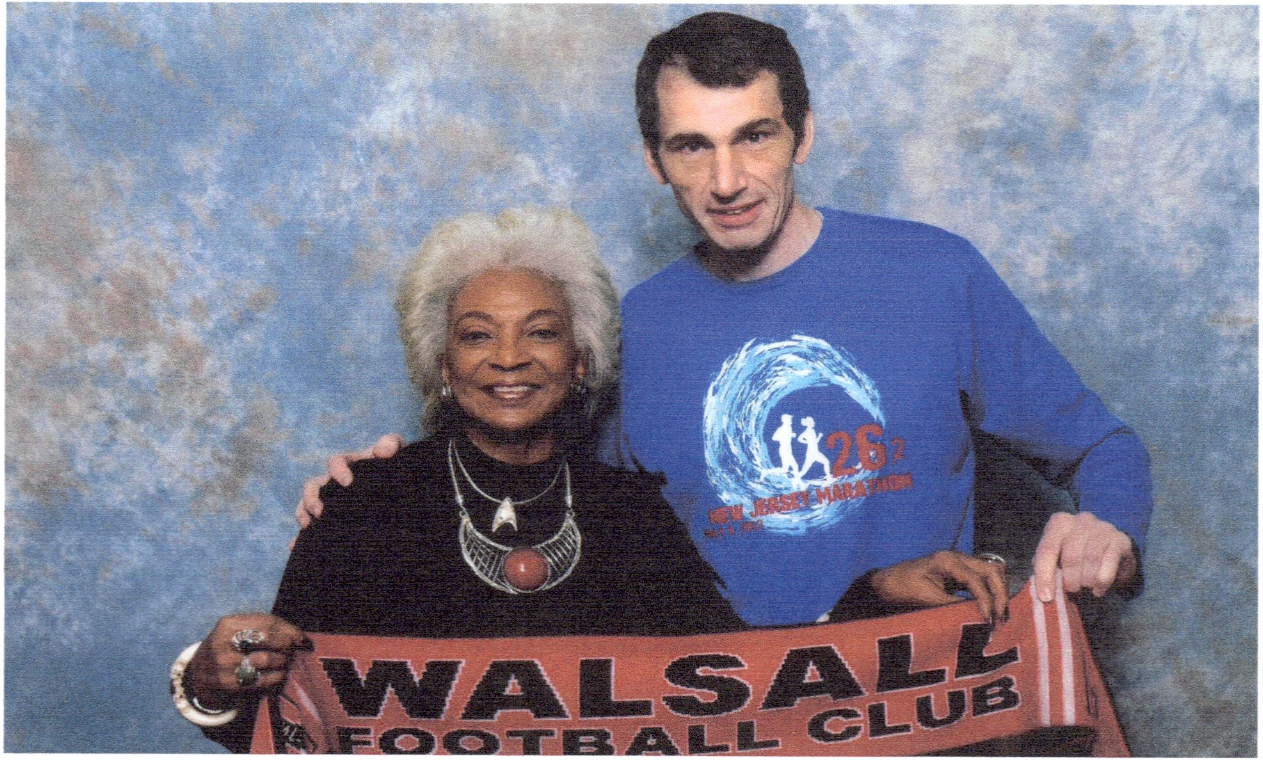

Nichelle Nichols

Nichelle Nichols hails from Chicago, Illinois, where she was discovered at the age of 15 by Duke Ellington while serving as choreographer and dancer in a ballet for one of his musical suites, and doing a stint as lead singer for his band.

When Gene Roddenberry cast Nichols as Lt. Uhura in his now legendary TV series *Star Trek*, she found herself in a role that would change her life. After seven blockbuster *Star Trek* motion pictures, she is in constant demand to appear before the millions of "Trekkers" who keep the dream alive around the world. Far from being her only role, she has also starred in the Sandy Howard Film *The Supernaturals*, and in the touring Broadway hit *Horowitz and Mrs. Washington*. Live theatre performance continues to be a favored venue for her. Twice she has been nominated for the Sarah Siddons Award for Best Actress for her performances in Jean Genet's *The Blacks* and *Kicks and Company*.

In 1991, Nichols became the first African American to place her handprints and signature in the concrete outside Mann's (Graumans) Chinese Theatre. Just a few short weeks later, in January 1992, Nichols was awarded a star on the Hollywood Walk of Fame. The occasions were marked by two especially treasured congratulatory messages: one from Whoopi Goldberg, and the other from Mae Jemison, the first African-American female astronaut. Both women credit her with the inspiration to begin their careers. Additionally, along with the

Enterprise crew, Nichols has been given an unprecedented accolade: an exhibit in Smithsonian's National Air and Space Museum.

A talented singer, writer, actress, and performer, her public service activities have been equally worthy of note. Nichols has served as a member of the Board of Directors for the National Space Institute (now the National Space Society), and been active in the leadership of the Space Cadets of America, an organization for young people interested in space and space careers. Through her consultant firm, Women in Motion, Inc., Nichols was instrumental in the NASA Astronaut Corps pioneering effort to break away from their all-white, all-male past. She received NASA's distinguished Public Service Award for her efforts and continued success.

In 1994 she published her autobiography, *Beyond Uhura: Star Trek and Other Memories*. She has also authored the first two volumes of what is expected to become a science fiction trilogy: *Saturn's Child* (1995) and *Saturna's Quest* (2002).

A frequent attendee at many *Star Trek* functions around the globe she joined others who had gone before in adding her picture with the scarf whilst here in London.

WALSALL FOOTBALL CLUB

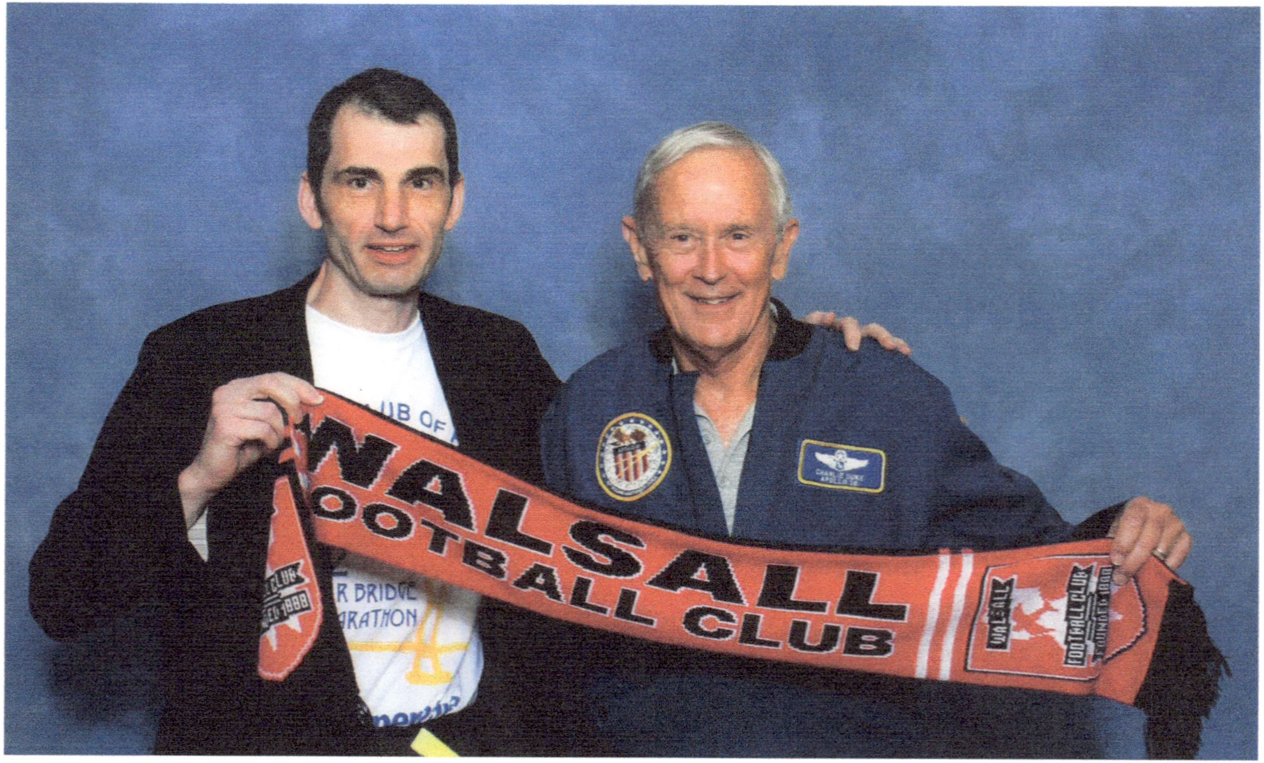
WALSALL
FOOTBALL CLUB

Charlie Duke

Charlie Duke was born in Charlotte, NC, in 1935. Led by a desire to serve his country, he attended the U.S. Naval Academy in Annapolis, Maryland. Following graduation, he was commissioned into the U.S. Air Force, and thus began a life-long love of flying. Over the years as fighter pilot, test pilot, and then encouraged by his commandant Chuck Yeager to become an Apollo astronaut, this love of adventure grew to the pinnacle of achievement when on April 20, 1972, he, along with John Young, landed on the surface of the moon. Their stay on the moon was a record-setting 71 hours and 14 minutes and in doing so he became the tenth and youngest person to walk on the Moon.

Duke and Young spent more than 20 hours exploring the moon. This involved emplacement and activation of scientific equipment and experiments, the collection of nearly 213 pounds of rock and soil samples, and the evaluation and use of Rover-2 (their lunar car) over the roughest and blockiest surface yet encountered on the moon. Charlie Duke filmed the only pictures made of the rover in action – its record setting speed was 17 kilometers per hour. During Apollo's three day return from the moon, Duke experienced a spacewalk with the third crew member, Ken Mattingly. The view over one shoulder was filled with a brilliant full moon and over the other hung a crescent earth – a thin sliver of blue and white. "Fantastic!" Charlie would exclaim again and again.

Apollo 16 returned to a hero's welcome, with Duke, Young and Mattingly each receiving NASA's Distinguished Service Medal. Since Duke's retirement from space exploration in 1975, he has been very active in business. He formed and was president of Orbit Corporation (a beverage company distributorship). He has been an active partner in real estate shopping centre development and was president and investor of several companies.

Duke also served in the Air Force Reserves as special assistant to the Commander of the USAF Recruiting Service, meeting all goals in recruitment of engineers and doctors. He traveled extensively speaking at schools and universities as part of Project Warrior. He was appointed by the National Aeronautics and Space Administration to the NASA Advisory Council. He is presently owner of Charlie Duke Enterprises (which has produced two space videos) and is president of Duke Investments.

A resident of New Braunfels, Texas, he is currently chairman of the board of directors of the Astronaut Scholarship Foundation.

Duke is one of the astronauts featured in the book and documentary *In the Shadow of the Moon*. At the end of the documentary, in response to Moon landing hoax theories, he says "We've been to the Moon nine times. Why would we fake it nine times, if we faked it?"

On a trip to Birmingham he proudly hailed the flag and the people of Walsall in his praise of the club.

WALSALL FOOTBALL CLUB

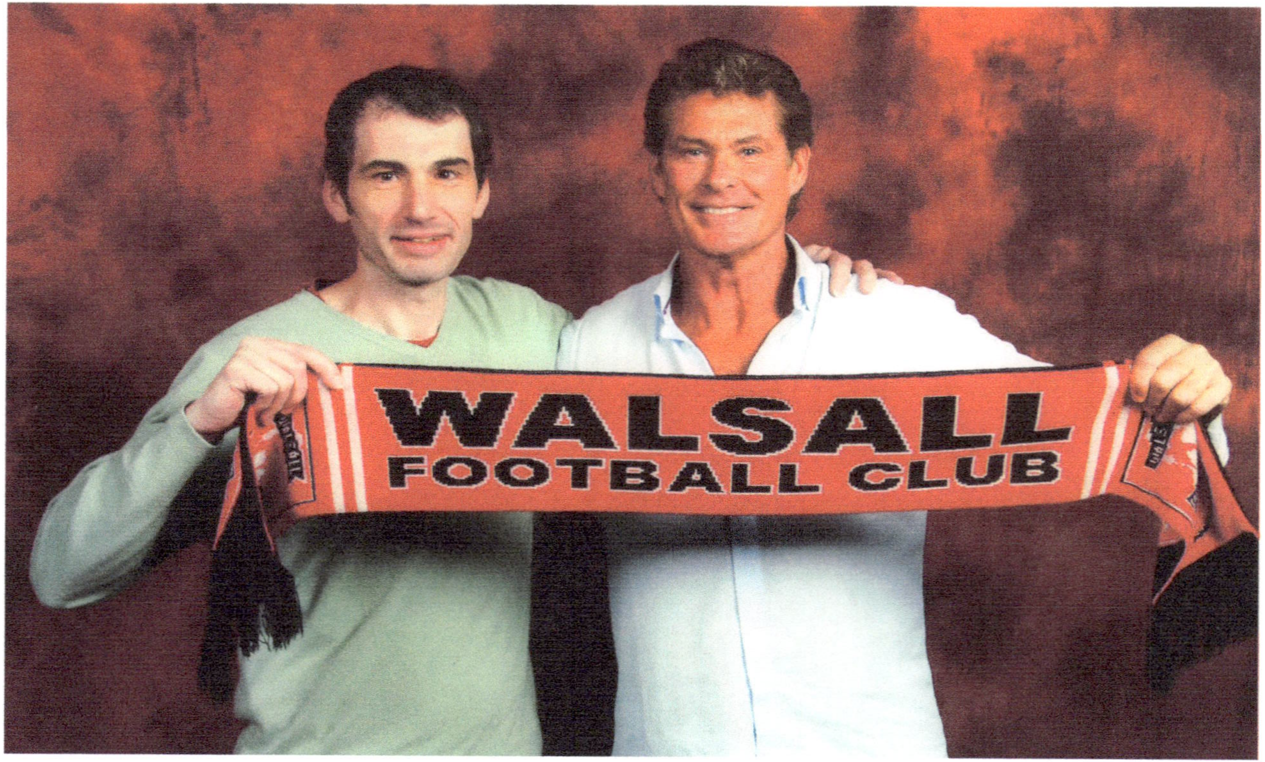
WALSALL
FOOTBALL CLUB

David Hasselhoff

Hasselhoff portrayed Dr. William "Snapper" Foster, Jr. on the serial *The Young and the Restless* early on in his career. He then went on to play the role of Simon in *Starcrash*. He launched his singing career with guest appearances on the first season of children's program *Kids Incorporated*, performing 'Do You Love Me.' He also guest starred on an episode of *Diff'rent Strokes* as himself in 1984.

However, it was not until he starred in the science-fiction series *Knight Rider* from 1982 to 1986 that his profile went global. He has described *Knight Rider* as more than a TV show: "It's a phenomenon. It's bigger than *Baywatch* ever was." On the success of *Knight Rider* – "It's because it was about saving lives, not taking lives, and it was how one man really can make a difference. And we had a blast making it, and we made sure nobody died on the show."

While his star status rose, fell and rose again in the US, Hasselhoff's popularity endured a little longer in Germany during the end of the '80s. Hasselhoff had one number-one hit in the German pop charts in 1989 ("Looking for Freedom").

Following a return to television on *Baywatch* which premiered in 1989 he enjoyed a larger audience. Although it was canceled after only one season, he believed the series had potential, so Hasselhoff revived it for the first-run syndication market two years later, investing his own money and additionally functioning as executive producer. His contract stipulated royalties to be paid to him from the rerun profits, which gave him the financial liberty to buy back the rights to *Baywatch* from NBC.

It was this second incarnation in which *Baywatch* was much more successful. It ran in syndication for another ten seasons. It was also well received internationally and has been shown in over 140 countries around the world. According to the Guinness Book of World Records, *Baywatch* is the most watched TV show in the world, with over 1.1 billion viewers. Hasselhoff explains the appeal of *Baywatch*: "I believe the camera photographs your aura, and it also photographs your heart. And I cast *Baywatch* that way. If you look at *Baywatch*, just about everybody on that show – even Pamela Anderson – has got a great heart."

In 1996, Hasselhoff was given a star on the Hollywood Walk of Fame. A year later he performed a duet with Filipino singer Regine Velasquez, which was used as the main theme for his movie *Legacy*.

On a visit to Birmingham he added another honour in becoming a scarf holder for Walsall, although he seemed to display some nerves prior to this shot.

WALSALL FOOTBALL CLUB

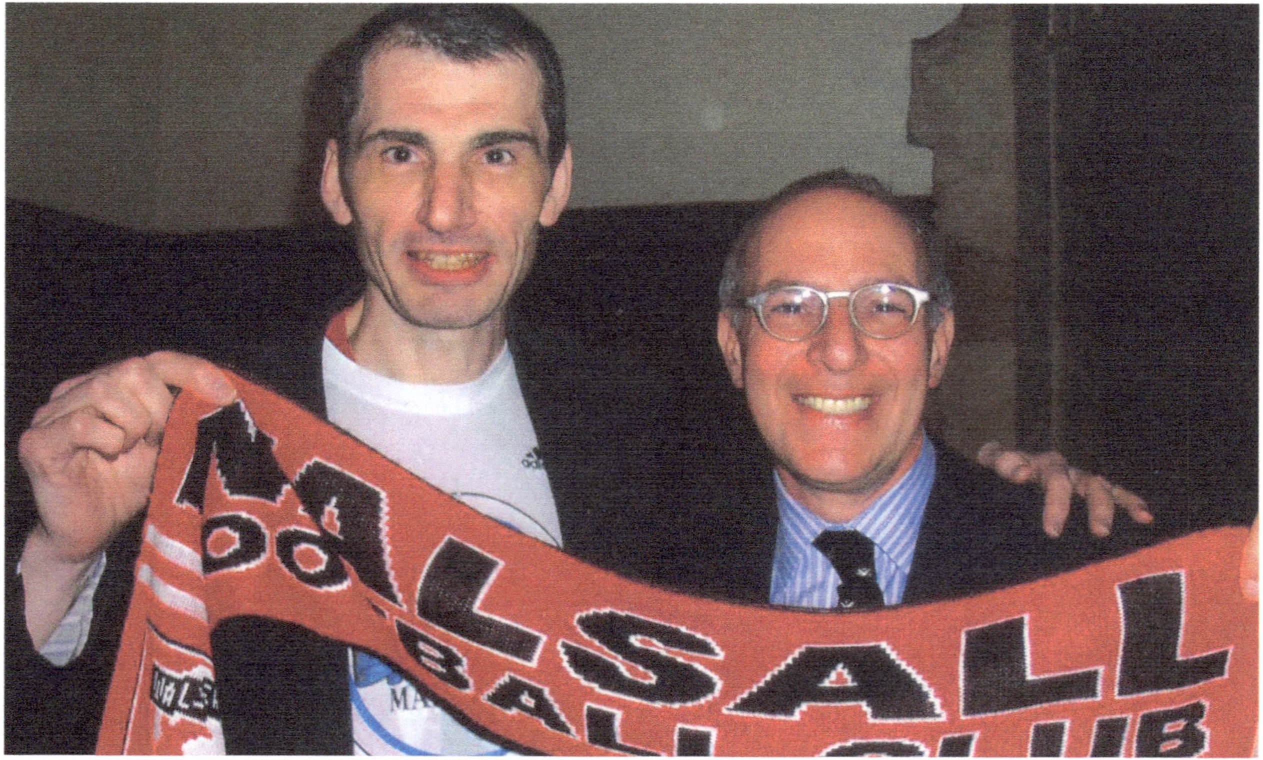
WALSALL

Loyd Grossman

After starting a career in journalism with Harpers & Queen and the Sunday Times he was diverted into television where as a writer, presenter or deviser he was involved in a wide range of programmes.

Grossman's television début came in 1987, as a roving presenter for *Through the Keyhole*, a programme examining the homes of the famous. Before leaving in 2003, Grossman made almost 400 appearances on the programme. Three years later, he became the first presenter of *MasterChef*, which he presented for 10 years (apart from a year off), also fronting the children's version for around five years. Other programmes include the *History of British Sculpture* and cookery show *Step up to the Plate* with Anton du Beke in which three amateur chefs competed against two professionals to produce the best three-course meal.

A little known fact is that he had a short-lived career as a singer with punk band Jet Bronx And The Forbidden, who reached number 49 in the UK singles chart in 1977 with "Ain't Doin' Nothing". He returned to playing music fairly recently, unable to leave it completely.

Loyd's knowledge of and fascination with food led him to create his own brand in 1995, which became Britain's most successful new premium food for shoppers and fans alike.

His lifelong interest in history, the arts and heritage has involved him in a number of organisations. He is a former

Commissioner of the Museums and Galleries Commission, a former member of English Heritage (where he was Chairman of the Museums Advisory Committee and the Blue Plaques Panel), a former associate of the Royal Commission on the Historical Monuments of England, a founding member of the Museums, Libraries and Archives Council, past Chairman of National Museums Liverpool and of the Public Monuments and Sculpture Association. He founded the 24 Hour Museum (now Culture 24) and was its Chairman until 2005.

In 2000, he was appointed to head the £40 million project to improve the quality of food served in British NHS hospitals and visited the Norfolk and Norwich University Hospital to raise awareness of the Better Hospital Foods project. His name has been lent to a number of cookery goods, particularly pasta and curry sauces, manufactured by Premier Foods. An advertisement campaign for his range of sauces began in the UK in 2008. Since their launch, the product has shifted more than one billion units.

Grossman won an edition of BBC's *Celebrity Mastermind* in December 2009. His specialist subject, not surprisingly, was 18th Century art and artists.

During a lecture talk in Southwell, Nottinghamshire he spoke eloquently about English churches in the Minster there, before mingling with the room and holding the scarf.

WALSALL FOOTBALL CLUB

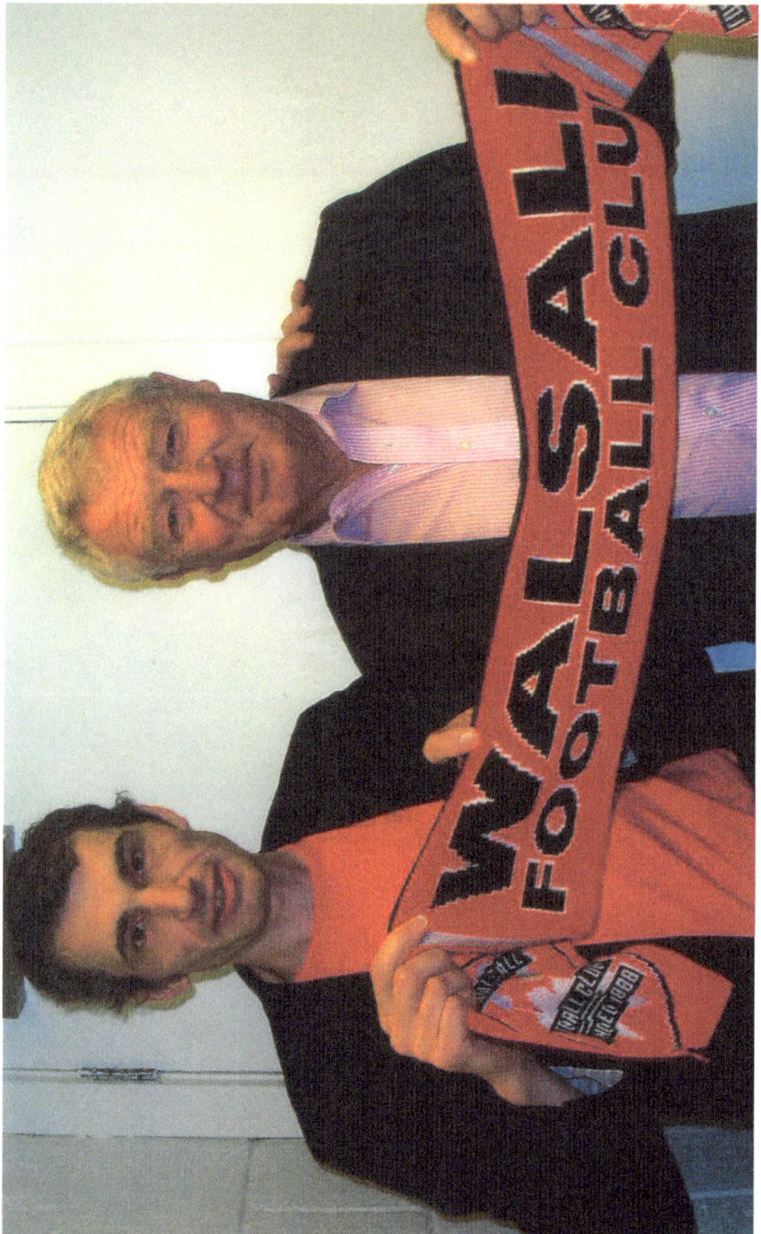

Paddy Ashdown

In 1972, Ashdown left the Royal Marines and joined the Foreign Office. He was posted to the British Mission at the United Nations in Geneva where he was responsible for Britain's relations with a number of United Nations organisations and took part in the negotiation of several international treaties and agreements between 1974 and 1976.

He was also involved in some aspects of the European Security Conference, also known as the Helsinki Conference.

After leaving the Foreign Office, he worked in local industry in the Yeovil area between 1976 and 1981, firstly with the Westlands Group (Normalair Garrett) and then with Morlands' Yeovil-based subsidiary called Tescan.

Tescan closed down in 1981 and, after a short period of unemployment, Mr Ashdown got a job as a youth worker with Dorset County Council Youth Service, where he was responsible for initiatives to help the young unemployed.

Elected as the Liberal candidate for Yeovil in 1979, he managed to raise the Liberal vote to its highest ever level. He then fought the next election in Yeovil and won with a 3,600 majority. Shortly after entering Parliament, he was appointed as the Liberal spokesman on trade and industry affairs within the Liberal/SDP Alliance team at the House of Commons.

His first shot at being a shadow cabinet member came about when he became spokesman for Trade and Industry and then

Education in 1987. In the election that same year, he increased his majority again to nearly 6,000 and was elected leader of the Liberal Democrats the following year. He was appointed to the Privy Council during 1989 and in the 1997 general election he further increased his majority to more than 11,000, thus making Yeovil a safe Liberal seat.

His decision to stand down came as a shock to many people when he announced it in January, some six months after the election. It appeared he felt he had taken the party as far as he could and wanted to give his successor time to build their own team before the next election.

Following his departure from British politics, he took up the post of the High Representative for Bosnia and Herzegovina in 2002, reflecting his long-time advocacy of international intervention in that region. He succeeded Wolfgang Petritsch in the position created under the Dayton Agreement.

Ashdown supports Yeovil Town F.C. and attends some matches, and was keen to hold the Walsall scarf backstage at the Lichfield Garrick theatre, before taking to the stage in his one-man show.

About the author

Acclaimed as Walsall's Running Ambassador, Mark Dabbs has competed in more than 70 worldwide marathons encompassing all six continents. He has met more than 120 Mayors as well as President Mandela, Prime Minister Gordon Brown and also Archbishop Desmond Tutu. Mark writes local history articles and cartoons for the Black Country Bugle and has also had three local history books published, as well as the romance novel *Untoward Occurrence*. In 2012 he was honoured to be chosen to carry the Olympic torch through the streets of his hometown. He is currently in the process of finishing his next novel, a thriller set in South East Asia, and trying to track down more faces to hold his scarf for the sequel to this project. For further details see www.markdabbsrunningambassador.co.uk

The proceeds of this book will be donated to St Giles Walsall Hospice which is a 12-bed in-patient facility based at the Palliative Care Centre in Goscote, near Walsall. The hospice offers specialist care for patients with cancer and other serious illnesses that are too poorly to remain at home, as well as respite stays and symptom relief. St Giles Walsall Hospice is a natural extension of this, and enhances services for local patients and their families while ensuring care remains free of charge to those who need it, thanks to the community support the charity receives.

See www.stgileshospice.com for ways to donate and support this worthy cause.

Acknowledgements

As always, for such an ambitious task as this one, the help and assistance of others has to be readily available, and without whom I could not have completed it.

I would like to thank the following people for their help and assistance with this project.

Firstly, to all the well-known faces that held my scarf I am most grateful, but especially to Lorraine Kelly, who even though I was delayed in meeting her at the studios, graciously waited before going home. Des O'Connor for entertaining me in his dressing room at the Garrick, Jayne MacDonald for spending time with us whilst we set up for the picture. To Angela Rippon, a legendary figure who was only too pleased to take time out of her schedule for me. Roy 'Chubby' Brown in allowing us to see him backstage moments before starting his show in Cannock – and not a swear word in sight. Honourable mentions go to Daniel O'Donnell for inviting me to his press launch at Birmingham, and Adam for coming along and being my photographer on a couple of occasions. Not forgetting Lord Archer who took me into his apartment and showed me around before taking the photograph. Ken Dodd, the Lord of Mirth who got me in to see him prior to my shift at the hospital, which saw me having to dash back and work the night afterwards – I must confess to being pre-occupied after a hilarious half hour with the man. My thoughts and sincere thanks also extend to those who are no longer with us but took part including Sir Henry Cooper, Geoffrey Hughes, Susannah York, Leslie Nielsen, Sir Patrick Moore, Kate O'Mara and most recently Lynda Bellingham.

Finally, to Sophie and Scarlett who have given me a new meaning and direction in life, I love them both very much and treasure my time spent with them always.

Lightning Source UK Ltd.
Milton Keynes UK
UKOW06f1124110215

246084UK00008B/19/P